UFO
CRASH
AT ROSWELL

UFO CRASH AT ROSWELL

THE GENESIS OF A MODERN MYTH

BENSON SALER, CHARLES A. ZIEGLER,
AND CHARLES B. MOORE

SMITHSONIAN INSTITUTION PRESS
WASHINGTON AND LONDON

Editor: Rosemary Sheffield
Designer: Linda McKnight
Indexer: Andrew L. Christenson

Library of Congress Cataloging-in-Publication Data

Saler, Benson,
    UFO Crash at Roswell : the genesis of a modern myth / Benson Saler, Charles A. Ziegler, and Charles B. Moore.
        p.   cm.
    Includes bibliographical references and index.
    ISBN 1-56098-751-0 (alk. paper)
        1. Unidentified flying objects—Sightings and encounters—New Mexico—Roswell.
    2. Myth—Miscellanea.   3. Folklore—Miscellanea.   4. Unidentified flying objects—
    Social aspects.   I. Ziegler, Charles A. (Charles Albert), 1927–   .   II. Moore, Charles B.,
    1920–   .   III. Title.
    TL789.5.N6S25   1997   97-8674
    001.942'09789'43—dc21   CIP

British Library Cataloging-in-Publication Data available

A paperback reissue (ISBN 1-58834-063-5) of the original cloth edition

Manufactured in the United States of America
10 09 08 07 06 05 04 03   5 4 3 2 1

⊗ The paper used in this publication meets the minimum requirements of the American
National Standard for Permanence of Paper for Printed Library Materials Z39.48-1984.

For permission to reproduce illustrations appearing in this book, please correspond directly with Benson Saler, Department of Anthropology, Brown 228, Brandeis University, Waltham MA 02254-9110. The Smithsonian Institution Press does not retain reproduction rights for these illustrations or maintain a file of addresses for illustration sources.

⊕ Printed on recycled paper

CONTENTS

CONTENTS

LIST OF ILLUSTRATIONS AND TABLES

Illustrations

Tables

ACKNOWLEDGMENTS

The authors wish to acknowledge the help they received in writing this book. Thanks are due to David Jacobson, David Kaplan, Lee-Ellen Marvin, Richard Parmentier, and Robert G. Todd for their cogent comments on Chapters 1 and 2. We are especially indebted to Robert Todd for providing us with reports, government documents, books, and other research materials from his voluminous files on Roswell. His help and advice were crucial in the timely completion of the investigatory phase of the work on Chapters 1, 2, and 3. We are deeply grateful to Albert Trakowski, John Peterson, Joseph Fletcher, Edwin Istvan, O. J. Tibbets, Herbert Crowe, Joel Carpenter, and Bernard Gildenberg, who provided their remembrances of relevant events and/or documentation used in preparing Chapter 3. For help in writing this chapter, thanks are also due to Captain James McAndrew, Office of the Secretary of the Air Force, for furnishing Balloon Group progress reports; to Karl Pflock for providing maps showing the location of the debris field; to Kevin Randle for generously supplying Weather Bureau Winds Aloft maps for 1947; and to John Lewis, National Severe Storms Laboratory, and Sam McCown, National Climatic Data Center, for supplying relevant meteorological maps and analysis.

INTRODUCTION

In the late 1940s, when sightings of unusual disklike objects moving across the sky first began to receive extensive media coverage, reporters coined the term "flying saucer" to convey to their readers the image of what observers of these phenomena said they had seen. Later, the term "unidentified flying object," or "UFO," became popular. Originally, "flying saucer" and "UFO" connoted only that the entity referred to did not appear to be either a known phenomenon of nature or a conventional aircraft, but with the passage of time both terms have become commonly used synonyms for "extraterrestrial spaceship." The gradual change in the meaning of these terms reflected the development of a "UFO community" made up of individuals linked by a common belief that at least some of the unusual objects that have been sighted over the years were spaceships manned by alien beings from a distant planetary system.

An idea of the size of the UFO community can be gained from surveys indicating that, at the present time, about one in four adult Americans avowedly believes that extraterrestrial beings have actually landed on Earth. Like most interest-linked communities, the commitment of its members ranges from passive belief in the traditional ideas of the UFO subculture to active participation in one of the many UFO organizations that have been established. Currently some of the larger organizations fund UFO studies, publish newsletters and journals, and coordinate the political activities of their members, such as, for example, petitioning the administration and Congress to declassify UFO-related government documents.

Few academics are overt members of this community, but the ability of these few to capture the attention of the media is vastly disproportionate to their numbers. For instance, the recent work of one such individual, a Harvard Medical School professor, was widely publicized when he indicated in articles and on television talk shows that his research (which was partially supported by federal funds) seems to show that more than a million people have been abducted by extraterrestrial beings. According to the professor, the abductees are carried aloft to a spaceship for examination and then returned to Earth with their memory of this event somehow clouded by the technological wizardry of the extraterrestrials.

The UFO community is now nearly half a century old, and thousands of sightings of UFOs have been reported during that period. However, the event that members of the community regard as the single most important UFO case is the alleged government cover-up of the recovery of a crashed flying saucer and the bodies of its crew at a site near Roswell, New Mexico, in 1947. This so-called Roswell Incident was first described in 1980 in a book in which it was asserted that the government had successfully hidden evidence of the incident for more than three decades. Coauthored by two writers who specialized in occult and "unexplained" phenomena, the book was dismissed by some critics as fictionalized history designed primarily to appeal to UFO buffs. Although it was ignored or rejected by most mainstream historians, the book became the *fons et origo* for a number of publications about the Roswell Incident that appeared over the next 14 years. Most of these publications supported the notion that the government was covering up the recovery of a crashed saucer, although a few skeptical authors derided that idea in their books and articles.

This controversy received widespread publicity in 1994 when New Mexico congressman Steven Schiff asked the U.S. General Accounting Office and the Air Force to search government files for Roswell-related documents. After a year-long investigation, a report that included reprints of ancillary documents totaling nearly 1,000 pages was released in 1995. Despite its impressive length, the report can be summarized briefly: there was no crashed saucer, no alien bodies, no cover-up.

These findings, publicized in newspapers and on television, were not accepted by the UFO community, as evidenced by articles, commentaries, and letters in UFO journals. Angry editorials in these journals characterized the massive government report as part of a continuing cover-up, a theme that some columnists in the mainstream press echoed. Indeed, the publicity engendered by the government investigation stimulated a resurgence of public interest in UFOs—an outcome that prompted the town of Roswell to hold "UFO Encounter '95." The festival, which attracted tens of thousands of visitors, celebrated the putative recovery of the crashed saucer and featured tours of the supposed crash site. Roswell now has several museums where, for a fee, visitors can see crash-related artifacts such as the pictures of extraterrestrials sketched by people who claim to have seen these beings. For those unable to visit Roswell, vials of earth from the crash site are available from mail-order entrepreneurs whose advertisements in UFO journals urge readers to spend $10 to purchase "your very own piece of UFO history."

Filmmakers and television producers also took advantage of the surge in public awareness of UFOs by releasing "docudramas" that portrayed the Roswell Incident as a government cover-up of the crash of an extraterrestrial spaceship. And in 1995 a film allegedly depicting government scientists as they conducted an autopsy on an alien body from the Roswell crash was aired repeatedly on national television.

In addition to the flurry of media attention in 1994–1995, the Roswell Incident has achieved worldwide notoriety through articles in international UFO journals and more than half a dozen books (some translated into 10 languages) that were published between 1980 and 1994. Almost without exception, these publications portray the events at Roswell as the cover-up of a crashed saucer.

Clearly, the Roswell Incident is multifaceted: it is an epiphany for millions of Americans who believe in the reality of extraterrestrial visitations; a pseudoevent for Air Force investigators who maintain that government files contain no evidence of a cover-up of a saucer crash; a cash cow for many people, including writers, filmmakers, and television producers; and a prodigy that has captured the interest of countless individuals around the globe. It is equally clear that—quite apart from the question of the objective reality of any extraterrestrial involvement—the Roswell Incident is a significant cultural phenomenon and, as such, can be analyzed using the theoretical tools and concepts of cultural anthropology. Indeed, such analysis is the purpose of this book.

A logical starting point for analysis is an aspect of the Roswell Incident that is not disputed by anyone, namely, that it involves something that happened in the New Mexico desert in 1947. It is our contention— and the theme of this book—that this objectively real "something" has been mythologized. In other words, as a cultural phenomenon, the Roswell Incident can best be understood as an example of a modern myth.

The relationship between the terms "UFO" and "myth" has been explored by others. The first substantive work based on this approach was the 1959 book *Flying Saucers: A Modern Myth of Things Seen in the Sky,* written by well-known psychoanalyst Carl Jung. In 1972 a noted Harvard University astrophysicist, Donald Menzel, expatiated on this idea in an article entitled "UFO's—The Modern Myth." And Curtis Peebles's 1994 book on UFOs, *Watch the Skies*, has a mythic theme. Between 1972 and 1995, about a dozen papers were written by folklorists who contended that some types of UFO narratives, such as abductee stories and reported sightings of unusual lights in the sky, can be categorized as modern legends or, in some cases, as ancient legends expressed in a modern idiom. The present book, however, is the first to analyze the mythlike aspects of the Roswell Incident.

Each of the separately authored chapters that follow is an elaboration of the Roswell-as-myth theme. Chapter 1 describes the mythologizing process, and Chapter 2 provides a detailed analysis of the myth itself. Chapter 3 examines the chain of events that seems likely to have formed the myth's historical core, and Chapter 4 explores the myth's religious dimension. The final chapter assesses the cultural implications of the findings in previous chapters, with emphasis on the link between Roswell and the media and what that link portends for the future.

The chapters speak for themselves and need no further preamble, but because the primary purpose of an introduction is to indicate what the reader can (and cannot) expect to find in a book, it is pertinent to emphasize that the focus of this book (as its title implies) is the Roswell Incident. Thus, other UFO phenomena are mentioned only insofar as they are relevant to this specific case. It also seems appropriate to end with an admonition. If you wish to learn what the Roswell Incident teaches us about extraterrestrial beings, you are well advised to seek elsewhere. If you are interested in what it tells us about ourselves and about the society in which we live, then read on.

CHAPTER ONE

MYTHOGENESIS

HISTORICAL DEVELOPMENT OF
THE ROSWELL NARRATIVES

CHARLES A. ZIEGLER

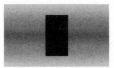n this analysis the word "myth" is used to describe a story that many people say they believe: a story about an alien spaceship that crashed near Roswell, New Mexico, in 1947. In common parlance, the word "myth" is often used to indicate that the statement or narrative to which it refers is false, but its usage in the social sciences does not require this connotation. As a popular appellation, "myth" thus has epistemological overtones that I wish to disavow at the outset. I make no claim to absolute certainty regarding the falsity of the story that extraterrestrial beings were involved in what has come to be called the Roswell Incident. What I do claim is that, without prejudging the factuality of the story, it can be treated and analyzed along lines that have become well established in cultural anthropology.

Myths sometimes form around a core of events that are commonplace or otherwise unremarkable, although the myths themselves may be fanciful in the extreme. Hence, in this chapter I begin my analysis by narrating the Roswell myth in its full-blown form and juxtaposing it with an account of some historically documented events that appear likely to have given birth to the myth. I then show how the account of these documented events evolved into the myth, a process of transfiguration that involved successive retellings in which some of the historically recorded events were retained, some were distorted or repressed, and entirely new elements were inserted.

My analysis continues in Chapter 2, in which I show that the Roswell stories are similar to traditional folk narratives in terms of transmission, structure, and central motif. In a second level of the analysis, I speculate about the motives of the persons involved in creating the myth and draw parallels to previous studies of mythmaking. Finally, because myths are usually symbolic expressions of themes that are important in a given culture, a third level of the analysis focuses on the functions and meaning of the Roswell myth in the context of some generally accepted ideas and values of our modern society. The questions I attempt to answer are these: How did this myth arise? Why do some people assert that it is credible? And what does the Roswell myth tell us about our culture?

At this point, it is relevant to note that for more than a decade a controversy has simmered between "true believers," who explain the events at Roswell in terms of a government cover-up of an extraterrestrial visitation, and skeptics who debunk that idea. In 1994 this debate erupted into national prominence when, at the request of a congressman, the U.S. General Accounting Office and the U.S. Air Force began investigating the government's role in the Roswell Incident. The involvement of a congressman and federal agencies in this debate has highlighted its political dimension. Hence, one of the themes I will explore is the degree to which the Roswell myth has become a vehicle for the expression of antigovernment sentiment.

THE FORM AND ACQUISITION OF THE MYTH

Before presenting the Roswell myth, I must first answer the question, Which Roswell myth? The myth appeared in crude but recognizable form in 1980 and has been evolving ever since. At various times in the succeeding years, the elements of its plot have differed considerably. These various transformations will be described, but I will first present the myth in its most recent form (circa 1996). To describe how I acquired this myth, it is pertinent to begin by describing some of the defining characteristics of any myth.

As used in this analysis, a myth is, among other things, a narrative that deals with a transcendental issue such as why and how the world and humankind came to be in their present form, the role of unearthly beings in human affairs, and the like; and it is a narrative that some people within the society say they find credible. In other words, a myth necessarily has (or had, in the case of antique myths) a constituency of true believers who, by virtue of a shared avowal of their belief, constitute a subculture. For the analyst, members of this subculture constitute a group of informants from whom the myth can be acquired. If the myth has reached maturity, it may be possible for the analyst to hear the complete myth recited by knowledgeable true believers or to read it in canonical form in their writings. On the other hand, a myth in the making, which by definition has not been canonized, will be more fragmented in recitals and in the writings of true believers, requiring some degree of collation by the analyst.

The Roswell myth falls in the latter category. It exists as a series of related propositions, explicit and implied, that are found throughout the subset of the UFO literature that describes the Roswell Incident in terms of an extraterrestrial visitation. This subset now includes more than a half dozen books and nearly 100 articles, commentaries, and letters in UFO journals. The myth that follows has been collated from these literary sources.

THE ROSWELL MYTH (1996)

In the first few days of July 1947, the spaceships of curious extraterrestrials flew over the New Mexico site of a 1945 atomic bomb test and over nearby military bases where secret rocket research was being conducted. During that time, one of the spaceships malfunctioned. Swooping low over the town of Roswell, it struck the earth glancingly on land owned by a local rancher, leaving behind gouged earth and material torn from the ship's hull by the impact, including fragments imprinted with alien symbols or hieroglyphics. The damaged craft rose into the air and traveled onward for a number of miles before crashing into the base of a cliff in a remote area, killing the crew.

Various portions of this sequence of events were observed on Army Air Force radars and by eyewitnesses whose reports reached authorities at the Roswell Army Air Field. Thus alerted, the military acted swiftly: a cordon of troops was placed around the impact sites; the wreckage and the small, humanoid alien bodies were removed; and all traces of the crash were expunged. The statements of eyewitnesses were also reported by the local radio station and newspapers, and on 8 July the public relations officer at Roswell Army Air Field issued a press release announcing the recovery of a "flying disk" that had been sent on to higher headquarters for examination. This official announcement attracted worldwide attention, but within hours it was repudiated at a press conference held by the general in command of the regional Army Air Force, who asserted that the alleged wreckage of a flying disk was merely the remains of a weather balloon.

This cover story, invented to cloak the recovery of an alien spaceship, was accepted by the media and by the public at large. Government officials took prompt action to repress further reportage by threatening eyewitnesses and local reporters with severe reprisals if they continued to reveal information about the flying disk. This was the beginning of a massive cover-up that for three decades succeeded in keeping the events at Roswell from being scrutinized by serious researchers.

In 1979 a former military intelligence officer at the Roswell Army Air Field, in defiance of security regulations, told UFO investigators that the wreckage collected near Roswell in 1947 was not that of a weather balloon and that the fragments he had seen and handled exhibited unusual properties, in terms of hardness and strength, that were not possessed by terrestrial materials. In the years that followed this revelation, researchers interviewed dozens of individuals who had firsthand or secondhand knowledge about the Roswell Incident. Their testimony, which appeared in a number of books and articles during the period 1980–1994, confirmed the crash of an alien spaceship and the recovery of alien bodies.

In 1994, exasperated by official silence about the true nature of the Roswell Incident, some New Mexico citizens petitioned their congressman to force the Defense Department to disgorge secret documents proving that officials were withholding evidence of the most important event in human history—extraterrestrial contact—because of a misguided government policy. That policy was due partly to the unwarranted fear that catastrophic panic and disorder on a global scale would follow the disclosure of such evidence, and partly to the desire of the military to keep secret the advanced scientific knowledge it had gleaned from the spaceship wreckage and the alien bodies.

The congressman succeeded in initiating an investigation by the General Accounting Office. Subsequently, that agency asked the Air Force to cull its files on the Roswell Incident. The result of those efforts was a report that attributed the wreckage found near Roswell not to a weather balloon but rather to the remains of balloon-borne radar reflectors, launched as part of a top secret project. Codenamed Mogul, the project aimed at developing a sonic technique for covertly monitoring the test of a Soviet atomic bomb. This most recent government pronouncement on the Roswell Incident was merely a restatement of the original cover story in a slightly modified form. Hence, the conspiracy of silence on the part of government officials continues to prevent the public from obtaining evidence of profound import—evidence that we, as intelligent life-forms, are not alone in the universe.

THE MYTH'S HISTORICAL CORE

In November 1946, New York University received a contract from the Army Air Force's Watson Laboratories in New Jersey to develop "constant-level" balloons capable of floating as long as 48 hours at preset heights between 10 and 20 kilometers (nominally 33,000 to 66,000 ft). It was hoped that the instrument payload would detect high-altitude sound waves over unprecedentedly great distances. The university formed a research team called the Constant Level Balloon Group to carry out this development, and late in the spring of 1947 six of its members, including the project engineer, were sent on a field trip to Alamogordo, New Mexico.

During the first week of June they launched three balloon trains, each supporting a low-frequency microphone, from the North Area of Alamogordo Army Air Field. The first of these balloon trains also carried three radar reflectors. The aim was to test the microphone's ability to detect distant, preset explosions. The radar reflectors were needed to enable ground-based radars to track the balloon train and ascertain its position at the time of the explosion. To ensure that heights approaching 66,000 feet (20 km) would be reached, the balloon trains consisted of linked clusters of about two dozen neoprene balloons, each 5 feet (1.5 m) in diameter. Such balloons, when used *singly* to carry a radiosonde (a miniature radio transmitter coupled to meteorological sensors) aloft, were popularly called weather balloons.

The radar reflectors, originally developed by the army during the World War II to measure the winds aloft for various purposes such as gunnery control for the field artillery, were unfamiliar to most local Army Air Force personnel, as were the balloon trains used to carry them to the stratosphere. In appearance, the radar reflectors were kitelike structures made of paper and tinfoil supported on a frame of lightweight sticks. They were inexpensive throwaway items, and unlike the radiosondes carried on conventional flights of single weather balloons, they were not readily identifiable as meteorological instruments. Moreover, the Balloon Group's balloon trains, which were designed to float at high altitudes, generally traveled farther from the launch site than single weather balloons did before bursting or losing enough gas to descend.

One such flight appears especially relevant to this history. In 1993, Charles B. Moore, the Balloon Group's project engineer, recalled some of the details of that flight. Moore remembered plotting on a map the ground track of a balloon train that was launched on 4 June 1947 and carried three radar reflectors. It was followed by a chase aircraft (a B-17 bomber) to the vicinity of the towns of Arabela and Bluewater, located about 75 miles (120 km) from the base. "The exotic names of these towns were new to me," Moore stated. "They stuck in my memory and I remember them well, but only because of their association with that flight." He also remembered that the balloon train was still airborne over Arabela when the B-17 crew terminated the chase. Moore's reconstruction of the ground track from the last sighting at Arabela indicates that the balloon train "encountered the usual low-level summer monsoon winds from the southeast that would have moved the remaining balloons to the northwest." This track places the impact site of radar reflectors and deflated balloon train at about 25 to 30 miles (40 to 48 km) to the north-northwest of Arabela. In this remote area a large parcel of land belonged to the J. B. Foster ranch operated by William W. Brazel.[1]

On 14 June, Brazel was making his rounds of the ranch accompanied by his 8-year-old son, Vernon. According to an interview Brazel gave reporters on 8 July, at about 7 to 8 miles (11 to 13 km) from the ranch house they encountered "bright wreckage made up of rubber strips, tinfoil, a rather tough paper, and sticks." This debris was strewn over an area about 200 yards (180 m) in diameter, but because he was anxious to complete his rounds, Brazel "did not pay much attention to it." He mentioned the incident to his wife, however, and nearly three weeks later, on 4 July, they and their 14-year-old daughter, Bessie, "went back to the spot and gathered up quite a bit of the debris." The following day, he visited the nearby town of Corona. There he heard for the first time about sightings of "flying disks," then being widely reported by the media, and he wondered if what he had found "might be remnants of one of these [disks]."[2]

To understand the context of Brazel's speculation about flying disks, it is necessary to recount the incident that one historian (Jacobs 1975:36) considers to be the beginning of the "modern era of [UFO] sightings in the United States." On 24 June (10 days after Brazel's discovery of the wreckage), Kenneth Arnold, a private pilot flying from Chehalis to Yakima, Washington, briefly sighted nine unusual objects flying at unprecedentedly high speeds. He told his story to reporters, who coined the terms "flying saucers" and "flying disks" to describe the objects that Arnold said he had seen. This sighting received extensive publicity, and during the weeks that followed, hundreds of people came forward with similar assertions that also received media attention. Brazel's later statements suggest that when he first heard about flying disks on 5 July, he thought of them in terms of some type of aircraft. And because he lived in the vicinity of an army air field, Brazel apparently suspected that the wreckage he had found was associated with a military project.

Indeed, a Gallup Poll taken at the time (Gallup 1972:666) indicates that virtually no one thought of associating flying disks with extraterrestrial spaceships, a linkage that is now made by a majority of Americans. Instead, most people attributed the reported sightings to illusions, hoaxes, misinterpreted or unknown natural phenomena, or secret military vehicles. The Cold War with the Soviet Union had already begun, so the latter possibility greatly exercised the Army Air Force's Technical Intelligence Division. From the intelligence perspective, the most likely explanation for the sightings, if real, was either an American secret project or a novel Soviet aircraft bent on surveillance or some more sinister purpose. There were precedents that preconditioned intelligence analysts to accept each of these suppositions as credible.

First, the possibility that the sightings could be associated with some domestic military project, unknown even to high-ranking military officers, had many precedents—most notably the wartime building of the atomic bomb. Today it is difficult to appreciate the almost surrealistic degree to which the policy of compartmentalization of secret information was then applied. For example, in 1946 the Joint Chiefs of Staff prepared a contingency plan for war with the Soviet Union that was later discarded because it was based on completely unrealistic assumptions about the atomic capability of the United States. According to historian Gregg Herken (1982:219), this gaffe occurred because the Joint Chiefs of Staff were not allowed access to the necessary atomic information, including the existing number and production rate of atomic bombs.

Second, the idea that the sightings were of a novel Soviet aircraft had its precedent in the wartime military intelligence experience with Japanese balloon bombers. Little more than two years separated the reports of unusual flying objects that alerted authorities to the Japanese balloon bomber offensive in 1944–1945, and the wave of reports in 1947 that were triggered by Arnold's sightings. In 1945, intelligence analysts had not ignored reports from people throughout the western United States who said they had sighted mysterious objects in the sky, and prompt investigation had revealed that the nation was being attacked with a hitherto unsuspected enemy weapon.[3]

Therefore, from the military standpoint, the wave of such sightings in 1947 could not be dismissed without first eliminating the possibility that they were due to some secret domestic project and then ascertaining whether or not they were caused by a new type of Soviet aircraft. The key to unveiling the Japanese threat in 1945 had been the recovery of the remains of crashed aircraft. That previous experience ensured that any reported finding of wreckage attributed to flying disks would receive the prompt attention of military intelligence officers.

It is against the historical background just described that the further actions of Brazel and other individuals, civilian and military, must be considered. Although Brazel had heard about flying disks on Saturday, 5 July, and speculated about the possibility that the crash of such a craft might have produced the wreckage he had discovered, he did not immediately report his find to authorities. He had no telephone, and apparently he did not think the matter was important enough to warrant a special trip into Roswell, which was 75 miles (120 km) away. Instead, Brazel decided to defer reporting his discovery until the following Monday, when he had to visit town to sell some wool.

While in Roswell, Brazel informed the sheriff, George Wilcox, that he had found some unusual wreckage that might be from a flying disk. Wilcox contacted authorities at the Roswell Army Air Field, and soon Major Jesse A. Marcel, the intelligence officer of the 509th Bomb Group, together with Captain Sheridan Cavitt, appeared and followed Brazel back to his home. When they arrived at the ranch, they picked up the remaining debris scattered on the ground and went to the ranch house, where Brazel handed over used feed sacks stuffed with the wreckage he and his wife and daughter had collected on 4 July.

For purposes of identification, Marcel attempted unsuccessfully to fit the pieces of debris together. Like other local officers, Marcel was apparently unfamiliar with radar reflectors, but according to an interview Brazel gave reporters on the following day, "they tried to make a kite out of it." Indeed, a kite is exactly what the sticks and paper composing the wreckage of a radar reflector would suggest to most observers. On two previous occasions Brazel had found the remains of a conventional meteorological weather balloon on the ranch, and he knew the latest wreckage was different: "What I found was not any weather observation balloon." The description he gave reporters bears out that assertion: "When the debris was gathered up the tinfoil, paper, tape and sticks made a bundle about three feet long and 7 or 8 inches thick [1 m long, 18–20 cm thick], while the rubber made a bundle about 18 or 20 inches long and about 8 inches thick [46–51 cm long, 20 cm thick]." Brazel estimated that the "entire lot would have weighed maybe five pounds [2 kg]."[4]

This description differs markedly in two ways from that of debris produced by a conventional weather balloon: much more rubber had been found than could be accounted for by a single weather balloon, and the small radiosonde carried by such balloons could not have produced the "tinfoil, paper, tape and sticks" that were collected. Although there were no identifying words on the fragments collected, there was "considerable scotch tape and some tape with flowers printed upon it that had been used in the construction."[5]

The last observation is significant because Moore later recalled that the radar reflectors he and his group had launched early in June had been constructed using "a scotch-like tape that had abstract pinkish-purple, flower-like designs printed or embossed on the back." These reflectors had been fabricated in the last years of the war, and the flowery tape was the legacy of wartime shortages and the expedient of using any available material that would do the job.[6]

Following the unsuccessful attempt to reconstruct the debris, Marcel took the material back to Roswell Army Air Field. While these events were transpiring on 7 July, the members of the Balloon Group were preparing to depart Alamogordo for New York City. Thus, the people in the area who were most competent to recognize the debris as the wreckage of a balloon train and a radar reflector were unavailable, and no one at Roswell Army Air Field was able to identify the debris when it arrived there. On the following day, 8 July, the base public relations officer issued a press release that stated: "The many rumors regarding the flying disc became a reality yesterday when the intelligence office of the 509th Bomb Group . . . was fortunate enough to gain possession of a disc through the cooperation of one of the local ranchers and the sheriff's office of Chaves County." The release went on to say that the wreckage "was inspected at Roswell Army Air Field and subsequently loaned by Major Marcel to higher headquarters."[7]

The wreckage had been flown to the Fort Worth headquarters of Brigadier General Roger M. Ramey, commander of the Eighth Army Air Force District, where it had finally been identified by Warrant Officer Irving Newton, the weather officer on duty at the time. Newton was able to recognize the debris as that of a balloon-borne radar reflector because he had used these devices during his wartime service overseas. In describing such a reflector to reporters, Newton said that it "looks like a six-pointed star, is silver in appearance and rises like a kite."[8]

On the evening of 8 July, Ramey was interviewed on a radio news broadcast. He announced that the alleged wreckage of a flying disk was actually the remains of a radar reflector and fragments of a weather balloon used to carry it aloft. To quell the media furor the incident had aroused, Ramey invited reporters to inspect the debris: "The wreckage is in my office now and as far as I can see there is nothing to get excited about."[9] The following day, newspapers around the country carried headlines such as FLYING DISK EXPLAINED. Subsequently, the historical Roswell Incident faded quickly from public memory and entered the limbo of overpublicized nonevents, where it remained for more than 30 years.

THE "REAL" COVER STORY

The foregoing history is based on three documents from around the time of the Roswell Incident (the Balloon Group's report and two newspaper accounts of interviews with Brazel and with Ramey and Newton) and on the remembrances of Charles B. Moore, who was a participant in some of the events recounted. Mine is not the only recent attempt to reconstruct the historical Roswell Incident.

Early in 1994, at the insistence of a U.S. congressman, an extensive investigation of this incident was undertaken by government historians. These researchers were granted security clearance to pry into the most highly classified files. And former government employees and military officers, whom they interviewed, were given releases by the Secretary of the Air Force to speak freely about what they knew of the Roswell Incident.

According to an early memorandum by Bruce Ashcroft (1994:1), a historian at the Air Force's Air Intelligence Agency, he and other workers searched, via electronic means, for references to Roswell or flying saucers in the Air Force History Office holdings "plus other base and USAF [U.S. Air Force] Museum archives, encompassing several million documents." Moreover, they carried out "an electronic search of the Air Force Historical Research Agency archives, again, several million pages of documents." They also interviewed a number of individuals who participated directly or peripherally in the Roswell Incident, as well as some of the officers who were involved in previous Air Force investigations of UFO phenomena. The Air Force version (McAndrew 1995) of the sequence of events composing the historical Roswell Incident—based on this massive research effort—is, in all essentials, the same as the foregoing narrative that I have just presented, with the exception of an addition that will be discussed. But first it seems pertinent to comment on the significance of the government's investigation.

As anyone who has written a supplicant's letter to a member of Congress knows, it is not easy to get the federal government to act, especially if the action requires funding. No estimate of the money spent on the government's Roswell investigation is presently available, but it is impossible to contemplate a year-long project involving staff members at a congressional member's office, the General Accounting Office, the Department of Defense, and the Department of the Air Force, as well as investigators and archivists at various document centers, without thinking that the cost would approach many hundreds of thousands of dollars. These expenses, of course, are taxpayer dollars—spent because of a myth. Therefore, the government investigation is, in itself, evidence that this particular myth has tapped powerful undercurrents in our society, a theme that will be discussed later.

As might be expected, the Air Force's version of the Roswell Incident cites reports in government files that provide additional documentary evidence for some of the events that I have just recounted. It refers to supporting testimony obtained by interviewing a number of key figures, notably Captain Sheridan Cavitt, the officer who accompanied Marcel when the latter picked up the wreckage from Brazel, and Warrant Officer Irving Newton, who later identified the material as the remains of a radar reflector. Air Force historians were also able to add another facet to the Roswell story; namely, they point to the possibility that a few days after Ramey disclosed the true nature of the wreckage, Army Air Force officers may have attempted to mislead the press about the purpose of the radar reflector flights. In other words, a cover story may have been promulgated to protect a secret military project. In order to evaluate this possibility, it is necessary to review briefly the nation's military posture at the dawn of the nuclear era.

When World War II ended, only the United States possessed atomic bombs, but the Joint Chiefs of Staff were acutely aware that this monopoly was ephemeral. They assumed (correctly) that the Soviet Union had mounted a secret crash program to develop a bomb and that the Soviets would do all in their power to keep hidden the crucial first proof-of-design test of their bomb, a test that would necessarily precede building a stockpile of such weapons. U.S. intelligence analysts wanted desperately to detect that test, because it would provide the essential "calibration point" they needed to assess Soviet progress and to predict Soviet capability to wage atomic war against the United States. Military leaders thus decided not only to use conventional espionage but also to develop technical surveillance methods to obtain that information. One such method, which could be implemented from sites outside the borders of the Soviet Union, was based on detecting the high-altitude sound waves produced by an atomic explosion.

This sonic method relied on the hypothesized existence of sound-refracting air layers at heights in the region of 66,000 feet (20 km), within which sound would travel thousands of miles with little diminution in intensity. To verify the reality of this "sound channel" and to use it later for monitoring purposes, sonic detectors had to be positioned within the channel on constant-level balloons capable of floating there for several days. Research on this sonic approach was initiated by the

Army Air Force's Watson Laboratories early in 1946 under the code name Mogul, and later that year New York University was awarded a contract to develop the necessary constant-level balloons. The university's balloon development contract was unclassified, but because of the immense strategic importance assigned to methods of gathering atomic intelligence, Mogul was classified top secret. (Indeed, because of security considerations, little was publicly known about such technical intelligence-gathering methods until quite recently. For a history of these methods, including those related to Mogul, see Ziegler 1988 and Ziegler and Jacobson 1995.) The possibility that the Roswell Incident involved a genuine cover story must be considered against this backdrop of cold war fears and secret projects.

On 10 July, two days after Ramey announced that the wreckage was the remains of a weather balloon and a radar reflector, a related article appeared in the *Alamogordo News*. Major Wilbur D. Pritchard, a Watson Laboratories project officer stationed at Alamogordo Army Air Field, was quoted in the article as saying that the balloon flights involving radar reflectors were for "training and experimental purposes." The article went on to say that the flights were conducted "with the hope of perfecting radar equipment to greater range."

Though not completely false, those statements fell short of the truth. And because Air Force historians found evidence that Pritchard was one of the very few people on the base privy to Mogul, the Air Force report on Roswell (McAndrew 1995:11) concludes: "This [newspaper] article appeared to have been an attempt to deflect attention from the top secret Mogul project by . . . offering misleading information. If there was a cover story involved in this incident, it is this article, not the actions or statements of Ramey." Nor was the article intended as a cover-up to hide the discovery of an alien spaceship. Investigators found no evidence "that indicated any [such] 'cover-up' by the USAF" (Weaver 1995:8).

From an analytical perspective the newspaper article of 10 July 1947 marks the end of the rather pedestrian events that appear to form the historical core of the Roswell Incident. Except for a few obscure references, this incident was never again mentioned in the UFO literature until its transfiguration into a myth began 33 years later.

GENESIS OF THE MYTH

An important aspect of the development of the Roswell myth is its cultural context, a theme that is discussed later. For present purposes it is sufficient to note that, over time, the meaning of the terms "flying saucer," "flying disk," and "UFO" changed as evidenced by polls (Gallup 1972:666; Kendrick 1992:346). In 1947 few people linked these terms to extraterrestrial visitations, whereas by 1992 a majority of Americans considered the terms to be synonyms for "alien spaceship." The gradual change in the meaning of these terms was paralleled by the creation and growth of a UFO community—individuals linked by a common espousal of the extraterrestrial hypothesis as an explanation for some of the thousands of UFO sightings reported over the years. It is beyond the scope of this analysis to describe the history of the UFO movement, which has been ably presented elsewhere (Jacobs 1975; Peebles 1994), but it is relevant to describe the evolution of "crashed-saucer stories."

Generically, the Roswell myth is a crashed-saucer story. A number of such tales surfaced between 1947 and 1980, when the first transfigured version of the Roswell Incident appeared. But only the story of the Roswell Incident developed all the elements needed to become a myth, including a large constituency of true believers. To understand both the timing and the content of the Roswell myth, it is instructive to examine the history of such stories.

According to Peebles (1994:47–50), the first crashed-saucer story to become the focus of widespread media attention was a tongue-in-cheek article written in 1948 by the editor of the local newspaper in Aztec, New Mexico, who stated that a saucer had crashed near the outskirts of town. The joke got out of hand, and the story about "little green men from Venus" was reported in more than 100 newspapers. It was, however, rejected as an obvious hoax by the nascent UFO community.

In 1950, perhaps prompted by the Aztec story, George Koehler of Denver radio station KMYR claimed to have seen alien bodies and the remains of two saucers that crashed near the southwestern border of Colorado. Koehler followed the Aztec story line by describing the aliens as 3-foot-tall humanoids from Venus, and he added the detail that their spaceships were powered by magnetism. Koehler subsequently admitted that he was joking, but not before his tale had inspired an imitator—one Silas M. Newton, self-styled Texas oil millionaire.

At a gathering of students at the University of Denver in March 1950, Koehler introduced Newton as a lecturer on flying saucers. In his talk, Newton described the experience of a scientist-friend, Dr. Gee, who had been asked by the military to examine three crashed saucers and 16 alien bodies. Journalist Frank Scully heard Newton's lecture and decided to write a book (Scully 1950) based on the revelations of Newton and Gee.

The book pointed to a government conspiracy to withhold evidence of extraterrestrial visitations, and it echoed some details of the previous stories: one of the three saucers had crashed near Aztec; the aliens were humanoids about 3 feet (1 m) tall, probably from Venus; and their spaceships were powered by magnetic lines of force. Scully's book, however, added three new elements: the metal of alien spaceships was much harder than anything known on Earth; alien orthography printed on booklets found in the wreckage was a pictorial-type script; and the reason that government officials denied they had evidence of extraterrestrial visitations was to prevent panic—a view that had been suggested earlier by Donald Keyhoe, an emerging leader of the UFO community. Keyhoe appears to have found the crashed-saucer stories unconvincing, but he believed that officials were not revealing all they knew about flying saucers because they feared the kind of panic that had followed Orson Welles's "War of the Worlds" broadcast in 1938 (Jacobs 1975:57).

Scully's book was widely reviewed and became a best-seller. The reviews were not uniformly favorable. *Time* (25 September 1950:75–76), for example, noted that "measured for scientific accuracy, Scully's science ranks below the comic books." The book's explanation of the magnetic propulsion used by the aliens was a special target of ridicule by scientists. Two years later, a journalist investigated the assertions in Scully's book. His report (Cahn 1952) showed conclusively that the book was based on a hoax. At this remove it is impossible to quantify the degree to which Scully's book had been accepted by the UFO community before it was exposed as a hoax. With the benefit of hindsight, one member of this community (Clark 1991:94) avers that "it generated little enthusiasm among the more sober ufologists." On the other hand, UFO historian Jacobs (1975:59) states that the book "had a large impact." Most commentators agree, however, that the exposure of the book as a hoax created within the UFO community a strong and long-lasting bias against crashed-saucer stories. Indeed, the UFO literature indicates that after the Scully debacle in 1952, crashed-saucer stories did not receive widespread consideration in UFO circles until the mid-1970s.

In those intervening two decades, spaceships launched from Earth probed the solar system. The idea that Venus was the home of humanlike aliens became as untenable as the notion, derided by scientists, that alien spaceships were powered by "magnetic lines of force." As elements of crashed-saucer stories, these ideas were finished, but as will be seen, other more scientifically neutral details that appeared in the prototypical Aztec story and in Koehler's and Scully's tales would be retained in crashed-saucer stories when they were revived.

With the passage of time the UFO community's bias against crashed-saucer stories waned. Also, during the 1960s and 1970s various events colluded to produce within the larger society a dramatic erosion of the credibility of government officials, giving new life to the old claim by ufologists that government officials conspired to withhold evidence validating the extraterrestrial hypothesis. The putative existence of such a conspiracy is a precondition for the credibility of a crashed-saucer story, because it provides almost the only plausible way for ufologists to explain the absence of saucer wreckage that would otherwise support their assertions that a crash had actually occurred. (Other explanations have been tried, however. Clark [1991:98] describes a report in which witnesses stated that before the wreckage of a saucer they had seen could be recovered, it was destroyed by other alien spaceships.)

With the Scully hoax a distant memory, the widespread lack of confidence in government provided a favorable context for the revival and acceptance of crashed-saucer stories. According to Peebles (1994:243), "a major figure in this acceptance was Leonard H. Stringfield," who in publications and lectures in 1977–1979 described a number of cases in which alien bodies and saucer wreckage were retrieved by the military. Stringfield also indicated that Scully's book was not a hoax but rather that it had been falsely discredited as part of a government cover-up of the recovery of crashed saucers. Stringfield's publications were favorably reviewed in UFO journals, and one editor (Creighton 1979) endorsed the idea that Scully was the victim of a smear campaign. Apart from proving that the UFO community was ready to reconsider crashed-saucer stories, Stringfield's most important contribution to the genre was the idea that such stories are unfalsifiable (i.e., if not discredited they are true, and if discredited they are also true, because discrediting is part of a government cover-up of the truth). As will be seen, the feature of unfalsifiability is one of the factors involved in the persistence of the Roswell myth.

By the end of the 1970s the stage had thus been set for a revival of the Roswell story. The initial version of the story was constructed by linking the historical Roswell Incident with two flying saucer reports that were formerly thought to be unrelated. First was the report by Mr. and Mrs. Wilmot of Roswell, who observed a saucerlike object passing over the town on the evening of 2 July 1947. The Wilmots did not report this sighting immediately but decided to do so on 8 July (indeed, their report appeared in the *Roswell Daily Record* of that date as part of the same story that carried the Air Force's announcement that a flying disk had been recovered). Second was a report by L. W. Maltais, who claimed that in about 1950 a close friend, soil conservation engineer Grady L. Barnett, had told of seeing small alien bodies and a crashed saucer while on a field trip in New Mexico several years earlier. Some nearby archaeologists had also observed the wreckage, but the military soon arrived and told Barnett and the other witnesses to leave and to say nothing about what they had seen. Barnett died in 1969, but Maltais kept his secret until 1978, when he revealed it to ufologist Stanton T. Friedman (Friedman and Berliner 1992b:4).

The catalyst that allowed Friedman to connect these two UFO reports to the historical Roswell Incident was Jesse A. Marcel, the former base intelligence officer at Roswell Army Air Field whose active duty in the Air Force ended in 1950. By the late 1970s, when he was first interviewed by Friedman and others, Marcel had apparently become interested in UFOs, for in telling his story to a *National Enquirer* reporter in 1979, he stated, "There's some credence in this UFO business. I believe in it" (Pratt 1994:122–124). He went on to say that the wreckage he had found at the Brazel ranch "was nothing that came from earth." To support that contention, he stated that when he held "a cigarette lighter to some of this stuff . . . it didn't burn" and that some small pieces would "not bend or break." He also noted that some material was imprinted with pictorial symbols he described as "hieroglyphics." Also, Marcel reportedly told Friedman and ufologist William L. Moore that thin metallic sheets of the debris were so hard that they could not be dented with a sledgehammer (Berlitz and Moore 1980:66).

After researching Marcel's story together with various aspects of the two UFO reports and the documentation on the historical Roswell Incident, Friedman and Moore enlisted the help of well-known occult writer Charles Berlitz to produce the book in which the first transfigured version of the Roswell Incident appears. (Friedman was apparently retained by Moore only as an investigator; Berlitz and Moore wrote the book.) Much of the narrative is based on informants' statements. Brazel had died in the 1960s, but Friedman and Moore located and interviewed a number of other people, including some of Brazel's children.

Berlitz and Moore's version of the Roswell affair is constructed from elements that can be placed in five categories: documented events of the historical Roswell Incident (which, for analytical purposes, are labeled "H" in the summary that follows); distorted versions of these historical events (labeled "HD"); ideas that appear in previous crashed-saucer stories (labeled "P"); beliefs that, according to Peebles (1994:52, 194, 213), were already common currency within the UFO community before 1979 (labeled "B"); and new ideas specific to this first version of the myth (labeled V-1). I will designate the following story, abstracted from Berlitz and Moore (1980), as Version 1. Quotation marks within the story indicate phrases used by Berlitz and Moore.

VERSION 1 (1980)

In the spring and early summer of 1947, saucer-shaped alien spaceships, intent on monitoring the scientific progress of humans, were drawn to the sites of atomic and rocket research near Alamogordo, New Mexico (B). On the evening of 2 July, one of these flying saucers swooped low over the town of Roswell and shortly thereafter was struck by lightning, causing parts of the craft to fall on the ranch operated by William Brazel (V-1). The stricken spaceship remained in the air and traveled more than 100 miles (160 km) before crashing in an area of New Mexico called the Plains of San Agustin (V-1). The abruptly terminated flight was observed on radar at the nearby White Sands Missile Test Range, where it was interpreted as a conventional airplane crash (V-1). A search for the crash site was ordered for the following day at first light (V-1). In the morning of that day, however, before military personnel could reach the site, Grady Barnett and a few archaeologists who were working in the area found the crashed saucer and alien bodies (V-1). The extraterrestrials were humanoids about 4 feet (1.2 m) tall (P). The military soon arrived, expecting to find a crashed airplane, but realizing it was an alien spaceship, they ejected the witnesses, with an admonition to remain silent about what they had seen (V-1). The military collected the wreckage and bodies and expunged all traces of the crash (V-1).

On that same day (3 July), Brazel found the wreckage that had been ripped from the spaceship by the lightning strike (HD). On 5 July he visited Corona, where he heard stories about sightings of flying saucers in the area, and he speculated that the wreckage he had found on the ranch might be from such a craft (H). The following day (Sunday, 6 July), he went to Roswell to report his discovery to Sheriff George Wilcox (HD). Wilcox notified authorities at Roswell Army Air Field, and the base intelligence officer, Major Jesse Marcel, accompanied by another officer, responded by visiting the ranch with Brazel to collect the wreckage (H). This consisted of a parchmentlike material and sticklike beams, some of which were imprinted with purplish symbols (H). The symbols were an alien pictorial form of writing, or hieroglyphics (P). Some of the lightweight metallic sheets of the material were much harder than any known terrestrial metal (P). Indeed, they could not be dented with a sledgehammer (V-1).

Marcel returned to the base with the wreckage and reported to his superiors that it could not be identified (H). Either as a result of lax security or as a ruse to divert attention away from the San Agustin crash site, the base public relations officer issued a press release about the wreckage Brazel had found (HD). The release, which appeared on 8 July, announced the discovery of the remains of a flying disk that had been sent on to higher headquarters (H). This announcement attracted worldwide attention, but within hours it was repudiated by General Roger Ramey, who commanded the Eighth Army Air Force District (H). Ramey stated in a radio broadcast that the wreckage was merely that of a "downed weather balloon" (HD).

This cover story, designed to cloak the recovery of an alien spaceship, was accepted by the media and the public (HD). The cover story points to a calculated government policy to deny the reality behind UFO reports (B). This policy is due partly to the fear that panic would follow any disclosure about alien visitations (P) and partly to national security issues—that is, the desire by the military to keep secret the advanced scientific knowledge it has gleaned from the spaceship wreckage and the bodies, knowledge that could provide "the ultimate secret weapon" (V-1).

Seven years elapsed before Version 2 of the myth appeared, and during that period, certain events occurred that influenced its form. In the larger society, public confidence in the truthfulness of government authorities continued to erode because of media disclosures of attempts by officials to hide some of their activities—as in the Iran-Contra affair, which began to receive public attention in May 1987. Within the UFO community, Berlitz and Moore's book on Roswell won adherents for the view that the Roswell Incident involved a government conspiracy to hide the recovery of an alien spaceship. Until 1987, however, evidence that might support this conspiracy theory was lacking. That year, Friedman, Moore, and television producer Jaime H. Shandera released a document describing Operation Majestic 12, or MJ-12. This document allegedly was a 1952 government report that had been prepared to brief President-elect Dwight Eisenhower on UFOs.

According to Moore, an anonymous donor had sent the MJ-12 report to Shandera in 1984. Moore further maintained that in 1985 he and Shandera had found in the National Archives another document, the so-called Cutler Memo, which seemingly validated the MJ-12 report (Nickell and Fischer 1991:120). Given that Moore avowedly had had these documents for several years, it might be suspected that the timing of the press release on 29 May 1987, announcing the existence of the MJ-12 report, had something to do with the denigration of officialdom then raging in the press because of the Iran-Contra hearings. The MJ-12 report's implication of yet another government conspiracy, much older than Iran-

Contra, was perhaps responsible for the wide coverage given the MJ-12 press release. Coverage appeared in the *New York Times,* the *Washington Post,* and a number of other news outlets that, according to ufologist Clark (1988:42), were "not ordinarily given to respectful treatment of . . . UFO claims."

Among other things, the MJ-12 report indicated that the military had retrieved a crashed saucer near Roswell in 1947. But it presented a picture of the transfigured Roswell Incident that is sufficiently different from that in Berlitz and Moore (1980) to warrant considering it a new version of the myth. Of course, it also contains ideas expressed in Version 1 and in earlier crashed-saucer stories. I will designate the following story, derived from the MJ-12 report, as Version 2. The elements are labeled as before, except that new ideas specific to this version are labeled "V-2." Quotations are from the MJ-12 report as reproduced in Hall (1991:107).

VERSION 2 (1988)

On or about 2 July 1947, a flying saucer malfunctioned and exploded as it flew over a remote region of New Mexico approximately 75 miles (120 km) northwest of Roswell Army Air Field, scattering wreckage on the land of a local rancher (V-2). Wreckage of the saucer was subsequently found by the rancher, who reported his discovery to military authorities (HD). On 7 July the military began a secret operation to recover the wreckage for scientific study (HD). During the course of this operation, a wider search via aerial reconnaissance revealed four alien bodies about 2 miles (3 km) east of the wreckage site (V-2). These were the bodies of "small, human-like beings" (P) that had ejected from the craft shortly before it exploded (V-2). The bodies were badly decomposed because of exposure and the actions of predators during the period of about a week that had elapsed before their discovery, but they were identifiable as nonhuman extraterrestrials (V-2). A special scientific team removed the bodies, and the wreckage was sent to "several different locations" (V-2).

Absent from the debris was any material recognizable as part of a terrestrial aircraft, and the propulsion unit was destroyed by the explosion (V-2). The wreckage did, however, provide examples of a form of alien writing (P). The nature of the wreckage suggested that the saucer was "a short range reconnaissance craft" (V-2). Secrecy was maintained partly to preserve national security (V-1) and partly to "avoid a public panic at all costs" (P). Civilian and military witnesses were debriefed, and the media were given a cover story that the retrieved object was a "weather research balloon" (HD).

Four years after the MJ-12 report surfaced, another version of the Roswell myth appeared in a book by two ufologists, Kevin D. Randle and

Donald K. Schmitt (1991). In the intervening years, skeptics had challenged the authenticity of MJ-12 documents (e.g., Klass 1988), but Friedman, Moore, and other leading members of the UFO community had vigorously defended the validity of the documents. Toward the end of that period, however, some individuals within the UFO community had also begun to doubt. Randle and Schmitt (1991:299) alluded to those misgivings, stating: "In the last few months [prior to the book's publication] the authenticity of the MJ-12 has been seriously questioned." They also declared that their book was "the result of an extensive and independent investigation" and that they had "purposefully refrained from using any of the existing literature" in reconstructing the events at Roswell (1991:37). More specifically, they did not cite the MJ-12 report as a source. Nevertheless, the scenario in their book is essentially a fleshed-out version of that in MJ-12. According to the authors, their scenario is based not on MJ-12 but largely on the reports of witnesses whom they interviewed in the course of their research. Their depiction of the transfigured Roswell Incident, which follows, is so close to Version 2 that it seems appropriate to call it Version 2-A, but for consistency I will use the designation Version 3. This version also includes many elements from Version 1 and previous crashed-saucer stories, which are labeled accordingly.

VERSION 3 (1991)

On the evening of 2 July 1947, a saucerlike alien spaceship swooped low over the town of Roswell (V-1). Shortly thereafter a malfunction caused the craft to touch down briefly on a ranch operated by William Brazel, where it left traces in the form of a blackened circle within which the sand had been turned into glass (V-3). Still malfunctioning after takeoff, the craft struck the ground glancingly. It left behind a gouge in the earth more than 150 feet (46 m) long, as well as material torn from the hull by the impact (V-3), including fragments imprinted with alien symbols or hieroglyphics (P). The damaged craft rose in the air and traveled onward for a few miles before crashing (V-3). The next day, 3 July, Brazel found the debris that had resulted from the craft's glancing contact with the ground (HD). On Sunday, 6 July, Brazel went into Roswell and reported his discovery to Sheriff George Wilcox (HD). Wilcox notified authorities at Roswell Army Air Field, and the base intelligence officer, Major Jesse Marcel, accompanied by another officer, responded by visiting the ranch with Brazel to collect the wreckage (H). The debris they found included lightweight metallic sheets that were much harder than any known terrestrial metal (P).

On 8 July, aerial reconnaissance revealed four alien bodies at a second site located about 2 miles (3 km) southeast of the debris field first found by Brazel

(V-2). At this site, the crashed saucer was jammed up against a ridge (V-3). Before troops on the ground could be directed to the site of the crashed saucer, Grady Barnett and some archaeologists who were working in the area stumbled upon the wreckage and the bodies (V-1). The four bodies had been exposed to the elements and to predators for several days (V-2). They were about 4 feet (1.2 m) tall and humanlike in appearance (P). The military soon arrived and ejected the witnesses, with an admonition to remain silent about what they had seen (V-1). The witnesses were threatened with severe reprisals if they failed to comply (V-3). The military collected the wreckage and bodies and expunged all traces of the crash (V-1). The bodies and some wreckage were taken temporarily to the hospital at Roswell Army Air Field, where a civilian visitor who saw the wreckage was ejected by the military police (V-3).

Partly because of lax security and partly because the commander of the 509th Bomb Group "felt the [local] community should know" of unusual events, an official press release was issued (HD). The release, which appeared on 8 July, announced the recovery of a flying disk that had been sent on to higher headquarters (H). Actually, parts of the wreckage had been sent to several locations for analysis (V-2). On that same day, the military carefully coached Brazel on a cover story to be given to the press (V-3). Thus, the Brazel interview published by the *Roswell Daily Record* on 9 July was a tissue of lies (V-3). The official press release attracted worldwide attention, but within hours it was repudiated by General Roger Ramey, who commanded the Eighth Army Air Force District (H).

Ramey stated in a radio broadcast that the alleged flying disk was merely the remains of a downed weather balloon (HD). The wreckage Ramey displayed to reporters in his office was indeed the remains of a weather balloon that had been substituted for the actual debris found by Brazel—this "fake" wreckage was part of the government's cover story (V-3). The cover story points to a calculated government policy to deny the reality behind UFO reports (B) for reasons of national security (V-1). The initial intent to hide the truth may have been benignly motivated, but the continuation of the cover-up to the present day must be decried, because it has denied us knowledge that would have "profound ramifications on our way of viewing the universe and humanity's place in it" (B).

Only a year elapsed between Version 3 and Version 4, the latter of which appeared in a book by Friedman and writer and UFO buff Don Berliner. During that interval, misgivings about the authenticity of the MJ-12 report and the Cutler Memo became more widespread in the UFO community. In their 1991 book, Randle and Schmitt had distanced themselves from these documents, and in the same month that their book was published, an article appeared that exposed the MJ-12 report and the Cutler Memo as forgeries and named William L. Moore (coauthor of Version 1) as the likely forger (Nickell and Fischer 1991).

Unlike previous attempts by skeptics to debunk MJ-12, this article was the result of an investigation by researchers with credentials in forensic analysis of documents, and it was carried out with the encouragement of the editor of a leading UFO journal. Hence, its findings were accepted by a number of ufologists, including Randle and Schmitt. The belief structure created over the years within the UFO community enabled its members to take the MJ-12 affair in stride. As with the Scully hoax, the MJ-12 forgeries appeared to be merely a part of a government conspiracy to discredit ufology. For example, according to Berlitz and Moore (1980:50), government authorities "encouraged the publication of [Scully's book] *Behind the Flying Saucers* as a subterfuge to discredit the initial [crashed-saucer] stories." The same rationale was proffered by a prominent ufologist (Rodeghier 1991:130) to account for the MJ-12 forgeries: "The intent was to confuse the UFO community, make us look gullible and, most important, to destroy the credibility of the Roswell event."

Nor did the exposure of the MJ-12 forgeries affect the status of Version 3 of the myth. Although Version 3 is a resurrected Version 2 (derived from the now infamous MJ-12 report), Version 3's avowed source was not MJ-12 but rather the reports of informants. Hence, Version 3's credibility within the UFO community remained unchanged. However, some ufologists, notably Friedman, were unconvinced by the core scenario of Versions 2 and 3, which placed Grady Barnett and the archaeologists not on the Plains of San Agustin but more than 100 miles (160 km) away on the ranch operated by Brazel.

The views of these ufologists were reinforced by the statements of a new eyewitness to the events that had occurred on the plains, Gerald Anderson, who came forth with his testimony after viewing a January 1990 television program about crashed saucers. Anderson asserted that when he was six years old, he and some family members were present on the plains with Barnett and the archaeologists. Anderson provided vivid details of the crash scene. Based on his testimony and on elements from previous versions of the myth, Friedman and Berliner (1992a) created the following reconstruction of the July 1947 events in New Mexico, which I will call Version 4.

VERSION 4 (1992)

In the spring and early summer of 1947, saucer-shaped alien spaceships, intent on monitoring the scientific progress of humans, were drawn to the sites of atomic and rocket research near Alamogordo, New Mexico (B). On the evening of 2 July a malfunction caused one of these craft to touch down briefly about 75 miles (120 km) from the town of Roswell on a ranch operated by William Brazel, where it left traces in the form of a blackened circle within which the sand had been turned into glass (V-3). Still malfunctioning after takeoff, the craft exploded, scattering wreckage on the ranchland below (V-2), including fragments imprinted with alien symbols or hieroglyphics (P). The next day, Brazel found part of the wreckage (HD). On Sunday, 6 July, he went into Roswell and reported his discovery to Sheriff George Wilcox (HD). Wilcox notified authorities at the Roswell Army Air Field, and the base intelligence officer, Major Jesse Marcel, accompanied by another officer, responded by visiting the ranch with Brazel to collect the wreckage (H). The debris they found included lightweight metallic sheets harder than any known terrestrial metal (P).

On 8 July, aerial reconnaissance revealed four alien bodies encased in "escape capsules" at a second site, about 2 miles (3 km) from the debris field first found by Brazel (V-2). About 1 mile (1.6 km) from the bodies, the main portion of the crushed saucer was found (V-4). The bodies were humanlike but "quite small by human standards" (P). The military cordoned the area with troops, collected the wreckage and bodies, and expunged all traces of the crash (V-1). The bodies and some wreckage were taken temporarily to the hospital at Roswell Army Air Field, where a civilian visitor who saw the wreckage was ejected by the military police (V-3). He was threatened with severe reprisals by a redheaded colonel if he revealed what he had seen (V-4).

"At about the same time" these events were transpiring on the Brazel ranch, the site of a second crashed saucer was discovered 150 miles (240 km) away (V-4). Grady Barnett and some archaeologists who were working in the area stumbled upon this crashed saucer on the Plains of San Agustin (V-1), where they were joined by Gerald Anderson and members of his family (V-4). They observed the bodies of three dead aliens and one alien that appeared to be alive (V-4). These aliens, like those found in the Roswell crash, were small and humanlike (P). The military soon arrived and ejected the witnesses, with an admonition to remain silent about what they had seen (V-1). They were threatened with severe reprisals by the military (V-3), including threats by a black sergeant and a redheaded captain, if they failed to comply (V-4). The military collected the wreckage and bodies and expunged all traces of the crash (V-1).

Because of lax security, an official press release was issued (HD). The release, which appeared on 8 July, announced the recovery of a flying disk that had been sent on to higher headquarters (H). Actually, the wreckage and the bodies from the crash site near Roswell and from the second crash site on the Plains of San Agustin (V-4) had been sent to several locations for analysis (V-2). On that same day, the military carefully coached Brazel on a cover story to be given to the press (V-3). Thus the Brazel interview published on 9 July was a tissue of lies (V-3). The official press release attracted worldwide attention, but within hours it was repudiated by General Roger Ramey, who commanded the Eighth Army Air Force District (H).

Ramey indicated in a radio broadcast that the alleged flying disk was merely the remains of a radar reflector and weather balloon (H). The wreckage Ramey displayed in his office was indeed the remains of a radar reflector that had been substituted for the actual debris found by Brazel, and this "fake" wreckage was part of the government's cover story (V-3). The cover story points to a calculated government policy to deny the reality behind UFO reports (B) for reasons of national security (V-1) and because of concern that "the public might panic" (P). The initial intent to hide the truth may have been benignly motivated, but continuation of the cover-up to the present day must be decried because it has denied us knowledge "of incalculable proportions," knowledge of "perhaps the most important event in the last thousand years" (B).

Almost two years elapsed before the next version of the myth appeared in a new book by Randle and Schmitt (1994), and this version was shaped largely by events that occurred within the UFO community during that interval. The conflicting scenarios in Versions 3 and 4 caused a schism in the ranks of ufologists and a split between two prominent UFO societies. According to Peebles (1994:271), "The differing versions of the Roswell Incident pitted Moore vs. Randle/Schmitt vs. Friedman/Berliner, and CUFOS [Center for UFO Studies] vs. MUFON [Mutual UFO Network]." Several conferences were held to resolve the controversy, and in 1992, at a solemn conclave jointly sponsored by CUFOS and FUFOR (Fund for UFO Research), the evidence for Versions 3 and 4 was reexamined.

The key to Friedman and Berliner's Version 4 was the testimony of Maltais (1991) and Anderson that placed Barnett and some archaeologists on the Plains of San Agustin. At the 1992 conference, Randle, Schmitt, and Carey (1992:19) argued cogently that Anderson's tale was "no more than a fabrication." These authors also indicated that they had evidence that Barnett never claimed (as Maltais had alleged) to have seen a crashed saucer. Insofar as something resembling a consensus resulted from this conference, it appears that Version 3 triumphed over Version 4. For example, the conference moderator concluded that Anderson's story presented "warning signs of a hoax" and that evidence for the Barnett story was "extremely soft" (Swords 1992:46, 47).

Nevertheless, despite a general trend of commentary favoring Randle and Schmitt, their Version 3 also came under fire. One ufologist (Whiting 1992:35) noted that "the basic weakness in the Randle-Schmitt argument is that it fails to provide a credible reason for moving . . . Barnett 150 miles [240 km] to the east," where, according to Version 3, Barnett and some archaeologists had stumbled upon the crashed saucer near Roswell.

Perhaps sensing that the tide of opinion was running in their favor, in their next book Randle and Schmitt (1994) produced Version 5 of the Roswell myth. In this version Barnett does not appear, thus eliminating the need to explain why he was near Roswell rather than on the Plains of San Agustin. However, new witnesses had come forth (or had been ferreted out by Randle and Schmitt), and their testimony indicated that an archaeological team did stumble upon the crashed saucer near Roswell. This, of course, was not the archaeological team of the Barnett-Anderson story (which had been largely discredited in the eyes of some ufologists) but rather a different group of archaeologists. Indeed, in their book Randle and Schmitt (1994:191) declare that, for lack of evidence, "Barnett's story and, in fact, the Plains [of San Agustin] scenario must be discarded." It was also necessary for them to change some details, such as the date of the crash and the shape of the alien spaceship, to conform to the testimony of their new witnesses. Despite these changes the core scenario of Version 5, which follows, is essentially a replay of Versions 2 and 3.

VERSION 5 (1994)

In the spring and summer of 1947, alien spaceships, intent on monitoring the scientific progress of humans, were drawn to the site of atomic and rocket research near Alamogordo, New Mexico (B). On 1 July, officials at White Sands Proving Ground began tracking these objects (V-1), which were recognized as alien spaceships by their high-speed maneuvers that were beyond the capability of any terrestrial airplane (B). And on 2 July, one of these craft, which appeared as "an oval object," swooped low over the town of Roswell (V-1).

On 4 July (V-5), one of these spaceships malfunctioned, causing the craft to touch down briefly on the ranch operated by William Brazel, where it left traces in the form of a blackened circle within which the sand had been turned into glass (V-3). Still malfunctioning after takeoff, the craft struck the ground glancingly. It left behind a gouge in the earth 500 feet (150 m) long, as well as material torn from the hull by the impact (V-3), including fragments imprinted with alien symbols or hieroglyphics (P). The stricken craft rose in the air and traveled onward for a while before crashing into the base of a cliff at a site about 35 miles (56 km) north of Roswell (V-5).

Radar operators at White Sands were monitoring the spaceship on the evening of 4 July (V-5). When it suddenly disappeared from the screen, they concluded it had crashed, and a search for the downed craft was ordered at first light (V-1).

The next morning, before the troops could arrive, some civilians, including a team of archaeologists who were working in the area, stumbled upon the crash site (V-1). The remains of the alien spaceship indicated that it was "narrow with bat-like wings" (V-5). Four alien bodies were found (V-2), and according to some witnesses, one alien was still alive (V-4). The aliens were humanlike beings about 4 feet (1.2 m) tall (P).

One of the archaeologists phoned Sheriff George Wilcox to report the crash (V-5). Troops soon arrived and ejected the witnesses, with an admonition to remain silent about what they had seen (V-1). The witnesses were threatened with severe reprisals if they failed to comply (V-3), including death threats (V-5). The military collected the wreckage and bodies and expunged all traces of the crash at that site (V-1). The bodies and some wreckage were taken temporarily to the hospital at Roswell Army Air Field, where a civilian witness was ejected by military police (V-3) and told not to reveal what he had seen (V-4). He was threatened with reprisals by a black sergeant and a redheaded captain if he failed to comply (V-5).

On that same day (5 July), Brazel found debris resulting from the craft's glancing contact with the ground (HD). On Sunday, 6 July, he went into town and reported his discovery to Sheriff Wilcox (HD). Wilcox notified authorities at Roswell Army Air Field that a second site with wreckage had been found (V-5), and the base intelligence officer, Major Jesse Marcel, accompanied by another officer, responded by visiting the ranch with Brazel to collect the wreckage (H). The debris they found included lightweight metallic sheets that were much harder than any terrestrial metal (P). Aerial surveys were made (V-2), and troops collected the wreckage and expunged all traces of the crash (V-1).

On 8 July an official press release was issued that announced the recovery of a flying disk that had been sent on to higher headquarters for analysis (H). Actually, parts of the wreckage had been sent to various locations for analysis (V-2). On that same day, the military carefully coached Brazel on a cover story to be given to the press (V-3). Thus the interview published by the *Roswell Daily Record* on 9 July was a tissue of lies (V-3). The official press release attracted worldwide attention, but within hours it was repudiated by General Roger Ramey, who commanded the Eighth Army Air Force District (H).

Ramey stated in a radio broadcast that the alleged flying disk was merely the remains of a downed weather balloon (HD). The wreckage Ramey displayed was indeed the remains of a weather balloon that had been substituted for the actual debris found by Brazel, and this "fake" wreckage was part of the government's cover story (V-3). This cover story points to a calculated government policy to deny the reality behind UFO reports (B).

Like Version 5, Version 6 of the Roswell myth also appeared in 1994—in a publication by Karl T. Pflock (1994b), writer and UFO researcher. His work was sponsored in part by FUFOR and, according to Pflock, was based on research he carried out over a 21-month period during which time he independently discovered that Project Mogul was linked to the Roswell Incident. The last 5 months of Pflock's research overlapped the Air Force's investigation of the Roswell Incident, and Pflock had learned that Project Mogul was an important focus of the government researchers, a fact that may have influenced the scenario of the transfigured Roswell Incident that appears in his report and that I have called Version 6.

To place Version 6 in context, it is necessary to sketch the history of the Mogul-Roswell connection. In Version 1, Berlitz and Moore (1980: 38) were the first to consider—and reject—the possibility that balloons launched from Alamogordo by New York University's Balloon Group may have been responsible for the wreckage found on the ranch operated by Brazel. These authors were, however, unaware that the unclassified work of the Balloon Group was a part of the highly classified Project Mogul. This link was first uncovered in 1990 by UFO researcher Robert G. Todd, who disseminated his finding in letters to ufologists. Later, in Version 5, Randle and Schmitt (1994:154) noted that balloons launched from Alamogordo in July 1947 by New York University personnel were part of the secret Project Mogul. But like Berlitz and Moore, they rejected the possibility that Mogul balloons could have been the source of the kind of debris found by Brazel.

Pflock (1994b:113), on the other hand, reached a different conclusion about the nature of the debris: "the great majority if not all," he declared, "was the wreckage of a huge [Mogul] balloon and instrumentation array launched from Alamogordo." In addition to this conclusion, Pflock's research led him to reject completely the MJ-12 report and the testimony of some of the key witnesses on which Berlitz and Moore, and Friedman and Berliner, had based their versions of the Roswell Incident (thus eliminating Versions 1 and 4). Pflock also found evidential problems with what he calls the "conventional wisdom" scenario (Version 3) and the "revisionist" account (Version 5). Indeed, much of Pflock's report is concerned with showing in detail the unreliability of the evidence that Randle and Schmitt cite for Versions 3 and 5. In the remainder of his report, Pflock presents his own scenario. Version 6 of the Roswell myth, which follows, is derived from that scenario.

VERSION 6 (1994)

During the first week of July 1947, a descending Mogul balloon and the attached instrument array struck the ground near Roswell on the Foster ranch operated by William Brazel (HD). "At about the same time," an alien spaceship crashed either because it malfunctioned or because it had a catastrophic encounter with the Mogul balloon (in which case, material torn from the hull of the spaceship was mixed with the Mogul wreckage) (V-6). In any event, the main portion of the spacecraft, along with its crew, struck the ground at a site removed from the site of the debris on the Foster ranch (V-6).

Sometime before 5 July, Brazel found the scattered wreckage, and on 7 July he went into Roswell and reported his discovery to Sheriff George Wilcox (H). Wilcox notified authorities at the Roswell Army Air Field, and the base intelligence officer, Major Jesse Marcel, accompanied by another officer, responded by visiting the ranch with Brazel to collect the wreckage (H). The debris they found consisted of parchmentlike material and sticklike beams, some of which were imprinted with purplish symbols (H). If some lightweight metallic sheets torn from the spacecraft were mixed in with the Mogul debris (V-6), they exhibited a hardness greater than that of any terrestrial metal (P). Nevertheless, all the wreckage at the "debris field" on the Foster ranch was the remains of a Mogul balloon, or "a great majority of it" was Mogul debris (V-6).

Marcel returned to the base with the wreckage and reported to his superiors that it could not be identified (H). Colonel William Blanchard, Marcel's commanding officer, reported the discovery of the unidentified wreckage to his superiors at Strategic Air Command (SAC), but before his superiors could respond, he learned that the main body of the spaceship and the bodies of three of its crew had been found (V-6). The crashed spaceship and bodies were found either as the result of a wider search made when collecting the wreckage scattered on the Foster ranch (V-2) or as a completely independent accidental discovery (V-6).

The military secured the area by placing a cordon of troops around the debris field on the Foster ranch, and the site was cleared of wreckage (V-1). The small, humanoid alien bodies (P) and some of the wreckage were temporarily taken to the Roswell Army Air Field hospital, where a civilian witness was ejected by military police (V-3) and told not to reveal what he had seen (V-4). He was threatened with reprisals by a black sergeant and a redheaded captain if he failed to comply (V-5). All three bodies "showed signs of exposure to the elements and the ravages of scavengers" (V-2). The wreckage and the bodies were flown to other locations for analysis (V-2).

"In a mistake born of hubris," Blanchard ordered the base publicity officer to issue a press release about the wreckage found by Brazel (HD). The release, which appeared on 8 July, announced the recovery of the remains of a flying disk that had been sent on to higher headquarters (H). Subsequent to the release, Blanchard notified authorities at SAC that a crashed alien spaceship and alien bodies had been discovered (V-6). Authorities at SAC put out a cover story (V-6)—that is, General Roger Ramey repudiated the official press release by announcing in a radio broadcast that the wreckage of the alleged flying disk was merely the remains of a downed weather balloon (HD). "Coincidentally or by design this tied in well with the Mogul cover-up" (V-6).

The Mogul group, fearing that the security of their top secret project might be compromised, had been "galvanized into action by Blanchard's press release" (V-6). Authorities at Alamogordo "staged a demonstration to divert attention from [the Mogul debris found near] Roswell" (H). This demonstration was reported in the *Alamogordo News* on 10 July (H). The dual cover stories (V-6) represent "excesses committed in the name of national security" (V-1), and the government's efforts, which continue to the present day, to keep hidden the true events at Roswell deny us "proof at last that we are not alone in the universe" (B).

Shortly after it appeared, Pflock's report (which presents Version 6 of the Roswell myth) was favorably reviewed in at least one UFO journal (Stacy 1994). But the general response by members of the UFO community apparently was quite negative. For example, one commentator (Davids 1995:38) described Pflock as "ufology's junior Phil Klass–wannabee," thus linking him to the bête noir of true believers (Phillip Klass is the author of several books and many articles debunking the claims of ufologists). Another commentator (Komarek 1994:1) suggested that Pflock's report encouraged skeptics by providing established debunkers with spurious research, and he went on to castigate Pflock, who in previous writings had identified himself as a member of the UFO community, as a debunker in disguise.

The Air Force report on Roswell appeared only a few months after Pflock's report and was uniformly condemned and rejected by the UFO community, as evidenced not only by letters to UFO journals but also in long, analytical articles published in the same journals (e.g., Davids 1994; Rodeghier and Chesney 1994) and in special reports (e.g., Friedman 1994; Randle 1995a). Many of the ufologists' objections to various aspects of the Air Force report apply with equal force to significant portions of Pflock's report. Hence, it seems reasonable to assume that Version 6 of the Roswell myth has been rejected by true believers, for now at least. Therefore, the myth with which I began this analysis, and that I believe to be currently accepted by most members of the UFO community, is a generic form of the core scenario found in Versions 2, 3, and 5, with the addition of the Air Force findings (which are themselves now part of the myth).

In thus tracing the evolution of the Roswell myth from its beginnings, I have attempted to set the stage for analysis. My approach depends on examining the six versions as a developmental sequence in which the considerable differences between the core scenarios of each version—which appear at first glance to confuse and obstruct analysis—actually provide essential clues that reveal the true nature of these tales.

CHAPTER TWO

ANALYSIS OF THE ROSWELL MYTH

A TRADITIONAL FOLK MOTIF CLOTHED IN MODERN GARB

CHARLES A. ZIEGLER

nvestigators who have attempted to deal with the UFO phenomenon have often noted that the only "things" available for analysis are reports and narratives *about* UFOs. Indeed, whatever influence the UFO phenomenon has had on human life over the past half century has been due not to UFOs but to such UFO stories. The stories are thus significant in themselves, quite apart from their epistemological status, and they constitute a worthy focus for analysis. The six transfigured versions of the Roswell Incident thus become data for an analytical approach that is somewhat akin to that of the literary critic, an approach that begins by determining the genre of the work being examined.

Libraries categorize books into two broad literary genres—fiction and nonfiction—simply because their authors identify them as such. For example, Margaret Mitchell's *Gone with the Wind* and Robert Wilcox's 1985 book, *Japan's Secret War,* will be found, respectively, in the fiction and nonfiction sections of libraries, because on the dust jacket of her book Mitchell declares that it is a novel, and Wilcox identifies his book as history. Yet Mitchell's book describes many events generally accepted as historical happenings, whereas Wilcox's book is largely based on events that most historians regard as fictional. Clearly, the categorization of a book by its author can be only the starting point for an analyst bent on understanding the nature of a literary work.

If we turn to the various versions of the transfigured Roswell Incident, we find that they appear in books shelved in the nonfiction section of libraries (except for Version 2, which stems from the MJ-12 document).

Indeed, their authors identify these books as investigative reports or histories of the events surrounding the Roswell Incident, and as evidenced by reviews, commentaries, and readers' letters in UFO journals, they are accepted as such by true believers. Skeptics have also accepted these books as investigative reports or histories but insist that the books are fatally flawed exemplars of their genre or, in some cases, that they are fictionalized accounts masquerading as histories—a purposeful deception designed to appeal to true believers and to general readers with an appetite for sensational literature.

Some skeptics (e.g., Taylor and Bennett 1985) have critiqued the general methodology that ufologists have used in constructing their reports and books, and others (e.g., Schaeffer 1981; Klass 1983, 1986, 1988, 1991) have reviewed some of the claims that ufologists have made in books they have written about the Roswell Incident. Such skeptics provide examples from these books to show that the authors, in structuring their narratives, omit data that is contrary to their argument, quote out of context, fabricate and/or use forged documents as evidence, make assertions without supporting evidence, and introduce information extraneous to their argument simply to sensationalize their text.

Other criticisms by skeptical reviewers are directed at the testimony obtained from informants that appears in the Roswell books. Using illustrative examples, the skeptics maintain that the authors of these books break all the generally accepted rules of investigative reporting and historical research because they misquote witnesses, ignore testimony that contradicts their claims, accept the testimony of witnesses who are preconditioned by the media and/or by the interviewers themselves, accept conflicting testimony of several witnesses on the same topic, accept internally contradictory testimony, cite testimony from anonymous witnesses as the sole evidence for some of their assertions, accept testimony contradicted by physical evidence, and display an overreliance on the background of informants as an indicator of truthfulness. In response, the authors of the Roswell books have published refutations of these allegations (e.g., Friedman 1991), and these refutations appear to have been accepted by most members of the UFO community.

As a result of partisan comments by true believers and skeptics, two views of the various books on Roswell authored by ufologists have emerged. The first is that they are histories that are substantially accurate, although differing in details. The second view is that they are histories debased by poor methodology and hence are unreliable, and to the extent that this debasement is purposeful, they are—in effect—fictionalized histories designed to appeal to a special readership. I believe that neither of these views captures the essential nature of the Roswell stories and that these stories display many of the features that are characteristic of a quite different literary genre: the recorded myth. Before discussing the grounds for reclassifying these stories as versions of a myth, however, it is pertinent to elaborate on the inadequacies of the two reigning views.

If the true believers are correct, the Roswell stories are accurate depictions of past events that meet accepted epistemological standards for investigative reports and are thus reliable histories. But this view is not consistent with the fact that most professional, mainstream historians do not appear to have considered them as reliable histories. The skeptics' view that they are simply flawed or purposefully fictionalized histories also fails to cover all the facts. Notably, this view does not explain why these stories are mythlike in structure and content (as I will later show) and why so many people, not all of whom are members of the UFO community, find them believable. Regarding the latter point, the recent Air Force report debunking these stories about Roswell was rejected not only in commentaries appearing in UFO journals but also in articles by columnists and editorial writers in some newspapers.[1]

A mythlike form and content coupled with relatively widespread credibility are not usually characteristics associated with the core stories found in histories that are considered unreliable because of flawed methodology (and when these characteristics do appear, the stories warrant the same kind of reconsideration I will apply to the Roswell stories). For instance, the previously mentioned book by Wilcox (1985) exemplifies the genre of flawed or unreliable history. Based on his historical research, Wilcox relates the story of a massive Japanese atomic bomb program during World War II that resulted in the successful production and perhaps testing of an atomic bomb before the war's end. Wilcox's book displays many of the methodological failings that skeptics claim to have found in the Roswell books, and his work has been largely discounted by historians, the scholarly community, and the general public. The core story in his book displays no mythlike features nor has it been found credible—the typical fate of flawed histories, but not of flawed histories that are myths.

At this point it is useful to further define "myth" and some related terms such as "folk narrative" and to discuss their status as cultural forms in modern industrialized societies. In the nineteenth century, scholars considered folk narratives to be orally transmitted, traditional tales that in contemporary nonliterate "primitive" societies were a vital part of the culture, whereas in contemporary literate European societies such tales were considered a kind of cultural fossil—a leftover from the preliterate past still preserved in the lower (peasant) stratum of society whose members were still largely illiterate. By the twentieth century, European peasants were mostly literate and Western cultures had seemingly outgrown the habit of creating folk narratives and other forms of folklore (e.g., traditional dances, games, gestures, and so on). Thus, by the 1930s one eminent cultural anthropologist, Ruth Benedict (1931:228), confidently stated that "folklore has not survived as a living trait in modern civilization."

In the ensuing decades, however, research by folklorists and cultural anthropologists demonstrated the falsity of this statement by showing that folklore was alive and well in modern industrialized cultures. By the 1980s, anthropologist Alan Dundes (1980:7) could write: "From this [new] perspective it would be absurd to argue that there is no folklore in the United States and that industrialization stamps out folk groups and folklore . . . for example, the folklore of computers."

Analyzing folklore in a modern Western setting required a reorientation of thinking in some areas, notably in the definition of "folk," and an abandonment of the convention of purely oral transmission as a defining characteristic of folk narratives (as opposed to literary and other forms of transmission made possible by modern technology). "Folk" is now defined as any group of people who share at least one common factor, and according to Dundes (1965:3), "Every group has its own folklore." In elaborating on this theme, Dundes (1980:6) avers: "It does not matter what the linking factor is . . . but what is important is that a group of people formed for whatever reason will have some traditions which it calls its own. . . . [A] member of the group may not know all the other members, but he will probably know the core of traditions belonging to the group, traditions which help the group have a sense of identity."

In other words, in modern Western societies groups may coalesce around a special interest (e.g., UFOs) that becomes the common linking factor. Over time, the interactions of group members create a unique "ideational system" that is based on this shared linking factor—that is, a system consisting of an integrated set of interest-related traditional concepts that constitutes a group subculture embedded within the culture of our larger society. One part of such a subculture usually consists of folk narratives—stories that stem from, and express traditional ideas about, the common linking factor of the group.

In this subcultural context, two types of folk narrative may emerge: those that are presented as fiction (e.g., jokes, cautionary tales, and parables) and are regarded as such by group members and outsiders alike; and those that are presented as fact and avowedly believed to be true by many group members, as evidenced by their letters, commentaries, articles, and books, but are not treated as factual in the annals of the larger culture (e.g., mainstream histories, encyclopedias, and almanacs), ostensibly because they do not conform to the scholarly epistemological standards for assessing historicity that prevail within our society. (It should be noted that the defining criteria for stories of the second type are independent of the objective factuality of the narrative.)

Analysts (see Bascom 1965) generally label folk narratives of the first type as "folktales," whereas those of the second type may be labeled either "legends" or "myths," depending on their content. In this regard, I have previously described myths as folk narratives that deal with transcendental issues such as the relationship between humans and unearthly beings. This characterization of "myth" is somewhat more inclusive than that of classicists who prefer to reserve this term for antique tales involving gods, spirits, and other religious themes, but it is more suitable for analyzing modern folk narratives that arise within our society, because it sidesteps the vexed question of what is and what is not "religious" (a question discussed in Chapter 4).

PARALLELS WITH TRADITIONAL FOLK NARRATIVES

As used in this discussion, the term "myth" refers to a type of folk narrative. I will begin my analysis of the six Roswell stories by assuming that they are versions of a myth—a tale that is not treated as factual in the annals of our society but is avowedly believed to be true by many of its members (the UFO community) and that deals with a transcendental issue (the knowledge that, as intelligent beings, we are not alone in the universe). This assumption allows us to seek parallels with other examples of folk narratives in terms of three elements: the transmission process, the structure of the narrative, and the central motif. To the degree that such parallels can be found, they support the validity of my assumption.

The Transmission Process

In what might be called the classical model of folklore transmission, a traditional tale is orally recounted to listeners who share a group culture that forms the cognitive context within which the tale is understood and appreciated. The storyteller is the active carrier of part of the group's traditions, and the listeners' contribution to the life of the tale is their continuing interest in hearing it told. The tale diffuses sporadically throughout a region when a storyteller moves to another place. New storytellers emerge from listeners in the new locale, and they in turn may also move to another place, and so on. In this way the tale may be eventually transmitted to another group that is culturally distinct from the group in which the tale originated. When that occurs, the tale is altered to fit the culturally preferred pattern of the new group.

The classical model is applicable to nonliterate groups. In partially literate societies, however, a more realistic model is one in which the oral communicative process is occasionally punctuated by literary transmissions. In other words, at some point a story might be written down and disseminated in books read by individuals, some of whom were or become storytellers who continue the chain of oral transmission. This model, in which links of oral transmission are temporarily interrupted by literary transmission, might be called the punctuated transmission model.

In such punctuated transmission, the act of writing the tales tends to change them in ways that differ from the changes they undergo during the oral transmission process. According to anthropologist Alan Dundes (1965:244), "there is a great difference between the conventions of writing and speaking . . . in writing one can see what one is saying and can 'correct' or improve it." Notably, when tales are written down, the process of rationalization—which proceeds but slowly as the stories are told and retold orally—is greatly accelerated. Nevertheless folklorist Francis Utley (1961:200) notes that although "print is a contaminator, a reverser and a freezer of versions . . . it does not necessarily destroy the oral process." Tales subjected to punctuated transmission can thus retain features that are characteristic of purely oral transmission.

The development of the Roswell myth can be best understood in terms of a modern type of the punctuated transmission model just described. I make the assumption that the core scenarios in the ufologists' Roswell books are versions of this myth, and that assumption requires abandoning the notion that these books are investigative reports or histories. The idea that these books were "authored," in the conventional sense of this term, by the people whose names appear on their covers (e.g., Berlitz and Moore, or Randle and Schmitt) can thus be dismissed. Instead, the role of these authors is similar in some ways to that of the folklorists who recorded the published versions of the folktales most of us learned as children. To formulate a realistic transmission model for the development of the Roswell myth, it is useful to examine the morphology of the books in which the various versions of the myth appear.

The core scenario in each of these books is largely based on the testimony of witnesses, and a relatively small portion is derived from archival sources. Significantly, virtually all the elements of a fantastical nature stem from testimony. The books rarely provide verbatim transcriptions of the testimony, but rather the authors tell us in print what they were told verbally by witnesses. Although "testimony" and "witness" are conventional terminology in an investigative report, they are inappropriate in discussing books that fall into what I have assumed to be the correct genre for the Roswell stories—the myth. Hence I will replace the term "testimony" with "personalized legend" and the term "witness" with "traditor," a term coined by von Sydow (1948:201) to designate an active carrier of a group's traditions who can verbally communicate them in an effective manner.

"Personalized legend" refers to a traditor's oral statement in which events that the traditor claims to have experienced are expressed in terms of ideas that are part of the traditional beliefs of the group (the UFO community) or ideas that are consistent with such beliefs. For example, when Major Marcel implied to his listeners that some of the wreckage he saw and handled was imprinted with indecipherable hieroglyphics and that some of the material was harder than any known terrestrial metal, his ideas about the nature of the wreckage were couched in terms of beliefs concerning alien writing and alien artifacts that had been common currency in the UFO community for nearly four decades.

Marcel and other traditors told their tales (usually in a one-on-one context) to a number of listeners, including the several authors of the Roswell books. Television programs about UFOs prompted some traditors to contact the authors, but other traditors responded to announcements in the Roswell books and in UFO journals asking for individuals involved in the Roswell Incident to come forth (e.g., see Friedman and Berliner 1992a:193). Still others, such as Marcel, told their tales to a local circle of UFO buffs and, through the grapevine, came to the attention of the authors. Finally, the authors actively sought out, through referrals from other traditors, individuals within the UFO community who were willing to talk about Roswell.

Some individuals who were not members of the UFO community but were known through documentary sources to have been associated with Roswell (e.g., Charles Moore and Bessie Brazel Schreiber) were also sought out by the authors. In using statements from these individuals, the authors assumed the role of gatekeeper by ensuring that the statements either were made to appear supportive of subcultural beliefs or were repudiated or omitted if found to be "unpleasant," that is, not consonant with such beliefs.

For example, Charles Moore has stated that the authors gave him misleading information. Moore's statements to the authors, couched in terms of that misinformation, thus appeared to support the notion that the balloon explanation of the wreckage found by Brazel was untenable (Moore et al. 1995:7; see also Appendix 2 of this book). And the authors rejected Schreiber's statements that they found "unpleasant," on the grounds that they conflicted with tales told by traditors. In the latter case the terminology of an investigative report was used: "Schreiber's testimony can . . . be shown to be in disagreement with other witnesses' statements" (Moore et al. 1995:9). In other words, the more fantastical elements in the testimony (personalized legend) of other witnesses (traditors) were used to discount statements that were made by individuals outside the UFO community and that did not fit the authors' vision of the Roswell Incident.

To the extent that the authors' gatekeeper role was consciously, even perhaps cynically, adopted, the examples cited above seemingly support the skeptics' view that the Roswell books are not only flawed but also fictionalized histories. However, an alternative view is that the authors' gatekeeper role was a virtually unconscious response on the part of individuals whose perceptions had been preconditioned by a group's subculture. The issue of the motives of those who originate folk narratives has, to a limited extent, been addressed by folklorists, and later in this chapter I review their comments and return to the question of deliberate deception versus culturally preconditioned responses.

The narratives of the traditors are, in effect, mini-legends that were collected and printed by the authors of the Roswell books. To this degree, the authors' role is analogous to that of other collectors of published folklore. But there the similarity ends, for unlike most collectors of folk narratives, the authors of the Roswell books were themselves members of the group subculture of which the collected tales were a part. Also, unlike the tales collected by folklorists, each of which is usually complete in itself, the personalized legends of the Roswell traditors are merely fragments of a larger picture—a picture assembled by the authors of the Roswell books, who selectively edited the personalized legends they collected and who juxtaposed them in their books in a way that conveyed the authors' conception of the Roswell Incident.

The editing performed by these authors went far beyond the polishing and rationalization that is usual when folklore appears in printed form. For example, Marcel's personalized legend (one of the few for which a separate verbatim account is available) includes the following statement about the ground beneath the debris field: "One thing I did notice—nothing actually hit the ground, bounced on the ground. It was something that must have exploded above ground and fell" (Pratt 1994:123). This part of Marcel's tale was accepted by the authors of Versions 1, 2, and 4 but was suppressed by the authors of Versions 3 and 5 in favor of the tales of other traditors who reported seeing a deep gouge hundreds of feet long in the earth beneath the debris field. The latter tales allowed the authors of Versions 3 and 5 to insert their own concept into the myth—that of a spaceship bouncing along the ground, shedding parts of its hull to create the debris field that Brazel found. In essence, unlike the authors of books of collected folklore, the authors of the Roswell books played an active role in creating the version of myth that appears in their books. Indeed, a more realistic term to replace "author" in discussing these books is "literary traditor."

In sum, the transmission model for the development of the Roswell myth is one in which traditors tell and retell their personalized legends to a series of listeners, including some who are literary traditors. The literary traditors collect the tales, edit them, and then—combined with suitable narrative material based on archival sources—these personalized legends are sequentially arranged in printed form in a way that presents the literary traditor's vision of the Roswell Incident. The book resulting from this process is read by individuals, some of whom are inspired to become traditors. Such individuals come forth with their own personalized legends about Roswell (which may repeat, usually in altered form, some portions of the tales of traditors that they have read and/or which may introduce entirely new elements). These personalized legends are recounted orally to listeners, including literary traditors who collect these tales, produce another Roswell book, and so on.

The model just described is a modern type of the punctuated transmission model previously discussed, although as I have indicated, the nature of the literary links in the above model differs in important ways from that of the conventional punctuated transmission model. Nevertheless, the two models are alike in that they both result in tales that retain some characteristic features of purely oral transmission that are found in the classical folk narrative, as I will next illustrate.

Structure of the Narrative

I have assumed that the Roswell books present successive versions of a myth—that is, a type of folk narrative. The various versions can thus be expected to display structural features that characterize the evolution of such tales: conformance with prevailing subcultural concepts, introduction of elements of fantasy, persistence of inventions and transformations, intensification of relations of dominance and subjugation, omissions of the "unpleasant," transposition of an element within a subplot, and rationalization of the plot. These seven features will be discussed sequentially and illustrated with examples.

Conformance with Prevailing Subcultural Concepts

Folk narratives stem from, and are supported by, the ideas and beliefs of the subculture. It would be expected, therefore, that subcultural ideas that remain unchanged will appear and reappear in successive versions of the myth. For example, the concepts labeled "B" and "P" in all six previously summarized versions of the myth represent such unchanging ideas (e.g., the government has conspired to withhold evidence of alien visitations from the public, aliens resemble small humanoids, and the like).

On the other hand, when some subcultural concepts change, we would expect the tale to reflect those changes. Indeed, the continuing credibility of tales that group members avowedly believe to be true (i.e., legends and myths) depends on the tales' remaining consonant with changing subcultural concepts. According to Dundes (1965:220), this phenomenon explains the "almost predictable alteration that takes place when the content of a tale is changed to fit the culturally preferred pattern." For example, such alteration occurred in the variants of the Roswell myth when the subplot of Barnett and the archaeologists stumbling upon the crash site on the Plains of San Agustin (introduced in Version 1) underwent a three-step change: in Version 3, Barnett and the archaeologists stumble upon the crash site on the Foster Ranch; in Version 5, Barnett and the archaeologists are eliminated, but new archaeologists are introduced who stumble upon the crash site "35 miles north of Roswell"; and in Version 6, the entire subplot is eliminated.

The changes in this subplot appear to reflect changes in part of the UFO subculture over the period in which the various versions appeared. More specifically, changes occurred in the entire belief structure about

Roswell that had been erected on this subplot (e.g., see Eberhart 1992). Those changes were engendered partly by the criticisms of skeptics and other outsiders (e.g., Schaeffer 1981; Klass 1986, 1991) and partly by revelations about MJ-12 and Gerald Anderson's story that were uncovered during internecine disputes.

Folklorist Gyula Ortutay (1959:176, 185, 187) has pointed out that the "appearance in the form of variants or [accepted] versions" is characteristic of forms of folklore and that some variants "are manifestations of the community's modifying activity." Indeed, the community, she says, "takes an active part in the act of creation and should therefore be regarded as a co-author." The changes in the subplot of Barnett and the archaeologists display this coauthor role of the UFO community in creating successive variants of the Roswell myth.

Moreover, Ortutay (1959:191) notes that there usually exists, "side by side with [accepted versions, or] variants, another category—namely, the *invariants* . . . which are felt by the community as being inconsistent with its traditions, mode of expression, and therefore refused." Such an invariant exists in the form of Version 6 of the Roswell myth, which has been generally repudiated by members of the UFO community for the very reasons cited by Ortutay.

Introduction of Elements of Fantasy   According to Dundes (1965:53, 54), one of the characteristics of folklore is its irrationality. By that, he means that folklore includes things like magic wands that "are not found in nature, in objective reality." Irrationality, of course, depends on the frame of reference. Thus, if the core scenarios of the Roswell books are versions of a myth, they would be expected to contain (as they do) descriptions of things that are so unusual and bizarre as to appear— to those outside the UFO community who do not share its traditions— irrational (things like small, humanoid aliens and material harder than any terrestrial metal).

In explaining the introduction of such apparently irrational elements into the Roswell myth, it is useful to begin by noting that folklore includes tales that Dundes (1965:220) says are "narratives of actual personal happenings," which are sometimes related by traditors (some analysts call such tales "memorates"). Much more commonly, however, a traditor's tale, although it may be based on actual personal happenings, is modified by the introduction of fantastical elements. Dundes avers that such tales, "through the powers of a process von Sydow calls fabulation, are transformed into fiction with little regard for fact." In the case of the

Roswell myth, I have labeled such fabulated tales "personalized legends."

The process of fabulation involves the fictionalization of a tale by inserting fantastical elements associated with a traditional belief structure (e.g., ghost stories) or with named persons (e.g., Robin Hood). In the basic folktale, which is considered to be fiction by both traditors and their listeners, the fantastical elements are not regarded as real objects or events. However, in tales that are legends or myths, the traditor intends that his listeners believe that the fantastical elements are real, and the listeners in turn claim to find them credible.

For now, I will defer discussion of the motives of the traditors in inventing such tales and the reasons why listeners avowedly believe them. Rather, I emphasize two points: First, storytellers have been around for millennia, and for millennia they have been inventing fantastical stories that many people have avowedly believed. Second, the introduction of fantastical elements into the Roswell myth is through a mechanism—personalized legends—in which fantastical elements are described in terms of the traditional stereotypes of the belief structure of a subcultural group. In other words, both the presence of elements of fantasy in the core scenarios found in the Roswell books, and their mode of introduction, are consonant with the assumed status of these scenarios as versions of a myth.

It is pertinent at this juncture to point out that because personalized legends are, by definition, expressed in terms of traditional stereotypes of a given subculture, they are necessarily similar in content. Therefore, members of the same subculture may—without prearrangement or knowledge of each other's stories—relate tales having similar elements of fantasy. The separate stories of such individuals may thus appear mutually supportive, an outcome that defeats the classical test for veracity—namely, that noncollusive witnesses are unlikely to tell the same lies. In this context, for instance, the similarities that appear in alien abduction stories told by individuals who demonstrably have had no opportunity to collude may indicate not that the stories are factual (as ufologists assert) but rather that the storytellers share the same UFO subculture.

Persistence of Inventions and Transformations   In a seminal study of the transmission and reproduction of stories, Bartlett (1920:32) found that "inventions and transformations, once introduced, show great tenacity." They are reproduced in successive retellings by the originating traditor because the traditor's viewpoint and attitude, from which the invention stemmed, generally remain unchanged. And they are retained in retellings by other traditors if they possess what Bartlett calls a normal "potency of reproduction." By that he means that the retellings are relevant to the plot, couched in familiar terms, and comply with the conventions of the subcultural group comprising the listeners.

The stories presented in the Roswell books contain inventions and transformations that display the kind of tenacity Bartlett describes. For instance, Version 1 fails to specify the number of alien bodies found. This number appears first in Version 2, which specifies a four-member crew for a flying saucer. This number is retained in Versions 3, 4, and 5 (in the rejected Version 6, only three bodies are found—a break with "received wisdom"). The number four was invented by the literary traditor who produced the MJ-12 document in which Version 2 is presented. The MJ-12 document was widely read by members of the UFO community, and the notion of "four to a saucer" was assimilated into the personalized legends of community members who became traditors and told and retold their tales to literary traditors, who in turn incorporated the tales in books on Roswell, and so on. Over time, the "storage" of the number four in these personalized legends (because it had the normal "potency of reproduction," as defined by Bartlett) ensured its persistence even though most members of the UFO community came to view its source, the MJ-12 document, as a forgery.

In this regard, the concepts that appeared in previous crashed-saucer stories, labeled "P" in the various summaries of the Roswell myth versions, also illustrate the persistence—despite a flawed source—of inventions of normal potency (e.g., aliens are small humanoids, alien writing is pictographic, and so forth). These inventions appeared first in stories that were admitted to be jokes by their originators or, in Scully's case, shown to be a hoax. Again, these inventions were stored in the traditions of the UFO group's subculture and 30 years later were repackaged in the personalized legends of traditors who told their tales to the literary traditors who produced the Roswell books.

Transformations also exhibit great tenacity for the same reasons as do inventions. According to Bartlett (1920:34), transformation occurs when the unfamiliar is replaced by the familiar. For example, in Version 1 the historically accurate but unfamiliar term "radar reflector" in General Ramey's statement is dropped, and Ramey is alleged to have said that the wreckage was nothing more than the remains of a "weather balloon," a device familiar to many Americans.[2] Bartlett (1920:43) points out that most transformations are akin to rationalizations in that they both result from "a common tendency to change all presented material into such a form that it may be accepted without uneasiness." The rationale for this particular transformation is, of course, that it tends to make Ramey's statement seem quite at odds with the nature of the wreckage described by Brazel—a result that reinforces the idea that Ramey's explanation is a cover story, which in turn reinforces the theme of a government conspiracy. The persistence of this transformation is evidenced by its repetition in Versions 2, 3, 5, and 6. (Interestingly, Version 4 accurately reports Ramey's statement.)

Intensification of Relations of Dominance and Subjugation Bartlett (1920:32) states that when a traditor tells and retells a tale, "relations of opposition, similarity, subjection and the like, occurring in the original, are very commonly intensified." This intensification is due to "a deep-rooted and widespread tendency to dramatization," according to Bartlett, who goes on to say that, "in particular, all those types of relation about . . . which feeling tends to cluster are readily exaggerated."

There is also a more generalized tendency toward exaggeration in folklore repetition, a tendency exemplified in the Roswell myth by the description of the gouge in the earth of the debris field, which is reported to be about 150 feet (46 m) long in Version 3 and 500 feet (150 m) long in Version 5. Moreover, the myth contains an example of the more specific kind of exaggeration to which Bartlett alludes—the intensification of relationships of subjection and dominance. The military personnel, and even specific army officers, are portrayed in the various versions of the myth as agents of a shadowy entity of great power—the government. The relationship of dominance on the part of government emissaries and subjection on the part of civilians putatively involved in the Roswell Incident is intensified in the personalized legends of traditors as they tell and retell their tales to successive literary traditors. In Version 1 the military personnel admonish civilian witnesses to remain silent; in Versions 3 and 4 the witnesses are told that severe reprisals will follow if they fail to comply; and in Version 5 their lives are threatened.

Omissions of the "Unpleasant" Bartlett (1920:34) avers that elements that he labels "unpleasant" usually drop out when tales are transmitted from one traditor to another. Such elements include "reports of incidents somewhat opposed to modern conventions," and Bartlett notes that "such relatively shocking incidents always tend to disappear." One such incident is introduced in Version 2 where the gruesome picture is presented of alien bodies that have been disfigured by weathering and partially eaten by predators. This incident is repeated in Version 3 but is dropped in Versions 4 and 5. It reappears in Version 6, but the rejection of that version appears to account for the incident's absence from the myth in its currently accepted form.

The above incident might be considered unpleasant by the public at large and not merely by members of the UFO community. A more significant form of omission occurs when elements are omitted because their "unpleasantness" is due to their violation of conventions specific to the group subculture. This kind of omission occurs, for example, when certain statements, both by traditors and by informants from outside the UFO community, are not couched in terms of the traditional stereotypes of the subculture. Such statements are likely to be omitted by literary traditors. Some examples of this gatekeeper role of literary traditors have already been cited. Another example that illustrates this role is the case of Captain Sheridan Cavitt.

Cavitt is mentioned in Versions 1, 3, 4, and 5 of the myth as the officer who accompanied Marcel when he went to the Foster ranch with Brazel to collect the wreckage. Like Marcel, Cavitt saw the debris field and handled the wreckage. His statements about this incident, therefore, would appear to be of enormous importance, if for no other reason than to confirm Marcel's comments about the "unearthly" nature of the wreckage. The significance of Cavitt's testimony did not escape the literary traditors who produced the Roswell books. For instance, in Version 4, Friedman and Berliner (1992a:134) wrote: "Cavitt is one of the few people still living who were involved in the retrieval of crash materials and who would have known a lot of details, rather than just a small part of the story."

It is unclear whether Cavitt was interviewed prior to the appearance of Version 1, but in any case no statements in that version are attributed to him. Version 2 appeared in the MJ-12 document, which is only a few pages long and contains no "testimony" of any kind. Cavitt was interviewed by the literary traditors who produced Versions 3, 4, and 5, but again no statements are attributed to Cavitt in Versions 3 and 4, and in Version 5 the only comments of Cavitt's that are cited are those in which he indicates that the wreckage he saw on the Foster ranch was not that of a Japanese balloon bomb or the remains of a German V-2 rocket (Randle and Schmitt 1994:140, 148).

No rationale is offered in Versions 3 and 5 to explain the omission of any substantive comments by Cavitt, but in Version 4 the literary traditors maintain that Cavitt "stonewalled" them. It seems unlikely that the paucity of statements by Cavitt in these versions was due to his inaccessibility. Between 1989 and 1993 the literary traditors who produced Versions 3, 4, and 5 avowedly conducted two face-to-face interviews and seven telephone interviews with Cavitt. Rather, it appears that most of his statements were ignored.

Cavitt's verbatim statements about Roswell are among the few available from a source other than literary traditors. In 1994, Cavitt was interviewed by Air Force representatives who provided him with a waiver from the Secretary of the Air Force to release him from any prior security oath. In the transcribed interview (Weaver 1995: attachment 17), his comments indicate that he had been contacted by UFO researchers and had willingly talked to them. His further statements concerning the wreckage *contradict* Marcel's statements about its unusual properties and, indeed, support the explanation originally proffered by General Ramey. Cavitt also indicates that he had never been told by anyone in the government not to talk about the incident, and he did not know that anyone considered the incident to be unusual until he was contacted by UFO researchers in the early 1980s.

It seems most unlikely that Cavitt would have failed to tell the literary traditors his views about the nature of the wreckage that he and Marcel collected. Hence, it seems reasonable to assume that his statements on this topic were omitted from various versions of the Roswell myth because they are "unpleasant"—that is, they contravene the traditional conventions and beliefs of the UFO community.

Transposition of an Element within a Subplot   The category involving transposition of subplot elements includes two subcategories: transferral, which Bartlett (1920:47) defines as an element that is "transferred bodily to some new position"; and reversal, which he says is "a reversal of the parts played by different persons." An example of the folk narrative characteristic of transferral can be found in versions of the Roswell myth that contain the subplot of the appearance of the saucer wreckage and alien bodies at the base hospital. This subplot can be traced to an individual who told his tale to a succession of literary traditors. It first appears in Version 3, in which this individual describes himself as a civilian who was visiting the Roswell Army Air Field Hospital when some of the wreckage and the alien bodies were taken there temporarily after being collected from the crash site.

In Version 3 this civilian describes his ejection from the hospital by the military police; in Version 4 he is ejected by the military police and accosted by an angry redheaded colonel who threatens him with severe reprisals if he reveals what he has seen; and in Versions 5 and 6 he is ejected by the military police, but the redheaded colonel is dropped and, instead, the civilian is accosted by a black sergeant and an angry redheaded captain who threaten him with severe reprisals if he reveals what he has seen. The threatening black sergeant and redheaded captain had appeared first in the story of Gerald Anderson, which is given in Version 4. Anderson's tale was rejected as a "fiction" by the literary traditors who produced Versions 5 and 6, but the ubiquitous black sergeant and redheaded captain reappear in Versions 5 and 6 in the story of another traditor.

This transposition also illustrates the previously described intensification of emotive elements in successive versions of a folk narrative. In European and American folklore, redheaded people are traditionally thought to have fiery tempers, and of course two irate people are more threatening than one. Thus, when the angry redheaded colonel was added to the subplot of ejection by the military police, the drama of the image escalated, and the replacement of the colonel with a threatening black sergeant and angry redheaded captain further intensified it.

The case of the archaeologists represents another example of transferral. The Grady Barnett subplot, in which archaeologists appear, was introduced in the personalized legend of a traditor in Version 1, which places Barnett and the archaeologists on the Plains of San Agustin. This subplot is repeated in Version 3, except that the group is moved to the Foster ranch; in Version 4 the group is back again on the Plains of San Agustin; and in Version 5 the Grady Burnett subplot is dropped entirely, for reasons explained previously. But the archaeologists are retained in Version 5 because they are transferred to the personalized legend of another traditor. In this instance, and in the case of the black sergeant and the redheaded colonel, the mechanism of transferral also provides a striking illustration of the feedback loop between the literary and oral links in the transmission process, a loop that was postulated in the modern type of punctuated transmission model proposed earlier. Because of feedback, it is virtually inevitable that the transposition of elements from the tale of one traditor to that of another would occur.

The second type of transposition—role reversal—is exemplified in the case of Brazel. In Version 1, selected parts of the Brazel interview published by the newspapers are quoted in a way that portrays him as a witness to unusual events who is striving to make them known to the world—a role diametrically opposed to that of Ramey, who is portrayed as a wily government emissary bent on shielding these events from public scrutiny through lies and misdirection. In Version 3, Brazel's role is reversed; he is now the messenger of deceit. Coached by the military, his role becomes like that of Ramey, and the information in his published interview is "a tissue of lies." This new persona for Brazel is retained in Versions 4 and 5.

This example of reversal, unlike the previous examples of transferral, involves the literary rather than the oral links in the transmission process. At this point it is necessary to interject an expository note. The characteristics of tale transmission described by Bartlett were derived from studies of purely oral transmission. The modern type of punctuated transmission model that I have proposed for the Roswell myth involves literary as well as oral links. As I have pointed out, however, the literary links differ significantly from conventional literary links represented by published collections of folklore. Rather, in my model the literary links involve literary traditors who play an active role in creating the versions of the myth that appear in their books. Hence, I believe it is reasonable to assume that features (such as role reversal) that characterize serial transmission by oral means also occur during transmission from one literary traditor to another, because the motivating factor—rationalization—is the same in both cases.

Rationalization of the Plot   Bartlett (1920:33) notes that, in his studies of the serial transmission of tales by oral means, rationalization of the plot in the sense of providing explicit reasons for each element of the narrative "was constantly illustrated." And, according to Dundes (1965:244), literary transmission accelerates the process of rationalization. In my proposed model, composed as it is of oral and literary links, rationalization permeates the entire transmission process. Indeed, rationalization is the motivating factor for some of the inventions, transformations, and transpositions that occur in various versions of any folk narrative.

Among the many rationalizations in successive versions of the Roswell myth are those involving the distortion of statements about events that are found in the relevant documents of that time (e.g., government reports, articles in the media, and the like), which for this analysis I will define as "historical events." Like many folk narratives, the Roswell myth has evolved around a core of historical events, and statements about some of those events are transmitted accurately from version to version because they fit the traditions of the relevant group subculture. Such statements are labeled "H" in the myth version summaries. For example, the official press release of 8 July announcing the recovery of a flying disk is accurately reported in all versions (except Version 2, in which it is not mentioned). However, many other statements about historical events, which are labeled "HD," are distorted to conform to the tales of traditors or to the inventions of literary traditors.

To choose just one example from many, consider the matter of dates. The date of the crash is 2 July in Version 1 because that date conforms to the UFO sighting reported by the Wilmots. Brazel, therefore, is alleged to have found the wreckage on 3 July. He is correctly described as visiting Corona on 5 July and first learning about flying disks there. But because it would be "unseemly" (once he suspected the wreckage to be from a flying disk) to delay reporting such an important discovery, he is described as rushing to Roswell on the very next day (6 July) to tell Sheriff Wilcox.

Actually, according to his contemporary account, Brazel found the debris on 14 June and considered the incident so trivial that he did not collect the wreckage until 4 July. He visited Corona on 5 July and learned about flying disks there, but apparently he considered them to be associated with an American military project. In any case, he did not consider the matter important enough to make a special trip on 6 July. Instead, he did so on 7 July, when he had to visit town to sell some wool.

In Version 1, the altered dates are simply presented as facts, and no reason is given for ignoring the historical dates that appear in the Brazel interview. But in Version 3, in which these distorted dates are repeated, two reasons are given that allow the actual dates to be ignored. First, the personalized legends of newly found traditors support Version 1's altered dates (which the traditors appear to have assimilated from reading Version 1). Second, the entire Brazel interview is dismissed as a "tissue of lies." These rationalizations are repeated in Versions 4 and 5.

In Version 5 the date of the crash is moved up to 4 July in order to conform to the personalized legends of another newly found group of traditors. Their tales provided other elements that allowed changes to be made in the core scenario that the literary traditors deemed desirable. These changes are necessary to compensate for the elimination of the discredited MJ-12 document and the Grady Barnett subplot. In Version 5 the dates of other events (e.g., Brazel's discovery of the wreckage) are "adjusted" to conform to the new date of the crash as part of the rationalization of the plot.

Interestingly, in Version 5 the Wilmots' UFO sighting is retained as part of the narrative even though it is no longer relevant, in the sense that it does not logically aid in establishing the plot, as it does in Versions 1, 3, and 4. But Bartlett (1920:33) points out that in folklore, relevance "must be used in its wider sense." And he goes on to say: "In a fantasy practically any sort of connection is enough to secure relevance." The Wilmot sighting is thus retained because of its psychological relevance to the literary traditors. Because it is a key event in Versions 1, 3, and 4, its absence would be missed, and its retention reinforces the general ambience of UFO activity in the Roswell area prior to the crash that is traditionally a part of the Roswell scenario. Hence, the apparent irrationality of retaining the irrelevant Wilmot sighting in Version 5 is—in the context of the group subculture—another example of rationalization of the plot.

The Central Motif of the Roswell Myth

In 1910, folklorist Antti Aarne produced the first tale type index. An updated and widely cited version of this index is that of Stith Thompson (1964). Other works (e.g., Thompson 1955) catalog, in abbreviated form, motifs gleaned from thousands of folk narratives collected worldwide. Such indexes reveal recurrent themes in folk narratives. For example, the Cinderella story (tale type 510 in the Aarne-Thompson index) embodies a motif thousands of years old; it appears in the folklore of many cultures and has been traced back to ancient Egypt.

Why do certain patterns continually recur? Quite apart from the phenomenon of diffusion from a common source, many scholars believe that the reinvention of specific themes can be traced to human nature. According to anthropologist Clyde Kluckhohn (1959:272), for example, "The recurrence of certain motifs in varied areas separated geographically and historically tells us something about the human psyche. It suggests that the interaction of a certain kind of biological apparatus in a certain kind of physical world with some inevitables of the human condition . . . brings about some regularities in the formation of powerful images."

In other words, for adult humans some experiences such as birth, puberty, and death are universal; others such as intrafamilial rivalry, mating, and parenthood are quasi-universal; and still others such as suffering deprivation, surmounting obstacles, and overcoming a powerful adversary are very common. Some motifs are associated with these widely shared experiences either directly or indirectly through symbolism. For example, according to some analysts, the virgin birth motif expresses symbolically one aspect of the intrafamilial rivalry between father and son. Thus it is not surprising to find such motifs appearing in otherwise disparate cultures. For instance, the motif of monster slaying—expressive imagery for overcoming a powerful adversary—is found in the folklore of many cultures, including that of the United States.

The presence of a widely repeated motif in a story suggests that the element may have been socially constructed. That is, its origin and persistence in the story may be traceable, not to some reality, but to its resonance with a significant panhuman experience. When such a motif occurs in a story that otherwise displays known characteristics of folk narratives (e.g., in terms of the transmission process, structure, and so on), its presence reflects negatively on the objective factuality of the story and reinforces the story's status as a type of folk narrative.

That an item of folklore may appear in more than one time and place has thus been useful to scholars in examining the historicity of a story. For example, in a seminal essay, Lord Raglan (1934) demonstrated that the biographical stories of a number of heroes such as Moses and King Arthur displayed certain similarities. Although some of these individuals might have been historical figures, the similarities showed that their life stories were not history but rather exemplars of a formulaic hero life cycle. Raglan argued that it was unreasonable to suppose that the 18 heroes he studied, who lived at different times and in disparate cultures, would have had such similarly patterned lives as their traditional biographies indicated.

Raglan's analytical approach is a very old one, long used by theologians. Dundes (1980:225), for instance, says that "the utilization of comparative folklore materials to illuminate the historicity of portions of the New Testament is by no means anything new." Dundes goes on to say that Celsus, writing an anti-Christian tract in the year 178, "compared the virgin birth of Jesus with Greek myths." Celsus was referring to the story of Perseus, born to Danaë while she was still a virgin. Christian writers like Saint Justin Martyr were well aware that the existence of Greek analogs weakened the credibility of the Jesus narrative. However, Saint Justin ([ca.178] 1948:249) argued, "When I hear it asserted that Perseus was born of a virgin, I know that this is another forgery of that treacherous serpent [the devil]." Justin thus asserted, according to Dundes (1980:226), "that such Greek myths had been invented by demons to counterfeit and thereby demean the true and miraculous events in the life of Jesus."

The form of Justin's rebuttal, which was written in the second century A.D., is the same as that of the previously cited explanation by ufologists that the Scully hoax was a subterfuge orchestrated by the government to discredit the early flying saucer stories and that the MJ-12 forgery was a government ploy "to destroy the credibility of the Roswell event." Discredited tales that weaken the credibility of a cherished narrative by embodying the same motif are explained by both Saint Justin and the ufologists as being inventions of a dark and malevolent entity. Furthermore, both Saint Justin and the ufologists maintain that such inventions are specifically designed by this entity to keep humans from acquiring wisdom or knowledge that is of transcendental importance to the human race. The identity of the form of the rationalizations used by Saint Justin and the ufologists is an important clue to identifying a significant motif in the Roswell myth—a motif that can be considered central in that it expresses the narrative's underlying rationale.

Thompson's mammoth index presents a number of motifs (e.g., A1111 and A1421) in which an essential item such as food or water is impounded or hoarded by a malevolent monster so that humankind cannot use it. A culture hero defeats or circumvents the monster to release or steal the item, which then becomes available to humankind. This theme is found in the stories of many cultures (e.g., in India, China, Japan, Papua, Melanesia, Tahiti, and North and South America). The hoarded item is usually a material good, but in some versions a nonmaterial good such as knowledge is sequestered. The cultures of the African Gold Coast provide a version that exemplifies the central motif of the Roswell myth. In Thompson's index it is A1481, in which the essential item that the monster impounds is wisdom (Thompson 1955:233).

Thus, the central motif of the Roswell myth is that a malevolent monster (the government) has sequestered an item essential to humankind (wisdom of a transcendental nature, i.e., evidence-based knowledge that we are not alone in the universe). The culture hero (the ufologist) circumvents the monster and (by investigatory prowess) releases the essential item (wisdom) for humankind.

Having determined the central motif of the Roswell myth, a further level of analysis is possible, according to Dundes (1965:122, 123). This analysis is based on the concept of a motifeme, or "unit of plot narrative structure." A tale can thus be defined as a sequence of two, three, or more motifemes. In applying this approach, Dundes notes that many tales "consist of a move from disequilibrium to equilibrium." Disequilibrium, a state to be feared and avoided, can often be seen as a state of lack or deprivation. This state gives rise to so-called hoarded-object tales, in which, Dundes says, "such objects as game, fish, food-plants, water . . .

are not available to the majority of mankind." He goes on to say that such tales "can consist simply of relating how . . . a lack was liquidated."

Dundes (1965:123) avers that one type of North American Indian tale "consists of just two motifemes: lack (L) and lack liquidated (LL)." As an example, he cites the Release of Impounded Water story found in the Malecite culture: "A monster keeps back all the water in the world (L). A culture hero slays the monster which act releases the water (LL)." It is obvious that the central motif of the Roswell myth can be similarly analyzed: A monster (the government) withholds essential wisdom from humankind (L). A culture hero (the ufologist) circumvents the monster to make wisdom available for human use (LL).

In the case of the Roswell myth, the significance of this kind of morphological analysis is twofold. First, it illustrates that the myth's central motif is thematically related to two-motifeme, hoarded-object folk narratives that are truly ubiquitous and geographically widespread (a fact that makes the historicity of this element of the Roswell myth suspect). Second, it provides a way of examining the cultural content of the myth that in turn provides insight into the myth's societal functions. Such functions, which bear on the question of why some people say they find the myth credible, are described later. As background for discussing the functions of the myth, it is useful to address first the issue of the motives of those involved in the mythmaking process.

MOTIVATIONS OF THE MYTHMAKERS

The motives of the folk who invent folk narratives is a topic that has been relatively unexplored. When scholars began to study folklore in the nineteenth century, much of their research was focused on origins—how and where a given tale arose. A plethora of now discarded theories was put forth, but scant attention was given to the motivation of the traditor who invented the initial tale, however added to and modified over time. Some of the European folk narratives collected in the nineteenth century were seemingly so ancient that their inventors were lost to history, and apparently scholars thought it fruitless to ponder the motivations of those individuals. This also seems to have been the opinion of anthropologists who began to study the myths of contemporary nonliterate "primitive" peoples in the late nineteenth century, and a disinterest in the motives of mythmakers has continued to characterize anthropologists' work on myths in this century.

Folklorists, of course, are well aware that folklore and folk narratives are a part of our present-day culture and that "new tales have been invented and may be invented at any time" (von Sydow 1948:190). Nevertheless, with some exceptions, they too have neglected to say much about the motives of the inventors of modern legends and myths. Folklorists have, however, addressed the issue of "creative lying" (e.g., see Bauman 1986:11–32), and their commentaries provide useful insights into the motives of traditors who deceive their listeners by presenting tales of fantasy as fact. (Why the listeners may say they believe such tales is a separate question, which is addressed in the next section of this analysis.)

The issue of motive goes to the heart of the matter in the case of a "technomyth" such as the Roswell myth. The content of the myth is expressed in terms of a scientific idiom, but according to the traditions of the relevant subculture, its presentation must also assume the form of an investigative report conducted along scientific lines and using screening criteria to evaluate the credibility of witnesses. Regarding the latter criteria, much of the belief structure of the UFO subculture rests on the notion that an informant who, in the words of one ufologist (Whiting 1992:34), is a "responsible member of society" will not make up fantastical tales and assert that they are true.[3] I postulate, however, that these informants are not witnesses but traditors whose testifying can be best understood as a "performance" and whose motives for relating their tales are similar to those of the traditors who, for millennia, have been inventing fantastical tales and sometimes presenting them as fact. To argue this point, it is useful to begin by discussing the invention of folktales, in which no deceit on the part of the traditor is involved.

In the case of the basic folktale, which is regarded as fiction by both the teller and the told, one of its chief functions is entertainment. The folklorist William Bascom (1954:343) notes: "Amusement is, obviously, one of the functions of folklore. . . . The same is true for the concepts of fantasy and creative imagination. The fact that the storyteller in some societies is expected to modify a familiar tale by introducing new elements or giving a novel twist to the plot is of basic importance to the study of dynamics and the aesthetics of folklore."

Hence, one motive for introducing fantastical elements into an existing story or for inventing a completely new fantastical tale is that listeners are entertained by it. But why should traditors care? A plausible assumption is that they receive psychological and economic rewards for being successful traditors.

This assumption is based on the so-called rational actor model of human behavior, in which an individual choosing between alternative courses of action (such as deciding to become a storyteller as opposed to other possible vocations or avocations) selects the one that maximizes return. The return can be a material (economic) or nonmaterial (psychological) good or a mixture of both. The model is silent, however, on the factors that lead an individual to prioritize returns based on physiological and psychological needs. It is outside the scope of this analysis—and would not add to the force of my argument—to attempt to discuss such needs or to elaborate on the motives of traditors in psychological terms, although I will indicate some of the psychological motives for storytelling that have been put forth. Hence, I use the word "psychological" simply as an inclusive term to describe all motives that are not economic. What is important to my argument is that, as a matter of common observation and inference, individuals perform many actions for noneconomic, or psychological, motives.

The nature of societal rewards for the storytellers of antiquity has been truly lost to history, but in the more recent nonliterate and partially literate societies that have been studied, it is known that traditors received some sort of economic benefit for their storytelling, and it is plausible to assume that the same was true in antiquity. Indeed, in some partially literate societies, oral storytelling was—and is—a recognized profession. In some cultures, religious leaders were often traditors, and if not rewarded directly in material goods for inventing stories, they benefited because their legends fostered the religious exercises from which they drew economic support.

In addition to economic motives, the extant descriptions of classical traditors exercising their skills suggest that they enjoyed telling their tales and that—in addition to any economic reward—they were paid for their storytelling by manifestations of wonder and approval on the part of their listeners. Classical traditors thus appear to have been motivated by a combination of economic and psychological rewards for inventing successful tales—that is, tales their listeners would pay to hear in terms of material goods and/or applause. Well-known variations in human nature suggest that the mix of economic and psychological payment that any given traditor found acceptable varied along a motivation-mix continuum from all-economic to all-psychological.

Regarding the all-psychological end of this continuum, it appears that some traditors invented "tall tales" and solemnly related them as fact for a variety of purely psychological rewards: for the pleasure of fooling the multitude (the traditor thus secretly becomes akin to the trickster, a well-known figure in folklore); for the enjoyment derived from the amazement of their listeners; for the sense of self-importance conveyed by the attention of others; and so on. In expanding on this theme, some folklorists maintain that one of the psychological benefits traditors derive from inventing fantastical tales is that the process provides them with an escape mechanism.

For example, Bascom (1954:343) deals with concepts of fantasy and creative imagination in folk narratives by asking why the teller introduces specific elements and twists into the plot. The answer, Bascom avers, is that by inventing fantastical tales tailored to personal needs, the traditor "attempts to escape from his geographical environment and from his own biological limitations as a member of [humankind]."

From the perspective of the present analysis, the point to be emphasized is that some traditors have engaged in storytelling for purely psychological motivations. More commonly, however, it appears that traditors have sought economic as well as psychological rewards for their storytelling and that this mix of motives has led some traditors to step over the line and present fantasy as fact—a deliberate deception.

For the basic folktale, which is avowedly fictional, the question of deception on the part of the traditor does not arise. It is possible that some of the fantastical legends and myths started out as tales that were originally presented as fiction by their inventors and were at first regarded as such by their listeners. But over time, perhaps centuries, the culture changed in ways that lent credibility to the tales, and they evolved into legends and myths by acquiring a coterie of true believers.

It is also known that fantastical tales now labeled as legends were invented by traditors who related them as factual with no intent to deceive, because they themselves believed in the objective reality of their fantasy. For example, about 2700 years ago a tale originated in Central Asia about a beast called the griffin, half lion and half eagle, that was said to guard gold deposits. This story was widely accepted as fact in antiquity, but by the 1600s European scholars regarded the griffin as an imaginary composite beast intended to symbolize the noble attributes of lion and eagle. Modern studies (Mayor 1994) have indicated that symbolism was not the intent of the originator of the griffin story, but rather the tale was based on the misinterpretation of the skeletal remains of *Protoceratops*, a beaked dinosaur whose bones were (and still are) frequently found mixed with alluvial gold deposits in Central Asia.

In addition, by assuming that some myths and legends were serially invented, it is possible to exculpate traditors of deceit in purveying fiction as fact. Suppose, for example, a traditor hears a group of fishermen describe a frightening encounter with a whale: "A fish so large that it *could* swallow a man and spit him out." The traditor then retells this story accurately, presenting it as an exciting factual tale. But listeners at the edge of the crowd, who hear the story in snatches, think that the traditor said that a huge fish *did* swallow a man and miraculously regurgitated him alive. This garbled version is handed on to another traditor who repeats it in good faith as a true story. After the tale is told and retold for a century or two, we have the story of Jonah presented as a real happening. Yet no one during the long and tortuous oral transmission process has deliberately lied.

Nevertheless, although it is possible to envisage ways in which fantastical tales could be invented and presented as fact without imputing deceit to the traditors involved in their creation, it is also the case that traditors have been suspected of knowingly presenting fantasy as fact. The issue of deceit, in the case of religious legends, has been addressed by students of theology.

For example, the biblical scholar Hermann Gunkel ([1901] 1975:2, 3) noted that "the senseless confusion of 'legend' with 'lying' has led good people to hesitate to concede that there are legends in the Old Testament. . . . There is no denying that there are legends in the Old Testament; consider for instance the [fantastical] stories of Samson and Jonah." Gunkel resolves the issue of deceit on the part of the inventors of these stories by declaring, "Such legends are not lies; on the contrary they are a particular form of poetry."

The legend-as-poetry explanation, however, smuggles some important assumptions into the argument. Notably, to exculpate the inventors of these tales from deliberate deceit, it is necessary to assume, first, that they presented the tales as poetical allegories in the service of "a greater truth" and, second, that they expected their listeners to interpret them as allegories and not as statements of fact. Regarding the second assumption, Gunkel ([1901] 1975:3) admits that the traditors' expectations—if such there were—remained unrealized: "The objection is raised that Jesus and the Apostles clearly considered these accounts to be fact and not poetry. Suppose they did; the men of the New Testament are not presumed to be exceptional men in such matters, but shared the point of view of their time." Nor, according to Gunkel ([1901] 1975:9), should the posited allegorical interpretation of biblical legends shake the faith of true believers: "We are able to comprehend this [literal interpretation of biblical legends] as the naive conception of the men of old, but we cannot regard belief in the literal truth of such accounts as an essential of religious conviction."

This explanation is convenient. That is, it eliminates the need to regard the inventors of biblical fantasies as liars, it allows scholars to patronize those who accept such tales as literally true, and because literal interpretation is not "an essential of religious conviction," it provides true believers with a way of maintaining their beliefs, in the face of biblical assertions "which go directly against our better knowledge" (Gunkel [1901] 1975:9). But because the inventors of biblical tales, together with their motives, are lost to history, Gunkel's explanation must remain forever speculative. Hence, it is equally valid to suppose that the inventors of biblical legends were motivated to purvey their fantasies as fact by the same mixture of psychological and economic rewards that appear to have motivated traditors for millennia.

With regard to the Roswell myth, two types of storytellers are involved: traditors who orally related their personalized legends about Roswell, and literary traditors who, as collators, editors, and gatekeepers, participated in the creation of the various versions of the myth that appear in their books. Like the creators of classical legends and myths, the Roswell traditors and literary traditors appear to be motivated by a mix of psychological and economic rewards. For the traditors these rewards fall near the all-psychological end of the continuum, whereas for the literary traditors they approach the all-economic extreme.

For example, Jesse Marcel had—for purely psychological rewards—related his tale to his friends, some of whom were UFO buffs, before he came to the attention of literary traditors. As his notoriety grew, he gave his story to the *National Enquirer,* a tabloid that admittedly pays its informants. It is possible that the expectation—if not the reality—of an economic return from the tabloids and from his later television appearances may have motivated Marcel, but like most of the Roswell traditors, he seems to have found his reward largely in the attention paid to him by his friends, the literary traditors, and the media.

It is noteworthy that the Roswell literary traditors are careful to point out in their books that they did not pay their informants (the traditors) and indeed required them to attest to this. The implication is that the stories must be true, because the traditors would have no motive for "fabulating" (von Sydow's term for injecting elements of fantasy into a tale) if they were not paid to do so. This reasoning is at odds with the common observation that individuals frequently perform actions for which no economic motive can be ascribed, and according to folklorists, one such action is the making up of tall tales and the presentation of them as fact.

Some members of the UFO community have evinced an awareness of the epistemological problems that ensue when attempting to evaluate the historicity of a traditor's tale based partly on the lack of an economic motive to lie. Ufologist Michael Swords (1992:42), for example, seems to allude primarily to noneconomic motives for fabulating when he states: "Let's not kid ourselves about not being able to imagine any motives for any UFO tale whatever." Nevertheless, despite an awareness of the problem, their own belief structure prompts those ufologists who are true believers to give credence to the narratives of a traditor who appears to be a "responsible member of society" and whose stories are consonant with the conventions and stereotypes of the subculture.

Analysts outside the UFO community, who do not share a faith in the criteria used by ufologists to judge the historicity of a tale, find it possible to hypothesize deception on the part of the Roswell traditors that ranges from embellishment to outright hoaxing. Jesse Marcel's story is representative of embellishment, and in the opinion of some ufologists, Gerald Anderson's tale "is seriously suggestive of a hoax" (Swords 1992:46). Indeed, some portions of those narratives have been shown to be false.

For example, Marcel's personalized legend—in a manner typical of such narratives—contains biographical information designed to establish his status as a "responsible member of society" and therefore to lend credibility to the rest of his tale. Such information can be checked using archival material, but despite an avowed espousal of the methodology of scientific investigation, ufologists (including the literary traditors responsible for the Roswell books) have long accepted Marcel's biographical assertions at face value. Recently, an independent researcher investigated those assertions. He found that the relevant military and college records reveal that Marcel embroidered the truth about his background (Todd 1995). Marcel's false statements augment his military and educational status and thus enhance the plausibility of his assertions about the extraterrestrial origin of the wreckage found on the Foster ranch—a pattern of embellishment that suggests deliberate deception.

Nevertheless, although false, a few of Marcel's assertions about his background tend to have a factual core.[4] That tendency is evident in the remainder of his tale, in which his description of the alleged unearthly properties of the debris is most circumspect. For instance, he indicates that it was reported to him by one of his men that thin sheets of the material could not be dented with a sledgehammer—he did not claim to have performed this experiment himself. He did state that he had placed some of the material in the flame of his cigarette lighter and it did not burn. Given that many conventional materials do not burn readily in the relatively low-temperature flame of a lighter, it is possible that his account of that experiment is factual. The fantastical element of his tale lies chiefly in his interpretation of what he saw and heard and in his assertion that the debris "was nothing that came from earth" (Pratt 1994:125).

Marcel's tendency to embroider his real educational and quite laudable military achievements does not, of course, demonstrate that other portions of his tale are untrue. But it does demonstrate a willingness to lie, to stretch the truth to make a good story better—an attribute that is the hallmark of legend-making traditors. It also lends support to the hypothesis that Marcel can be characterized as an embellisher who, chiefly for the psychological reward derived from the response of his listeners, may inject elements of invention or fantasy into the narrative of a remembered experience. In von Sydow's terms, he is a traditor who transforms a mundane memorate into a tale of wonder by fabulating. In Marcel's tale, the fantastical elements thus stem from the salient beliefs of a specific subculture, in this case the subculture of the UFO community.

Unlike Marcel's tale, that of Gerald Anderson seems to be regarded by some ufologists as mostly pure invention. It contains a relatively small amount of verifiable information, some of which has been discredited by ufologists (see Randle, Schmitt, and Carey 1992; Swords 1992). Much of Anderson's story is a detailed account of fantastical objects and events that he says he witnessed directly. He apparently did not receive much economic benefit from his story. According to ufologist Fred Whiting (1992:34), "Anderson has never asked for money for relating his experience, and he has granted very few interviews with the media. In short, Anderson has demonstrated no reason for lying." Although Anderson's expectation of an economic return may have exceeded the reality and thus could have been a motivating factor, his rewards appear to have been largely psychological, stemming from the attention he received. He told his tale to a succession of interviewers and ufologists, reportedly he submitted to both hypnotic regression analysis and a lie detector test, and his story and his name figured prominently in a number of articles in UFO journals and in the book in which Version 4 of the Roswell myth appears.

Anderson apparently recounted his story convincingly. I have stated previously that traditors do not testify, but rather they perform. Anderson's truthful demeanor may have resulted from a sincere belief in his own story, or it may have owed much to his skill as a competent actor, a skill that characterizes the successful traditor. For example, one story-teller—whose tale of a close encounter with a flying saucer was found credible by his friends and associates—has been described by UFO investigator Frank Drake (1972:248) as "a completely believable witness." Drake goes on to say: "There was not one statement or voice inflection that sounded phony. He was bright, articulate and completely credible. His story held together no matter how circuitously I came back to complex points." This individual was eventually shown to be a hoaxer, an outcome that led Drake (1972:257) to conclude that some people have "a need . . . a desire to pull the wool over other people's eyes and do it very cleverly."

If the assessment of ufologists such as Swords is correct, Anderson's story, like that of Drake's hoaxer, seems to fit the pattern of tales told by the traditor-as-trickster, a storyteller who quite deliberately sets out to present fantasy as fact, primarily for the psychological rewards derived from fooling others. Indeed, in the light of the history of folklore, in which the trickster is a ubiquitous persona, Whiting's remarks that Anderson, lacking an economic motive, had "no reason for lying" is touchingly ingenuous. The lengths to which some individuals will go, solely for the psychological reward of tricking the multitude, attests to the value they place on that noneconomic return for their efforts. The so-called crop-circle phenomenon (see Schnabel 1994) is a recent example of a considerable physical effort put forth over a number of years by tricksters whose chief reward was psychological in nature.

The personalized legends of most of the remaining traditors that appear in various versions of the Roswell myth suggest a level of deceit approaching embellishment rather than hoaxing. Their reward for telling their stories seems to have been chiefly psychological. The same cannot be said, however, about the literary traditors to whom they told their tales. The literary traditors are obviously linked to an economic return, namely, the royalties from the Roswell books. To explore this link, it is pertinent to note briefly the relevant background of the seven literary traditors involved in producing the various versions of the myth.

Charles L. Berlitz (Version 1), grandson of the Berlitz who founded the well-known language school, graduated from Yale, where he specialized in language studies. Later, he became a lecturer and writer on occult topics. His books include *The Mystery of Atlantis* and *The Bermuda Triangle*. The latter book, although widely condemned by skeptics as being based on a nonphenomenon produced by an incorrect use of statistics (e.g., see Kusche 1975), was translated into 23 languages and sold more than 10 million copies worldwide.

William L. Moore (Version 1 and allegedly Version 2) graduated from Thiel College in 1965 and in 1978, after a career in teaching and labor relations, became a lecturer and writer on unexplained phenomena. His first book, *The Philadelphia Experiment,* was written "in consultation" with Berlitz and appeared in 1979. It describes a purported 1943 Navy experiment on making a ship invisible, an experiment that government officials allegedly conspired to keep hidden. According to one reviewer (Kusche 1979), the book provides "no substantial evidence" that the experiment ever occurred. Nevertheless, the book achieved a wide readership and was translated into more than a dozen languages. Moore is a state section director of MUFON and is affiliated with several other UFO organizations.

Kevin D. Randle (Versions 3 and 5) describes himself as a captain in the Air Force Reserve who "brings military intelligence training to his work as an investigative journalist." He has written 3 books and more than 50 magazine articles on UFOs. In addition, between 1984 and 1992 he wrote the astonishing total of 82 novels of adventure and science fiction, bearing such titles as *Mind Slayer* and *Galactic Silver Star,* which appeared as paperbacks. He is a special investigator for CUFOS.

Donald R. Schmitt (Versions 3 and 5) describes himself as a medical illustrator with training in criminology, sociology, and theology. He has coauthored two books and written dozens of magazine articles on UFOs and has worked on the script of several television documentaries on UFOs. He was the director of special investigations for CUFOS, but he recently resigned from this position when a reporter revealed that he had lied about his background. Schmitt claimed to be a medical illustrator with a bachelor's degree and to be working on his doctorate; actually he has been a rural mail carrier with the U.S. Postal Service since 1974, and he has no degree. He is a member of the board of directors of CUFOS.

Stanton T. Friedman (Version 4) received B.S. and M.S. degrees in physics from the University of Chicago in 1955–1956 and later worked in the nuclear industry. In the 1970s he began lecturing on UFOs, and he has worked on the scripts of several documentary films on UFOs. He has authored dozens of articles about UFOs, many of which appeared in UFO journals, and he coauthored a book on UFOs. He is a regional director of MUFON.

Don Berliner (Version 4) received a B.S. in Business Administration from Ohio State University in 1953. After a short career as an accountant, he became a professional writer. He has authored hundreds of magazine articles and 21 books on aviation and space and coauthored a book on UFOs. He is a founder and an executive committee member of FUFOR.

Karl T. Pflock (Version 6) graduated from San Jose State University in 1964. He subsequently worked in industry and government (including a stint as Deputy Assistant Secretary of Defense) until 1992, when he decided to devote himself to writing full-time. He has authored several works of fiction and nonfiction, and with a grant from FUFOR he wrote *Roswell in Perspective*. He is affiliated with several UFO organizations.

All of these literary traditors benefited economically by participating in the creation of the Roswell myth, all write professionally and derive part of their incomes from their publications on UFOs, and except for Berlitz, they are all closely affiliated with UFO organizations. Apart from Pflock (who has received only a grant for his work thus far), all the literary traditors receive royalties from one or—in the case of Friedman, Randle, and Schmitt—two books on Roswell. To assess the significance of the economic return from such books, it is useful to examine Friedman's account of how *The Roswell Incident,* by Berlitz and Moore (1980), came to be published. Friedman wrote his account a few months after the book appeared. The information he provides is invaluable as the basis for inferring the motives of the literary traditors involved in the process by which Version 1 of the Roswell myth was invented.

Friedman begins by addressing two issues: his competence to talk knowledgeably about the Roswell book, and the unsavory reputation of one of its authors, Charles Berlitz. In Friedman and Moore (1981:133), Friedman states: "Some may wonder at my writing a paper about *The Roswell Incident* when the listed authors are William L. Moore and Charles Berlitz. What did Friedman have to do with the stories? A related question I have been asked is: What reliability can the story have if the co-author is Charles Berlitz, who wrote about the so-called Bermuda Triangle and other supposed mysteries?" Friedman answers the first question by explaining that it was he who found Marcel, whose story provided a government linkage, and Maltais, who provided the Grady Barnett story. Friedman passed their stories on to Moore, who decided to conduct further research on Roswell. Moore joined Friedman as a coinvestigator, apparently on the understanding that Friedman would receive a share of the royalties and any initial advance on a projected book.

Friedman then brings up an obvious question: If he and Moore did all the research, where did Charles Berlitz fit into the picture? Given that

Berlitz had a "reputation for sensational, but inaccurate reporting" (Friedman and Moore 1981:136), why did they seek him out to coauthor the book? Friedman goes on to answer this question in terms that are strictly economic (1981:139): "The major involvement by Mr. Berlitz was in getting the book published in the first place. . . . Charles has carte blanche with several publishers. Sometimes they don't even read his outlines, but pull out the checkbook and say, 'How much do you want?'—in 5 or 6 figures."

Friedman noted that the English publishers had met with Berlitz, who had submitted a four-page outline, before research was complete or any manuscript prepared. The publishers agreed to a payment of £50,000 (then more than U.S.$100,000) for the privilege of publishing the book because, according to Friedman, they knew that the Berlitz name would make it a success. In further expatiating on why he undertook the difficult and often frustrating investigative work required for such a book, Friedman says, "The book advance and later royalties justifies the goal" (Friedman and Moore 1981:137).

It seems reasonable to infer that the expectation of an economic reward motivated Berlitz, Friedman, and Moore to produce Version 1 of the Roswell myth. In the case of Berlitz, who appears to have had little interest in UFOs per se, perhaps the only motive was economic. Friedman and Moore, on the other hand, had long been members of the UFO community. They benefited economically from their work on UFOs, but it seems plausible to assume that they obtained psychological rewards from this work as well, perhaps by assuaging their curiosity about UFOs or from the satisfaction engendered by promulgating a message they believed to be important.

For example, Friedman states, "I am convinced that the evidence is overwhelming that planet Earth is being visited by intelligently controlled vehicles whose origin is off the Earth. In other words, *some* UFOs are extraterrestrial spacecraft" (Friedman and Moore 1981:152). This last sentence is the very definition of "true believer" that I have used in this analysis in relation to the UFO community. It seems probable that, like Friedman and Moore, the literary traditors who produced later versions of the myth, all of whom are long-standing members of the UFO community as well as professional writers, were motivated by a mix of economic and psychological rewards.

Of course, it is fruitless to speculate about the exact ratio of the mix for each individual, but it is significant that Friedman and Moore were, for economic reasons, willing to compromise the perceived reliability of their book by bringing in Berlitz. This willingness suggests that economic considerations were uppermost in their minds. Given that the other literary traditors write professionally, it seems probable that they too approach the all-economic end of the motivation-mix continuum.

Regarding the issue of deliberate deceit on the part of the literary traditors, it is apparent that the literary traditors have a much stronger economic motive to lie than do the traditors on whose tales their books depend. For instance, the sales of the first Roswell book by Randle and Schmitt have already exceeded 160,000 copies (Sender 1995:23). It seems that the royalties from some of Berlitz's sensationalized books have run to six figures, and to state the obvious, many a "responsible member of society" has been known to lie for a lot less. Indeed, there is evidence that one literary traditor, Donald R. Schmitt, who coauthored the books in which Versions 3 and 5 of the Roswell myth appear, made false biographical statements. Like Jesse Marcel, Schmitt apparently lied about his background to lend credibility to his assertions about UFOs.

As in Marcel's case, Schmitt's biographical assertions had long been accepted at face value by other ufologists, including his coauthor, Kevin D. Randle. It was only recently, after a journalist (Sender 1995) investigated these claims, that their falsity was discovered. Randle (1995b:1–2) was putatively so shocked by Schmitt's deception that he felt impelled to issue a statement addressed "To Whom It May Concern," in which he indicated that Schmitt had lied repeatedly about his educational background and, when confronted, had told more lies. This pattern of deception extended to his work on UFOs as well, for, according to Randle, research that Schmitt claimed to have done was not carried out. Randle also indicates that Schmitt revealed himself as a pathological liar, one who seeks only self-promotion. To explain the more than five years Randall spent collaborating with Schmitt on the research and writing needed to produce two books and many articles on Roswell, Randle was faced with the invidious choice of playing either a fool or a knave. That he found the former role the more congenial of the two is evident from his explanation—namely, that he had been gulled.

In a kind of non sequitur, Randle concludes his commentary by insisting that Schmitt's lies did not appear in the books on which they collaborated. Paradoxically, however, deceit on the part of the literary traditors did not have to take the form of direct lies, because the fabulations of the traditors provide most of the fantastical elements needed to sensationalize the books. Rather, the literary traditors' deception—if such there is— lies chiefly in the artful juxtaposition of the traditors' personalized legends so as to convey the preferred picture and in the omission of information that would mar that picture.

Are the literary traditors—as some skeptics assert—merely cynical manipulators motivated by greed, who knowingly purvey fiction as fact simply to sell their books? Perhaps. But an alternative hypothesis is that they are true believers whose perceptions are filtered through the ideas, values, and norms of their subculture. Skeptics point to the fantastical tales in the Roswell books as evidence of a cynical sensationalism on the part of the literary traditors, but the presence of these tales may merely demonstrate conformance with the conventions of the subculture. The screening criteria used by true believers in any kind of subculture (e.g., religions) to judge the credibility of stories involving their special interest are chiefly determined by the subculture itself. Such criteria thus constitute a kind of subcultural Rorschach test that reveals more about the belief structure of the group than about the historicity of the stories. Hence, the inclusion in the Roswell books of tales that seem fantastical to those outside the UFO subculture may simply mean that the literary traditors are the true believers they claim to be. Then again, maybe not.

The answer to the question of whether the literary traditors are greedy cynics or true believers, although of intrinsic interest, would not affect the status of the Roswell stories as versions of a myth. Hence, it is irrelevant to the theme of this analysis. What is significant in the analysis presented in this section is that the available evidence seems to show that classical traditors, who invented fantastical tales and sometimes presented them as fact, and the creators of the Roswell stories are alike in benefiting from their traditorial efforts by receiving a mix of psychological and economic rewards—a finding that is consonant with the treatment of the Roswell stories as versions of a myth. And if the rational actor model of human behavior is accepted, it can be inferred that the motivations of these classical and modern mythmakers are alike, as well.

FUNCTIONS OF THE MYTH

Dundes (1965:277) likens the traditors, who recount folktales, myths, and other forms of folklore, to singers and asks, "Why does the singer sing and audiences listen?" The answer to the first part of this question is that singers sing because they are paid to do so, and in the previous section I have argued that the motivations of the creators of the Roswell myth are akin to those of classical traditors in this regard. But why do audiences listen, or in Dundes's words, "What does folklore do for the folk?" The answer, Dundes declares, is that folklore performs diverse functions, including "promoting a group's feeling of solidarity, providing socially sanctioned ways for individuals to act superior to or to censure other individuals, serving as a vehicle for social protest, [and] offering an enjoyable escape from reality."

Anthropologists have tended to focus on myths as an especially significant form of folklore and have ascribed various functions to them. For example, they are said to act as the spoken counterpart to rituals, as a symbolic outlet for sociopsychological tensions, and as a mechanism for mediating crucial binary oppositions such as life-death. One of the more widely cited views is that of anthropologist Bronislaw Malinowski (1954:108), who maintains that myths function as "a warrant or charter" for beliefs.

Most commentators agree that any given item of folklore is unlikely to serve all these functions, but those that it does fulfill can usually be determined by the way the item is used in situational contexts. For example, the patronizing tone of articles in UFO journals (e.g., see Friedman 1991; Pflock 1994a), written in response to comments by skeptics who debunk the Roswell myth, leaves little doubt that the myth is "providing socially sanctioned ways for individuals [ufologists] to act superior to or to censure other individuals [skeptics]." Such articles also indicate that by acting as the focus for a debate that clearly delineates the differences between "us" (ufologists) and "them" (skeptics), the myth is "promoting a group's feeling of solidarity," and the relevant group in this case is the UFO community. The comments evoked by the Roswell books, evidenced by letters published in UFO journals, suggest that a number of people like to read about Roswell, in part, because the myth offers "an enjoyable escape from reality." Perhaps the two most significant functions of the Roswell myth are that it acts as "a warrant or charter" for beliefs, and it serves as "a vehicle for social protest."

Regarding myth as a charter for belief, the Roswell myth is a kind of epiphany for true believers. For example, Jerome Clark (1988:42), the editor of the *International UFO Reporter,* calls Roswell "the most crucial case of all time," and according to Fred Whiting (1992:33), a FUFOR official, "the reality of the UFO phenomenon can rise or fall on this case alone." Indeed, the Roswell myth is of central importance to the UFO community because it acts as a linchpin, holding together much of the belief structure on which the community is based.

The defining belief, the belief that makes one a true believer and member of the UFO community, is the notion that alien visitations have occurred; hence, we humans are not the only intelligent beings in the universe. During the first three decades of the modern UFO era, an ever-present issue that tended to undermine this belief was the lack of a proven case of such visitation. Early leaders of the UFO movement had predicted that a case of this sort would soon appear, but such assurances had begun to wear thin when, in 1980, the advent of the Roswell myth dramatically altered this situation.

I have shown that the Roswell myth is thematically akin to a two-motifeme, hoarded-object tale in which the object is wisdom (i.e., evidence-based knowledge that we are not alone in the universe). The myth asserts that this wisdom has long been hoarded by the government and that the investigatory efforts of ufologists have, in effect, largely circumvented government security and thereby made this wisdom available to humankind.

Any doubts about UFO phenomena that are engendered in true believers because of the comments of debunkers, the ambiguity of UFO sightings, and the continuing lack of unambiguous physical evidence pointing to an extraterrestrial origin for UFOs are assuaged by the Roswell myth. This validating function of myths has been described by Bascom (1954:345): "When dissatisfaction with or skepticism of an accepted pattern or doubts about it arise, there is usually a myth or legend to validate it." This role of the myth is similar to that ascribed by Malinowski (1954:101), who noted that a myth "expresses, enhances and codifies belief." He also pointed out that myths are a guide for action.

The Roswell myth does appear to have inspired certain actions on the part of the adherents. Excepting Version 2, all versions of the myth end with a condemnation of government secrecy and an explicit or implicit call for the government to admit to a Roswell cover-up. Leaders of the UFO community have responded to the mandate inherent in the Roswell myth by applauding and, perhaps to some extent, orchestrating the demands that resulted in the investigation by the General Accounting Office (GAO).[5] Another action in response to the myth was undertaken by the officials of CUFOS and two other UFO organizations in December 1994. They called on UFO community members to sign a so-called Roswell Declaration that embodied an appeal for an executive order to declassify any government information on UFOs, with special emphasis on Roswell information. The explanation accompanying the declaration noted that a listing of the total number of signatories from each of the 50 states as well as from other countries would be delivered to the offices of all members of Congress and to the White House. The explanation further indicated that this action was aimed at rectifying the fact that protest against government sequestration of UFO information had never been galvanized into a large-scale grassroots movement.[6]

The Roswell myth is thus a textbook example of the Malinowskian assertion that such tales may be used by subculture members as both a charter for beliefs and a guide for action. Another function for myths, however, is sometimes imposed upon them by the nature of the larger society itself. In societies in which some group is oppressed, the group's myths, legends, and other forms of folklore tend to reflect that condition and to become mechanisms for ameliorating it.

"One of the most important functions of folklore," according to Dundes (1965:308), "is its service as a vehicle for social protest." He avers that wherever there is oppression by a ruler or by an institution, it is often through folklore that "the anger of the folk is vent upon the often frighteningly unassailable person or institution." Most commonly, the "frighteningly unassailable" institution is a government. Indeed, the link between antigovernment sentiments and folklore has long been recognized—and not just by folklorists. For instance, Wang (1935:161) cites the use of folklore by an analyst in India, early in this century, to indicate the level of anti-British feeling. Wang also documents the longtime use of folklore by political leaders in China to gauge the level of antigovernment sentiment on the part of the peasants.

In the case of the Roswell myth, the hoarded-object theme clearly indicates antigovernment sentiment. In the typical hoarded-object tale, the entity doing the hoarding is implicitly malevolent and is generally described by the native word for "monster." It is, of course, in the nature of monsters to be "frighteningly unassailable"; hence more credit redounds to the culture hero who circumvents the monster and releases the hoarded object. The Roswell myth can thus be seen as an affirmation that the government is a malevolent monster and that ufologists are heroes. The myth also demonstrates that the monster can be defeated.

The antigovernment sentiment in the Roswell myth is the expression of a theme that has been present in the UFO movement almost from its inception and one that can be traced throughout its history (see Jacobs 1975; Peebles 1994). In the late 1940s one of the early leaders of the then embryonic UFO community, Donald Keyhoe, adopted a distinctly antigovernment position, and this stance has characterized most of his successors. Crashed-saucer stories, of course, are necessarily permeated with antigovernment sentiments because, as I have previously pointed out, government sequestration of the crashed saucer is virtually the only plausible explanation for the lack of physical evidence that a crash occurred. For example, Scully's book—the first book-length treatment of crashed saucers—contains virulent attacks on the government. Air Force activities like the Project Blue Book and other forms of government involvement with UFOs, such as the Condon investigation, exacerbated rather than ameliorated the occurrence of outbursts of antigovernment sentiment in the UFO community. The Roswell myth is simply the latest and most effective vehicle for members of that community to use in protesting against the government.

This antigovernment sentiment within the UFO subculture found no echo in the larger national culture until the late 1960s. From that time onward, however, a series of events such as the Watergate and Iran-Contra affairs eroded public confidence in government, a trend that placed the public's views about the trustworthiness of government on a converging course with the views of ufologists.[7] In 1994 and 1995 the election of a Republican majority in Congress, the rise of the militia movement, and the acts of domestic terrorists have all been ascribed to antigovernment feelings. A flood of recent books by political analysts expresses findings similar to those of Patterson and Kim (1994:266): "The signs are all around: Americans are fed up with the status quo. They're coming to sense that the traditional institutions—the political parties, the Congress, the White House—are failing them." Indeed, the Roswell myth appears to be one such sign, an indicator of a deep and widening rift in our society between the government and the governed.

The Roswell myth is thus in the mode, as it were. That may explain why some previously cited mainstream columnists have echoed the dissatisfaction of ufologists with the GAO-instigated Air Force report on Roswell. The remarks by the columnists do not necessarily suggest that they have become true believers. Rather, it appears that they are seizing the opportunity to express an innate antigovernment bias. And to the extent that they espouse the ufologists' position, it appears that they are acting in accord with the old saying, The enemy of my enemy is my friend.

The GAO investigation of Roswell was a win-win situation for the UFO community. On the one hand, its mere occurrence publicized the UFO movement and dignified the assertions of ufologists as allegations that are taken seriously by the government. On the other hand, the inevitable failure of the government to demonstrate that there was no Roswell cover-up was—equally inevitably—seen by ufologists as a continuation of the cover-up.

I argue that both outcomes were inevitable. If government knowledge of a bona fide alien visitation has been successfully concealed for nearly a half century, the reasons for the cover-up must be so compelling that the chances are vanishingly small that the government would now release this knowledge at the promptings of ufologists. And if Roswell did not involve an alien visitation, there is no form of evidence the government could offer that would convince ufologists that there was no cover-up, no saucer, no alien bodies. The latter may be rephrased as a query: Can ufologists define the nature of the government evidence they would be willing to accept as conclusive proof that there was no cover-up, no alien visitation? The answer, I believe, is no, because any such evidence can be regarded as an element of a further cover-up.[8] In other words, the Roswell myth will live on, partly because it is unfalsifiable—an attribute that it shares with the central myths of most theologies—and partly because it serves various functions for those who claim to find it credible.

There may be another attribute that the Roswell myth has in common with theological myths, namely, functioning as an expression of humanity's relationship to the cosmos. Some commentators (e.g., O'Hara 1989; Schultz 1989) maintain that in modern industrialized societies the doctrine of scientific materialism has eroded the ability of traditional theological myths to function in this way and that those individuals who are not satisfied with such traditional myths create or espouse new myths that fulfill that function. Books (e.g., see Thompson 1991; Lewis 1995) and magazine articles have echoed this theme and linked UFO phenomena with religion. For example, the author of one such article (Mansueto 1994:66) declares, "Whatever the physical reality of UFO's and aliens may be it is easy to see the religious dimension of the phenomena." He goes on to say that tales of alien encounters or "finding the Other" provide a glimpse of the cosmos "that transcends the daily intercourse of human existence."

The possibility of a link between UFOs and religion is also suggested by the similarities between the UFO movement and the more traditionally based angel movement. The latter has manifested itself in the recent popularity of publications and television shows about angels. According to a television commentator (Patsuris 1994:16), "These days angels tread fearlessly from Broadway to the bestseller list, from magazine covers to greeting cards, from the silver screen to the TV screen." She quotes a television producer who jokingly declared, "Angels are hot as hell." Angels are equally hot in publishing: over the last five years a literature consisting of several hundred books and articles about angels has been created.

Most of the books are collections of what might be called angel sightings—that is, reports by individuals about encounters with angels.

It is evident from even a casual perusal of any recent book on angels (e.g., see Freeman 1993) that angel sightings and the individuals who report them appear to satisfy the screening criteria that are used to judge the credibility of a UFO report. These criteria have been summarized by ufologist Fred Whiting (1992:34): "We expect the individual [making the report] to be a responsible member of society . . . to have a reputation for truth and honesty in his community . . . to be cooperative with responsible investigators. . . . We expect witnesses' accounts to be basically consistent. . . . We would suspect a witness who seeks monetary gain or extensive media coverage."

As has been previously noted, the application of these criteria did not screen out the tales of Gerald Anderson and Frank Kaufman—individuals whom some ufologists later came to regard as hoaxers. Hence, the fact that the tellers of angel tales and the tales themselves may satisfy these criteria provides no assurance that these are stories about real happenings, although they are presented as such.

But if angel sightings are hoaxes, that fact will never be known, because unlike the UFO movement, the angel community has not engendered a countervailing group of skeptics who debunk the tales of those whose lives have been "touched by angels." It seems reasonable that UFO tales attract debunkers and that angel stories do not. The technological nature of UFOs and the presentation of UFO tales as "investigative reports" invite the scrutiny of outsiders and, in effect, challenge them to subject the tales to generally accepted standards for judging historicity. Conversely, the religious nature of angels and the presentation of angel stories in the form of uplifting anecdotes that are biblical in tone predispose outsiders to ignore them as accounts of religious experiences for which the question of historicity is largely irrelevant.

Nevertheless, despite differences in context and presentation, UFO and angel stories share striking similarities. Both involve elusive entities that carry out their terrestrial activities unobtrusively without leaving behind physical evidence of their existence or their unearthly status, and at the deepest level, both convey the same fundamental message—we are not alone. Also, UFO and angel stories are alike in fostering communities of true believers, some of whom have demonstrated their faith by forming networks to watch for the entities (UFOs or angels) on which their respective communities are based. In both communities, members are kept apprised of putative sightings by organizational journals (e.g., *Interna-*

tional UFO Reporter and *Angel Watch Journal*). And in both communities the belief structures, although otherwise disparate, are alike in being based largely on the notion that a "responsible member of society" is not likely to present a tall tale as fact.

It is tempting to speculate that UFO and angel tales are essentially the expression of the same theme in different idioms (technoscientific and generic-religious). If that is so, then for some members of their respective communities, the tales may be substitutes for the myths of a traditional theology. As a UFO story, the Roswell myth may thus serve religious as well as the previously described secular functions.

To assert that the Roswell myth may serve various functions implies nothing about its objective truth or falsity, but it *does* imply the existence of function-related motives for professing to believe it is true. In effect, the Roswell myth provides adherents with a mechanism for achieving one or more goals (e.g., group solidarity, antigovernment protest, cosmic understanding, and so on). To adherents who seek to achieve such goals, this functional aspect of the myth is a powerful incentive to espouse it. Folklore is replete with examples illustrating the power of a legend or myth to create a coterie of adherents in the face of physical evidence of its falsity that seems incontrovertible to those outside the subculture that gave birth to the tale (e.g., see Degh and Vazsonyi 1971:284). Function-related incentives are even more powerful when they are operant in the context of epistemological uncertainty that exists when—as in the case of the Roswell stories—the hypothesis on which the narratives are based is practicably unfalsifiable. Hence, it is not surprising that some people claim to find the Roswell myth credible.

A CULTURAL PERSPECTIVE

The Roswell-as-myth approach used in this analysis differs significantly from the approach adopted by true believers and by skeptics, who are alike in focusing on the crashed saucer and alien bodies as the things that need to be explained or explained away. The only "things" available for study in this case, however, are not a crashed saucer and alien bodies but rather books containing stories about a crashed saucer and alien bodies. Because it is these stories that have affected our society, it is the stories themselves that need to be explained.

The primary data on which this analysis is based, therefore, are the various stories about the Roswell Incident contained in the books that I have cited. My purpose has been to understand how these stories came to be written, why they differ, why some people claim to find them credible, and what they tell us about our culture. The answers to these questions, which are scattered throughout my analysis, constitute what might be called a cultural perspective on Roswell.

This perspective does not require the analyst to establish the truth or falsity of a narrative in order to classify it as a myth. The stipulative definition of "myth" used in this analysis thus makes no reference to the objective factuality of the tale. However, relevant historical facts have led me to suggest that certain mundane events (described in greater detail in Chapter 3) are both likely and sufficient to have given birth to the Roswell stories.

If these events form the historical core of the Roswell stories, then all else they contain is attributable to the performance of various storytellers. In this context the term "performance" refers to a mode of communication in which the narrator's skill and effectiveness in eliciting the interest and approval of the target audience are highlighted, rather than the factuality of the information conveyed. This mode of communication generally results in the accretion of imaginative narrative elements around the core of real happenings, and it is, of course, one of the time-honored ways in which legends and myths have been created down through the ages.

The hypothesis that alien life-forms may exist is by no means implausible. In fact, this hypothesis has gained luster from recent discoveries indicating that planets orbit some sunlike stars and that an ancient form of life may have existed on Mars.[9] But it would seem an unnecessary elaboration to posit the intervention of real alien beings merely to account for stories about alien beings, because in the absence of physical evidence to the contrary, such stories may be attributed to the human capacity for telling (and for believing) tall tales, a capacity that has been demonstrated over and over again for millennia.

On the other hand, I have repeatedly pointed out that there is no practicable way to falsify the hypothesis that an alien visitation lies at the heart of the Roswell Incident. Indeed, in the introduction to my analysis, I specifically disavowed the notion that I could assert with certainty that the events at Roswell did not involve alien beings from a far world. What I believe my analysis does show is that, whatever its nature, the reality underlying the Roswell Incident has played a seminal role in the making of a modern myth.

CHAPTER THREE

THE EARLY NEW YORK UNIVERSITY BALLOON FLIGHTS

CHARLES B. MOORE

he New York University (NYU) Constant Level Balloon Group was organized in November 1946. Its mission was to develop and launch balloons that would carry Army Air Force instruments aloft to various levels near the base of the stratosphere for the long-range detection of nuclear explosions and rockets.

In early 1947, while awaiting the delivery of the polyethylene balloons that were planned for use in these flights, tests were performed using long trains of meteorological sounding balloons made of neoprene. Three ascents were attempted from Bethlehem, Pennsylvania, but were not successful, in part because of strong winds at the surface. As a result, in June the flight operations were transferred to Alamogordo Army Air Field in New Mexico, where three full-scale flights were launched.

One of those flights, undocumented NYU Flight #4, was last reported over the Capitan Mountain–Arabela area in central New Mexico. From a recent examination of the June 1947 reports of winds aloft and of the ground tracks of the two subsequent NYU flights, it appears that Flight #4 is a likely candidate to explain the debris later recovered on the Foster ranch, about 25 miles (40 km) to the north-northwest of Arabela.

In this chapter, I provide a possible reconstruction of the ground track of Flight #4 to show the likelihood that it landed on the Foster ranch on the afternoon of 4 June 1947. Next, I discuss five points that demonstrate that the wreckage found on the ranch (as described in contemporary documents) matched the debris that would have been produced by this balloon train after touchdown.

BACKGROUND

In November 1946 the Research Division of NYU entered into contract W28-099-ac-241 with Watson Laboratories of the Army Air Force's Air Materiel Command. The program specified in the contract aimed at the design, development, and flying of constant-level balloons to carry instruments at altitudes from 10 to 20 kilometers (nominally 33,000 to 66,000 ft).

To fulfill this contract, Athelstan Spilhaus, the NYU director of research, recruited several of the meteorological personnel who had worked for him during the recent war, in Colonel Marcellus Duffy's Army Air Force Liaison Office to the U.S. Signal Corps on matters related to meteorological instrumentation. He selected Charles S. Schneider to be the assistant project director; and I, then a beginning graduate student in physics, became the project engineer. Other members of the early group were James Richard Smith (a graduate student in meteorology), Murray Hackman (a radiosonde specialist), Richard S. Hassard (an electrical engineer), and Paul Morrell (a fieldworker). An extensive record of the work on this project is available in C. S. Schneider's periodic progress reports to Watson Laboratories (Schneider 1947a–c).

At that time, the only balloons available to carry instruments aloft were the meteorological sounding balloons (popularly called weather balloons) that were used primarily to carry radiosondes aloft for the weather services. When released after inflation with a lifting gas, these balloons usually rose until they burst, often at altitudes above 60,000 feet (18 km). Because the neoprene films that composed the envelopes of these balloons were elastic, the balloon volumes increased as the balloons rose into less dense air. There was no feasible way to limit that expansion at some desired, intermediate level.

Although efforts had been made previously to tow aloft an extensible balloon that had just the right inflation to support its load and then to release the tow balloon at some desired altitude, solar heating made that technique unusable. After the main balloon was left on its own and the forced ventilation (caused by its being dragged upward by the tow balloon) ceased, absorption of solar radiation by the balloon envelope would heat the lifting gas, causing it to expand and thereby increase the net lift. As a result, the balloon would rise at rates of up to 100 feet per minute (0.5 m/s) in the troposphere. When the tow technique was used at night, on the other hand, radiation from the balloon would occur, cooling the lifting gas and causing the balloon to descend. Consequently, these meteorological balloons were not suitable for constant-level flights.

At the outset of the NYU effort, we recognized the need for light-weight, constant-volume balloons with envelopes made of transparent films (to minimize absorption of sunlight) and equipped with some device for dropping expendable ballast to reduce the load whenever the balloon descended below the desired floating altitude. The Japanese had flown paper and silk balloons with expendable ballast across the Pacific late in the war (see note 3 for Chapter 1, and Spilhaus, Schneider, and Moore 1948), but we rejected the Japanese approach because their balloons were opaque and very heavy. We concluded that they would require excessive amounts of ballasting to maintain a constant level.

In November 1946, after a study of the plastic films with the desired properties for the balloon envelopes, we selected polyethylene and began a search for a fabricator. Engineers at PLAX Corporation, an extruder of polyethylene film, referred us to Harold A. Smith of Unexcelled Chemical Corporation, Mamaroneck, New York; we began negotiations with him in late December. Smith constructed the first polyethylene balloons during the following spring, but the first ones that were suitable for flight were not delivered until late June 1947.

During that interval, another, larger balloon development program known as Project Helios was under way. Jean Piccard at the University of Minnesota and Otto Winzen at General Mills Aeronautical Research Laboratories had obtained support from the Office of Naval Research for Piccard's planned ascent to 100,000 feet (30.5 km) under a cluster of about 80 plastic balloons. The flight was to carry out a wide range of scientific experiments, including the release of a free-fall missile. In early 1947, Winzen preferred Pliofilm, a Goodyear vinyl product, as the material for the construction of Piccard's balloons and was uninterested in fabricating polyethylene balloons for NYU. However, after some tests in the spring of 1947, Winzen discovered that Pliofilm degraded quickly after exposure to sunlight. Thereafter, he too began to use polyethylene, and in June 1947 he fabricated 25 small polyethylene balloons (7 ft, or 2.1 m, in diameter) of the Piccard design for use by our Balloon Group.

These balloons were delivered later that month—the first ones were flown in a cluster of 10 that we launched from Alamogordo Army Air Field on the morning of 3 July. Flights of such polyethylene balloons, however, were not involved in the Roswell Incident. Instead, it is the earlier flights of neoprene weather balloons that appear to be relevant to the Roswell Incident, as is shown in the following account of our Balloon Group's activities in the spring of 1947. To aid the reader, a list describing the early NYU flights to which numbers were assigned is provided (Table 1).

THE FIRST NYU BALLOON FLIGHTS

The Army Air Force's scientific director for our Balloon Group program, James A. Peoples, was under considerable pressure during early 1947 to get acoustic monitoring equipment aloft for tests of the long-range detection program of which our effort was a part. Accordingly, while awaiting the delivery of the first nonextensible polyethylene balloons, Peoples requested that we use standard meteorological balloons to carry aloft test models of the low-frequency microphones that were being developed for the detection program. To carry the relatively heavy loads, we adopted a technique used by cosmic ray physicists, involving a cluster of radiosonde balloons arranged in a long, vertical train. This approach was suggested to us by Serge Korff, one of our professors, who had used this technique for lifting cosmic ray measuring instruments aloft prior to World War II (Clarke and Korff 1941).

In early April 1947 the British military prepared to destroy German naval installations on Helgoland, an island in the North Sea, with explosives (Cox 1949). On 3 April 1947, in preparation for monitoring the acoustic signal produced by the explosion, we launched a vertical train of 14 meteorological balloons from the football field at Lehigh University at Bethlehem, Pennsylvania.

This cluster of balloons, configured as shown in Schneider (1947a:35), was 330 feet (100 m) long and was to have been towed to 30,000 feet (about 9 km) by two lifting balloons, which were then to be cut free. The lift of the remaining balloons was set to equal the weight of the load and of some sand ballast; the plan was to have the train float at the approximate altitude where the tow balloons were released. We had no experience in handling long balloon trains with appreciable lift and had to improvise some auxiliary rigging to hold the balloon train down during its assembly. These auxiliary lines remained on the train after launch and fouled both the lifter balloons and the parachute that was to have carried the ballast when it was dropped. As a result, the balloon train rose to 46,000 feet (14 km) before the tow balloons worked their way free. The remaining balloons then descended as rapidly as they had ascended (at around 1,000 ft, or 300 m, per minute) and landed in the ocean near Sandy Hook, New Jersey.

After this flight, which we called NYU Flight #1, we assigned a flight

TABLE 1

Summary of New York University's First Balloon Flight Attempts
for Watson Laboratories in 1947

Flight #	Date and release time	Launch site	Description of balloon(s)	Equipment description
1	3 April, 1412 EST	Bethlehem, Pa.	14 balloons in train, each 350 g	Radiosonde and sand ballast
2	18 April, time unknown	Bethlehem, Pa.	23 neoprene balloons in train	Sonobuoy, radar targets, radiosonde, and sand ballast
3	8 May, time unknown	Bethlehem, Pa.	23 neoprene balloons in train	Same as Flight #2
4	4 June (probably around 0300 MST)	Alamogordo, N.Mex.	28 neoprene balloons in train	Same as Flight #2, plus liquid ballast dribbler but minus radiosonde
5	5 June, 0516 MST	Alamogordo, N.Mex.	28 neoprene balloons in train	About same as Flight #2, plus liquid ballast and minus radar targets
6	7 June, 0509 MST	Alamogordo N.Mex.	28 neoprene balloons in train	Same as Flight #5, but dribbler lost at launch
7	2 July, 0521 MST	Alamogordo, N.Mex.	16 neoprene balloons in Helios cluster	Microphone, radiosonde, and ballast
8	3 July, 0303 MST	Alamogordo, N.Mex.	Ten 7-ft-diameter GMI (General Mills, Inc.) balloons in Helios cluster	Microphone, radiosonde, and ballast
9	3 July, 1930 MST	Alamogordo, N.Mex.	16 neoprene balloons in Helios cluster	None launched
10	5 July, 0501 MST	Alamogordo, N.Mex.	15-ft-diameter polyethylene balloon	Microphone, radiosonde, and liquid ballast
11A	7 July, 0508 MST	Alamogordo, N.Mex.	15-ft-diameter polyethylene balloon, plus 7 small GMI balloons	Microphone, radiosonde, and liquid ballast

Maximum altitude	Theodolite tracking	Aircraft tracking	Flight duration	Recovery site and amount	Comments
46,000 ft	76 min	None	115 min	No recovery	Failure due to poor rigging, poor technique.
No data	None	None	No data	No data	No flight; telemetry failure.
No data	None	None	No data	No recovery	Balloons broke free.
No data	Theodolite to Arabela	B-17 to Arabela	Unknown (calculated duration: 466 min)	Foster Ranch?	Telemetry failed over Arabela; B-17 pilot then terminated tracking.
About 57,000 ft	259 min	B-17, 343 min	343 min	25 mi east of Roswell; 100%	First successful flight with telemetry and a heavy load.
About 60,000 ft	166 min	B-17, 66 min	166 min	18 mi southeast of launch site; 100%	Altitude control damaged when launched.
48,500 ft	346 min	C-54, 412 min	412 min	East of Cloudcroft, N.Mex.; 1%	Best flight possible with neoprene balloons.
18,500 ft	64 min	C-45 for last part of flight, 30 min	195 min	No recovery	First polyethylene balloons, leaky and smaller than advertised. Balloons dragged on desert but were not recovered.
No data	None	None	No flight	No flight	Flight canceled because of V-2 rocket accident at White Sands Proving Ground.
15,100 ft	82 min	None	>512 min	No recovery	Reported 11 hr later over Albuquerque, then Pueblo, Colo.
17,000 ft	209 min	C-54, 559 min	559 min	19 mi west of Roswell AAF; no recovery	First successful constant-level flight. Interesting path over mountains. Longtime suspect as source of Roswell Incident.

number to each of the flights on which we planned to carry instruments, but if no altitude data were obtained, the flights were not documented and were not listed in the flight summary (see Table 7 in Moore, Smith, and Goldstein 1948). As another result of this experience, we redesigned our launching technique for the next flights by assembling the balloon trains with large aluminum rings, as shown in Schneider (1947a). The rings, made from thick-walled aluminum tubing 4 inches (10 cm) in diameter, were used both as junctions in the flying line and as anchor points through which a doubled nylon line could be run to hold the train before launching and then could be removed by holding one end at the start of the flight. All of the subsequent flights with meteorological balloons in 1947 were launched using this technique.

On 18 April we attempted to launch Flight #2 from Lehigh University to monitor the Helgoland explosion, but after the balloons were inflated, the launch was canceled because of high winds and the malfunction of the telemetry receiver in the airplane that was to track the balloons. We released the balloons and took the instruments back to NYU. The configuration for Flight #2 was shown in Schneider (1947a) and is reproduced in Weaver (1995: attachment 25).

As our progress report for May 1947 (Schneider 1947b) indicates, we inflated a new set of balloons for Flight #3 from Bethlehem on the early morning of 8 May, but after the balloons were inflated, the winds picked up and the balloons broke free before we could attach the instrument payload. It became clear that we needed a launching site with better wind conditions. We also needed a launch site with less air traffic than that around New York City. Accordingly, Peoples arranged for the next set of flights to be made from Alamogordo Army Air Field in New Mexico, where a Watson Laboratories field station was already in operation.

THE JUNE 1947 BALLOON FLIGHTS FROM ALAMOGORDO

In preparing for the Alamogordo expedition, we planned to launch three balloon trains with the same configuration as Flight #2, but modified to use 25 neoprene balloons, weighing 350 grams (about 12 oz) each. Arranged along a 650-foot (200-m) vertical line, the balloons were separated from one another by 20 feet (6 m) of nylon line. Each of these trains was to be towed aloft by three 1,000-gram neoprene balloons, which were to be cut free by a pressure switch when they rose above 45,000 feet (13.7 km).

In an effort to prolong the duration of these balloon flights, we attempted to compensate for any diffusive losses of lifting gas from the balloons in flight by arranging for a slow reduction of the loads they carried with devices that we called dribblers. To accomplish this, we modified the Flight #2 configuration by attaching a plastic reservoir filled with a special kerosene at the bottom of the train. A pressure switch on each reservoir was arranged to allow the kerosene to leak (or, in our jargon, to dribble) out slowly after the balloon altitude exceeded 34,000 feet (10.4 km). For these ballast drops aimed at prolonging the flights, we used a special "compass fluid" kerosene that remained liquid at around –60°C, the temperatures encountered at the tropopause. We replaced the dribblers with more sophisticated servo controls on the flights we launched in August and September 1947.

To minimize the amount of equipment to be transported to New Mexico by plane, Peoples decided to obtain the height measurements needed for the acoustic measurements by tracking the balloons with the Watson Laboratories SCR-584 radar operating in the North Area of the Alamogordo Army Air Field. This radar had been installed to track the German V-2 rockets being launched from White Sands Proving Ground, just across the Tularosa Valley from the Army Air Field.

As I remember, in place of the bulky and heavy receiving station needed to record the pressure signals from balloon-borne radiosondes for our preferred height-determination method, we took to New Mexico several lightweight ML-307B, corner-reflecting radar targets to be carried on our balloon trains so that they could be tracked by the SCR-584 radar. I was familiar with these targets because I had worked with Major Joseph O. Fletcher's people in Colonel Duffy's group in 1944 when the targets were being tested and young weather officers were being trained to use antiaircraft radar for measuring winds aloft. (The idea of tracking balloon-borne retroreflectors by radar had originated with then-Captain Fletcher in 1943 while he was assigned to the Massachusetts Institute of Technology [MIT] Radiation Laboratory in Cambridge. For an account of the target development, see Appendix 1 of this book.)

From our recent reconstruction of the events, it appears that, for the 1947 Alamogordo expedition, Peoples located a supply of some ML-307 radar targets that were left over from the developmental effort at Evans Signal Laboratory in 1944 and 1945. As best we have been able to determine during my recent discussions with Fletcher and with one of his project officers, Edwin J. Istvan, these targets were preproduction prototypes, fabricated by a vendor in the Manhattan garment district. Istvan has stated that the wind loads on the early balloon-borne ML-307 targets caused the first commercial models in 1944 to break up in flight, so design modifications were necessary.[1] These changes for the B model of the targets included an adhesive tape reinforcement of the laminated aluminum foil-paper panel attachment to the balsa wood stiffeners. The manufacturer apparently used some tape that he had in stock; this tape, which was not used in the later production models, had a distinctive pinkish purple pattern of an abstract flowerlike design printed on its backing. Several of the NYU Balloon Group members still remember these colored markings on the targets we used in Alamogordo in 1947. The significance of the markings puzzled us each time that we prepared a target for flight.

Our host in Alamogordo was Albert Crary, a Watson Laboratories geophysicist working for Peoples. Crary had the use of a hangar in the North Area. His mission there was to record and then to analyze the acoustic disturbances produced by ground-based explosions at various ranges, by bombs being dropped in the ocean off Bermuda, and by the V-2 rocket ascents at White Sands. His diary (Crary 1947) contains the only record now existing for some of these events. According to Crary's diary (1947:10), the advance party for the balloon operations arrived in late May 1947:

> May 28 Wed. B-17 in from Watson with Mears, Hackman NYU and Alden. They plan to test fly balloons tomorrow. Other gang with recording equipment due to leave Watson Lab Sat. Got everything ready for HERMES rocket tomorrow. Dona a[nd] White Sands. Finished theoretical calculations of T-X solutions of sky waves.

> May 29 Thurs. Mears and Hackman got balloon ascension off about 1 pm today without plane to follow it. Don and Godbee out to Dona. Bill E[dmondson] and I out to E White Sands to record HERMES Set for 1100 AM, postponed repeatedly, finally fired at 0730 p.m. Rocket off course, landed near Juarez, Mexico.

The balloon ascension on 29 May appears to have been a test flight that did not carry any instruments, because the necessary recording equipment had not arrived. Hackman, the radiosonde specialist, could not have inflated or launched a full-scale balloon cluster on his own, for he was the only member of the NYU Balloon Group at Alamogordo. Given that the plan was to use the Watson Lab radar to track our instrumented flights, I think that this flight was a test of the radar tracking and that it was not successful. In 1947 we never were able to get adequate tracking information from the SCR-584 radar at Alamogordo Army Air Field. The operating crew was not experienced in tracking corner reflectors, and the maximum range of that radar was only 70,000 yards (39.8 miles, or 64 km), much less than the distances traveled by most of our balloons. Because this first test flight did not carry an instrument payload, it was not assigned a number. Neither was it was documented in the NYU records, because no altitude or test data were obtained.

The Cluster Flight on 4 June 1947

Crary's diary has the only record for cluster flight on 4 June 1947. Crary (1947:10) reported that on the arrival of the rest of the party a few days beforehand:

> June 1 Sun. C-47 [arrived] with Moore, Schneider, and others from NYU, also Ireland, Minton, Olsen. NYU men worked on balloons today in north hangar.

> June 2 Mon. Changed shooting plans to coordinate with balloon flights. Balloons all ready to go—receiver in plane and receiver on ground. Edmondson with GR 8 to Roswell PM—Godbee and Reynolds with GR 3 to Silver City. Vivian working on amplitudes of Flight 5—Eileen on April 7 rocket.

> June 3 Tues. Up at 230 AM ready to fly balloons but finally abandoned due to cloudy skies. I went out to Tularosa Range and fired charges from 6 on to 12. Missed 530 shot—trouble getting ordnance man—

> June 4 Wed. Out to Tularosa Range and fired charges between 00 and 06 this am. No balloon flight again on account of clouds. Flew regular sonobuoy mike up in cluster of balloons and had good luck on receiver on ground but poor on plane. Out with Thompson pm. Shot charges from 1800 to 2400. [The sonobuoy mike was a low-frequency microphone from a Navy antisubmarine sensor that Crary and Peoples were using while their own sensors were being developed.]

Crary's contradictory diary entries concerning the 4 June balloon flight are puzzling. My examination of his original handwritten entries suggests that Crary copied them later from other notes; the entries from 2 June through the first half of 5 June appear to have been written at one sitting, with the same pencil and without any corrections or false starts. During the hectic operations in June, he apparently used field notes to record events as they occurred and then transcribed them later into his diary. This is evident in some later entries, where the events of an entire week were lumped together. (See Crary 1947: entries for 23–28 June and

30 June–5 July.) One interpretation of the 4 June entry is that the launch scheduled for making airborne measurements on Crary's surface explosions after midnight was canceled because of clouds, but when the sky cleared later, the cluster of the already inflated balloons was released. Obviously, the initial cancellation and the later launch were recorded in his field notes sequentially, as they occurred, and later he transcribed into his permanent diary, without elaboration.

As is described in the NYU report (Moore, Smith, and Goldstein 1948:27), our term "cluster" denoted the use of multiple balloons. The long, vertical trains used on all the flights during the first expedition to Alamogordo were identified as clusters in that report, as were the later arrangements in which the tether lines were all the same length and each was attached to a ring at the top of the load line so that the balloons touched at their equators. We called this second arrangement the Helios Cluster, after Jean Piccard's balloons, and used it for the first time during the second expedition in July 1947. We found launchings with it to be much easier than with the "cosmic ray trains" because the rigging was simpler, the launching stresses were much less, and the problems with the surface winds decreased.

In our preparations for these flights, we had planned to use the Flight #2 configuration with the dribbler ballast droppers and with the radar targets in place of a radiosonde. Crary's diary indicates that we had spent the two days after our arrival at Alamogordo in preparing for a full-scale flight, so we would not have improvised on the morning of 4 June. After the gear was ready and the balloons were already inflated, we would have launched the full-scale train, complete with the targets for tracking by the Watson Lab radar.

According to the progress report for May 1947 (Schneider 1947b), NYU Flight #3 from Bethlehem, Pennsylvania, on 8 May had been the last attempt to carry instruments aloft before 4 June. The next ascent after 4 June took place on 5 June and was recorded as NYU Flight #5 in the NYU report (Moore, Smith, and Goldstein 1948: table 7). On this basis, it is clear that NYU Flight #4 was launched on 4 June. There is no mention of this flight in the NYU flight summary, because no altitude data or ground track were obtained, but it was assigned a number before the launch because it was to carry a Watson Lab instrument.

I have a distinct memory that James Richard Smith, better known as J.R., watched the 4 June balloon train through a theodolite on a clear, sunny morning and that Captain Larry Dyvad, our contact with the Watson Lab SCR-584, reported that the radar had lost the targets while J.R.

had them in view. It is also my recollection that the balloon train was tracked to about 75 miles (120 km) northeast of Alamogordo by the B-17 crew. As I remember this flight, the B-17 crew terminated their chase while the balloons were still airborne (and while J.R. was still watching them through the theodolite) in the vicinity of Capitan Peak, Arabela, and Bluewater, New Mexico. I, as an easterner, had never heard of those exotically named places, but their names have forever afterward been stuck in my memory. This flight provided the only connection that I have ever had with those places. From the note in Crary's diary, the chase was terminated because of the poor reception of the telemetered acoustic information by the receiver aboard the plane.

We never recovered any of the equipment from that flight, in part because we had not made any advance arrangements to chase it. We had not equipped it with reward tags; we did not use such tags on our early flights because we had no need to recover the expendable equipment, which was usually damaged when found. However, after the failure of the sonobuoy transmissions, Peoples asked that we make efforts to recover the equipment from the next flight so that he could diagnose the problems.

The 4 June flight also resulted in a change in our tracking method. Because the inadequate tracking by the Watson Lab radar had prevented us from obtaining altitude information from that flight, we convinced Peoples to let us carry radiosondes on the subsequent flights. It is significant that the sketch of the balloon train for Flight # 5 (Moore, Smith, and Goldstein 1948: fig. 31) shows a radiosonde but no radar targets. After Flight #4, we no longer relied on radar tracking for our primary performance and location information. All of our numbered flights thereafter carried radiosondes, even though we had to improvise various means for recording the telemetered information until we could obtain the proper receiving equipment from New York.

Many years later, in 1992, I learned that in an interview to the *Roswell Daily Record* on 8 July 1947 (reproduced in McAndrew 1995: app. 1), a rancher named W. W. Brazel was quoted as saying he had found some "bright wreckage" on the J. B. Foster ranch, about 30 miles (48 km) southeast of Corona, New Mexico, on 14 June of that year. Brazel said that the debris consisted of "rubber strips, tinfoil, a rather tough paper" and "considerable scotch tape and some tape with flowers printed upon it had been used in the construction." Brazel continued, "When the debris was gathered up the tinfoil, paper, tape and sticks made a bundle about three feet long and 7 or 8 inches thick [1 m long, 18–20 cm thick], while the rubber made a bundle about 18 or 20 inches long and about 8 inches thick [46–51 cm long, 20 cm thick]. In all, he estimated the entire lot would have weighed maybe five pounds [2 kg]."

In 1994, I learned about a 1979 interview with William Moore in which Bessie Brazel Schreiber confirmed her father's description. However, her account provided some additional information: two aluminum rings about "4 inches [10 cm] around" were also found at the site.

It now seems likely that Brazel found some of the wreckage from NYU Flight #4. He and his daughter provided a good description of the scattered debris that would have been produced by one of our balloon trains with the Flight #2 configuration (sans radiosonde) after it returned to Earth with some of the balloons still inflated. As the lower end of the train dragged across the shrubs on the ground, it would have shed, over an extended area, the debris of several targets and the dangling remnants of other balloons that had burst aloft.

NYU Flight #5

The information on NYU Flight #5 was recorded in the NYU flight summary and in Figures 31, 32, and 33 of the NYU Constant Level Balloon Project report (Moore, Smith, and Goldstein 1948). To avoid confusion with the figures that are part of the present chapter, I will refer to those earlier ones as NYU figures. NYU Figure 31 depicts the flight train, NYU Figure 32 gives the ground track for the flight, and NYU Figure 33 gives the reported time-altitude information.

The atmospheric pressure information from which the altitudes were calculated for Flight #5 was obtained by the manual recording of the changes in the audio signal telemetered from the radiosonde, which transmitted a carrier frequency at 72 MHz. This carrier was modulated at an audio rate ranging from about 10 to 200 Hz by the resistances of temperature and of humidity sensors that were connected to the transmitter input sequentially by a pressure switch (termed a baroswitch). When the atmospheric pressure changed as the balloons rose, the baroswitch moved a pen arm across a segmented commutator to make the connections. After four sequential connections to the humidity sensor, each followed by a temperature input, the next switching connected a fixed resistance to the transmitter, which provided a reference signal. By counting the tone changes in the received signal caused by these pressure-driven switchings, we could deduce the atmospheric pressure and, from the Standard Atmosphere Tables, get an approximate value for the balloons' altitude at each switching.

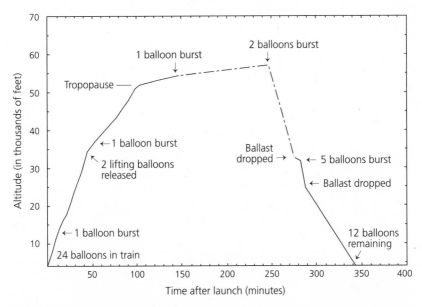

Figure 1. Corrected time-altitude plot for NYU Flight #5, launched at 0516 MST, 5 June 1947, from Alamogordo Army Air Field.

Problems with this technique developed in our constant-level flights because radiosondes were designed originally for use on ascending balloons only. Ambiguities arose when a balloon leveled off and then started a descent. If more than four humidity switchings occurred between reference signals, the observer on the ground could not know whether the balloon was ascending, descending, or oscillating in altitude when the next reference signal was received. Furthermore, because we had not been allowed to bring to Alamogordo our heavy but useful recorder for the radiosonde signals, we had difficulties in keeping track of the switchings, so that errors both in the recording and in the subsequent analysis were possible. Because of the uncertainties in the manual record, two different interpretations (which I refer to interpretations 1 and 2) of the altitude information were presented in NYU Figure 33. As is discussed below, with hindsight and the experiences gained in many subsequent flights, I now think that a different interpretation (interpretation 3), shown in Figure 1, is more likely for the Flight #5 time-altitude information.

On the other hand, the ground track in NYU Figure 32 was obtained from the B-17 crew orbiting beneath the balloon train and from J. R. Smith's theodolite observations. To verify its worth, I have examined the

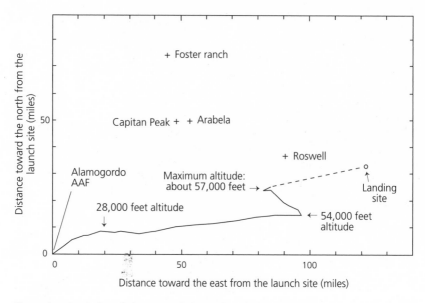

Figure 2.   Ground track for NYU Flight #5, launched at 0516 MST, 5 June 1947, from Alamogordo Army Air Field.

possible ground tracks that would result from the use of the greater altitudes suggested in the midportions of interpretation 3 with the reconstructed theodolite elevation angles extracted from interpretations 1 and 2. Both of these sets of data would place the balloons, while still at their maximum altitude, almost directly over the spot where they later landed. With such a location over the recovery site at the start of the final descent, no further displacement to the east could have occurred during the final descent, despite the strong tropospheric winds observed during the ascent.

Such a cessation of the winds aloft is unlikely, but the ground track shown in NYU Figure 32, and here in Figure 2, is consistent with the actual recovery site, about 25 miles (40 km) east of Roswell. That location is certain because the B-17 pilot followed the balloon train until it descended to Earth, just east of an oil derrick where drilling operations were in progress. The drillers started chasing the balloons, which were dragging the payload on the ground. To stop the drillers, the pilot buzzed them repeatedly at 50 feet (15 m) or so until they desisted. In the meantime, several of us were pursuing the flight in a weapons carrier and were able to arrive at the oil rig before the B-17 returned to Alamogordo. We recovered all of the equipment from that flight and took it back to Alamogordo so that Peoples could evaluate the battery condition in his instruments.

Crary's diary (1947:10–11) has the following entry for that day:

> June 5 Thurs. Up at 4 to shoot 2 charges for balloon flight. Whole assembly of constant altitude balloons sent up at 0500. Fired charges at 0537 and 0552 then was buzzed by plane to return. Receiver at plane did not work at all. Ground receiver worked for a short time but did not receive explosions. B-17 and most of personnel out to Roswell—recovered equipment some 25 miles east of Roswell. Out at 10 this morning. Got TNT and went out to range. Fired shots 12 to 18 every hour. Last of bombing tests this week.

NYU Flight #6

The events associated with NYU Flight #6 and the end of our first Alamogordo visit were described in Crary's diary (1947:11) by the following entries:

> June 6 Fri. NYU personnel getting ready for flight tomorrow. Conference about noon—Hackman with radiosonde, Olsen a[nd] Godbee with receiver to Roswell—also Smith on theodolite. Regular equipment in plane. Edmondson and Reynolds to operate equipment at labs—receiver with GR 8. Worked on adapting GR 8 this pm and this evening. Fired some shots pm at Site 4 but no transmitter for Sonobuoy. This pm put McCurdy low frequency amplifier in circuit before GR 8 and have plenty of signal.

> June 7 Sat. Balloon flight off about 530. Dribbler broken on takeoff. Balloons rose to 60,000'+ or –, broke lift balloons then train came down somewhere in mountains. Recordings at north hangar and at Roswell—but plane did not receive. Shot at 6, 630, 7, 730, 8 and 830 at Site #4. Plane out to find balloons but no luck. All of the NYU personnel and John Alden off in a B-17—Lewis, Gallagher. Went over to Alamogordo with Ireland, Minton, Olsen and Mears but no train today. Making reservations for tomorrow.

> June 8 Sun. Rancher, Sid West, found balloon train south of High Rolls in mountains. Contacted him and made arrangements to recover equipment Monday. Got all recordings of balloon flights. Took Ireland, Mears, Minton, Olsen to Alamogordo to catch train this p.m.

The airplane mentioned in Crary's diary was a B-17G, tail number 44-85680, which was assigned to us from the 4149th Army Air Force Base Unit, Olmstead Army Air Field at Middletown, Pennsylvania. In this period, it was used as an airborne receiving station for the telemetered acoustic data, as a balloon tracker, and as transportation for the project.

Flight #6 was the first NYU balloon flight to carry a reward tag, and we paid the reward offered for its recovery. As described in our progress report for June 1947, we sent a check from NYU to A. P. Crary on June 16 for the "equipment recovery reward." The use of a reward tag for Flight #6 was inspired by the strenuous effort made to recover Flight #5 two days earlier. Reward tags were not used normally with radiosondes nor were they used in our earlier flight attempts from Pennsylvania, because we expected those balloons to fall into the Atlantic Ocean.

From the information that I have been able to reconstruct, after the acoustic equipment failed during the ascent of Flight #4, we made a major effort and recovered Flight #5 ourselves so that Peoples could check the condition of the transmitter batteries. Because this flight landed east of Roswell, more than 140 miles (225 km) by road from the launch site, we immediately recognized that subsequent flights might travel farther and that our only chance of obtaining any information on their fate was to attach reward tags with our address to the balloon train. The tags were aimed at giving the finder an incentive to contact us. The first tags, attached to Flight #6 and launched on 7 June, were handwritten. The printed tags that are shown in the later NYU reports were produced back in New York during August 1947 in preparation for the third expedition back to Alamogordo in September.

After our problems in trying to record manually the radiosonde signals from Flight #5, on the next day (6 June), we borrowed a Brush oscillograph from Peoples and were able to jury-rig a recorder for the pressure signals. This solution was not entirely satisfactory because, at its slowest speed, the oscillograph fed chart paper at the rate of about 6 inches (15 cm) per second and often ran out of paper; the record from the next flight (#6) was discontinuous because of the frequent need to reload paper. Nevertheless, a somewhat better record was obtained than was possible during Flight #5. The NYU technical report (Moore, Smith, and Goldstein 1948) describes Flight #6 with a plot of its ground track in NYU Figure 34, with its time-altitude curve in NYU Figure 35, and with the essentials listed in the flight summary.

With 49 years of hindsight, it appears to me that there are some problems with these illustrations. Crary's diary reports the maximum altitude for Flight #6 as about 60,000 feet (18 km); NYU Figure 35 gives it as 72,500 feet (22.1 km). The last point in the ground track is at a greater range and at an azimuth of about 12° or 13° greater than that for the location reported for the site where the debris from this flight was recovered. In the following sections, reinterpretations of the data for Flights #5 and #6 are presented that are now based on my later education into high-altitude ballooning.

A Reexamination of the Data for NYU Flight #5

Inspection of the ground track shows that winds changed the directions and speeds of the balloons shortly after their rate of rise decreased to low values. From the record, it appears that the decrease in the rise rate was not due to the loss of lifting balloons, because none of them burst or were released at this time. It is more probable that the lower rise rates resulted from the balloons' entering the thermally stable air in the stratosphere. The temperature of the air in the lower stratosphere increases with altitude, often as much as 1°C per 1,000 feet (300 m), whereas near the top of the troposphere it cools by about 3°C for each 1,000 feet of rise. On the other hand, helium, being monatomic, has a lower specific heat than does diatomic air and, on expanding with increasing altitude, cools by about 4.2°C per 1,000 feet of rise in both regions of the atmosphere. As a result, the helium in a rising balloon tends always to be colder than the surrounding air, which reduces its buoyancy until heat from the surrounding air leaks across the balloon envelope and reduces further cooling.

Because of the differences in "thermal lapse rates," the contrast between the temperature of helium in an ascending balloon and that of the surrounding air increases markedly after the balloon rises into the stratosphere. This phenomenon immediately reduces the buoyancy of the balloon, which in turn decreases its rate of rise. The observed decrease in the rate of rise that occurs just above the 52,000-foot (15.8-km) altitude is therefore a good indicator that Flight #5 had entered the stratosphere.

Initially, the mean winds in the transition region at the base of the stratosphere were from the southeast at about 15 mph (6.7 m/s). Later, just before the train started its final descent, the balloons entered a level where the winds came from the east. Because east winds were not encountered at any lower level during this flight, this indicates that these east winds were encountered because the balloons had reached a new, higher level.

Interpretation 3 (Figure 1) is a plot of the probable performance of the balloons in Flight #5 and is based on the recognition that they had ascended to their highest level during the flight while they were being carried westward by the winds in the stratosphere. This plot makes more sense than do the time-altitude curves given for interpretations 1 and 2 in

TABLE 2

Winds Aloft Encountered by NYU Flight #5 on 5 June 1947

Time (min)	Altitude (ft)	Rise rate (fpm)	East (mi)	North (mi)	Wind speed (mph)	Wind from azimuth (°)
0	4,069		0.00	0.00		
		793			15	240
10	12,000		2.17	1.25		
		625			48	231
14	14,500		4.63	3.24		
		450			39	235
20	17,200		7.78	5.45		
		650			52	251
25	20,500		11.91	6.88		
		660			38	262
30	23,800		15.05	7.34		
		667			41	254
36	27,800		18.96	8.44		
		756			29	275
45	34,600		23.31	8.03		
		300			42	261
49	35,800		26.06	8.47		
		333			48	279
52	36,800		28.42	8.10		
		240			63	275
57	38,000		33.64	7.64		
		257			69	262
64	39,800		41.59	8.76		
		280			74	257
69	41,200		47.64	10.13		
		233			57	263
75	42,600		53.26	10.84		
		300			100	266
81	44,400		63.19	11.60		
		420			92	265
86	46,500		70.80	12.23		
		314			63	259
93	48,700		78.07	13.63		
		383			65	264
99	51,000		84.55	14.30		
		200			38	267
105	52,200		88.37	14.47		
		50			17	270
135	53,700		96.92	14.49		
		53			9	144
150	54,500		95.63	16.26		
		30			9	115
180	55,400		91.41	18.18		
		27			9	129
210	56,200		88.05	20.90		
		25			13	131
230	56,700		84.72	23.81		
		18			11	82
247	57,000		81.72	23.37		
		−792			14	244
259	47,500		84.32	24.66		
		−519			27	258
343	3,870		120.74	32.55		

NYU Figure 33; their presentation of balloons floating at some intermediate altitude after some of the lifting balloons burst is unrealistic. From
our later experience, we know that these balloons would either continue
to rise or to descend without floating at some constant level. In fact, the
slow stratospheric ascent depicted in interpretation 3 is exactly the performance that we were trying to achieve with the use of the dribbler ballast dropper.

On the other hand, as discussed earlier in the section on NYU Flight #
5, I find no reason to modify the original ground track shown in NYU
Figure 32 and reproduced here as Figure 2. An independent check for the
validity of the balloons' displacement in the stratosphere to the left of
their track in the troposphere is given by the location of the landing site
relative to the trajectory earlier in the flight. If the balloons had not entered the stratosphere but had continued in the upper troposphere, they
would have passed about 17 miles (27 km) south of the actual landing site
and would have landed more than 150 miles (240 km) to the east at the
end of the 343-minute flight. The location of the actual recovery site attests
to the correctness of the ground track in regard to the horizontal movements of the balloon train while it was in the stratosphere on 5 June 1947.

Table 2 lists the winds calculated from NYU Figure 32 and the calculated rates of rise for the balloon train from Figure 1. These data show
that the tropospheric winds were quite strong on 5 June. The wind
speeds increased with altitude, exceeding 80 mph (36 m/s) just below the
tropopause. The mean wind above 25,000 feet (7.6 km) was about 60
mph (27 m/s) from an azimuth of 265°. These winds indicate an appreciable horizontal pressure gradient aloft at some levels in excess of 1 mil-
libar per 100 kilometers (62 mi), with low pressures to the north. Furthermore, the shear between the winds below 25,000 feet and those
above that level suggest a lower-level, horizontal atmospheric thermal
gradient oriented with lower temperatures to the northeast. However, the
increase of the wind speeds with altitude from 28,000 feet (8.5 km) to the
tropopause indicates that the horizontal temperature gradient in this
layer was directed with low temperature toward the north. These orien-
tations are different from those that occurred during Flight #6, launched
two days later. Their significance is discussed later.

A Reexamination of the Data for NYU Flight #6

As discussed in the earlier section on Flight #6, the ground track in NYU
Figure 34 does not fit the location reported for the flight debris recovery.
If the ground track were correct and errors were made in reporting the

recovery site, the actual site would have been deeper in the mountains, in an area almost inaccessible from High Rolls, where Sid West, who recovered the equipment, resided. However, there was a road directly south from High Rolls that passed near the location where West reported having recovered the debris from this flight. Accordingly, I place more trust in his report for the impact location than in the end point for the ground track shown in NYU Figure 34.

On examining the track, I noted that all of the azimuths appeared to be rotated clockwise about 12° or 13°, suggesting that perhaps someone made an unnecessary correction to the original azimuths measured during the flight. The magnetic declination for Alamogordo at that time was about 12.5°. It appears to me that someone in the NYU data reduction section may have added the magnetic declination to the azimuths reported for the theodolite measurements when the analyst learned that the theodolite orientation was made using a compass but he or she did not know that this correction had already been made. In any event, replotting the ground track data after subtracting 12.5° from the azimuth for each location rotates the track counterclockwise so that the last point on the track is almost on the azimuth of the reported recovery site. However, that last point is about 20 percent more distant from the launch site than is the recovery site. But the maximum altitude of 72,500 feet (22.1 km) given in NYU Figure 35 is about 20 percent greater than the peak altitude of about 60,000 feet (18 km) given in Crary's diary for this flight.

Figure 3 in this chapter was prepared by use of the corrected azimuths and by scaling the horizontal distances by the factor (60,000 – 4,069)/(72,500 – 4,069), where 4,069 is the altitude in feet of the theodolite at Alamogordo. With these corrections to the Flight #6 ground track, the last point on the new ground track lies just upwind (i.e., southwest) of the probable actual recovery site. Another advantage of scaling on Crary's maximum altitude is that it makes the tropopause heights agree with those inferred during Flight #5. Furthermore, the direction (85°) from which the stratospheric wind was blowing in the revised ground track (Figure 3) is the same as that found at the maximum altitude reached by Flight #5. For these reasons I think the revised plot is probably more nearly correct than the one given in NYU Figure 34. The origin of the altitude error in plotting is not clear; Crary obviously obtained his value for the maximum altitude from us, because we received the radiosonde signals during the flight, but for some unknown reason, the NYU data analysts chose a different interpretation, one that now seems

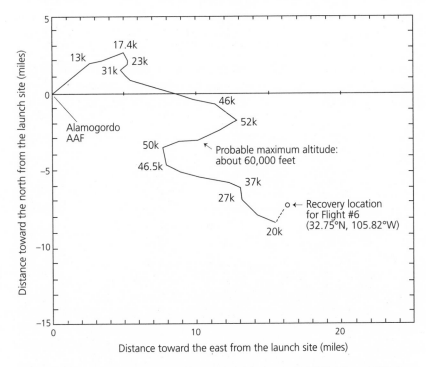

Figure 3. Ground track for NYU Flight #6, launched at 0509 MST, 7 June 1947, from Alamogordo Army Air Field. The azimuth and altitude data recorded for this flight have been modified so that the ground track fits the location where the balloon train was recovered. The numbers followed by the letter *k* along the track give the calculated altitudes in thousands of feet.

unlikely. Table 3 lists the winds aloft that I calculated from the revised data for Flight #6.

Weather in Central New Mexico, Early June 1947

After a long search, several of the weather records for central New Mexico in early June 1947 have been located. John M. Lewis of the National Severe Storms Laboratory at Norman, Oklahoma, obtained Northern Hemisphere surface and 500-millibar atmospheric pressure maps from the U.S. Navy Fleet Numerical Weather Central for the first week of June 1947. Excerpts from the 12Z (Z = Greenwich Mean Time; 12Z = 0500 Mountain Standard Time, or MST) for 4 June 1947 are shown in Figures 4 and 5. These maps show an extended low-pressure region extending

TABLE 3

Winds Aloft Encountered by NYU Flight #6 on 7 June 1947

Time (min)	Altitude (ft)	Rise rate (fpm)	East (mi)	North (mi)	Wind speed (mph)	Wind from azimuth (°)
0	4,069		0.00	0.00		
		727			17	234
12	12,700		2.69	1.99		
		439			11	256
16	14,500		3.40	2.17		
		572			21	253
21	17,400		5.03	2.67		
		572			4	334
31	23,100		5.33	2.05		
		618			2	20
40	28,600		5.25	1.82		
		654			9	54
44	31,300		4.77	1.47		
		654			10	311
50	35,200		5.54	0.80		
		654			25	285
54	37,800		7.13	0.37		
		627			22	286
60	41,600		9.23	−0.23		
		1,022			34	282
64	45,600		11.42	−0.70		
		934			16	307
71	52,200		12.87	−1.81		
		726			9	64
82	60,000		11.41	−2.53		
		−672			12	67
89	55,000		10.08	−3.08		
		−545			23	85
92	53,400		8.93	−3.18		
		−613			13	73
98	49,700		7.73	−3.54		
		−467			10	349
105	46,500		7.96	−4.69		
		−722			10	295
111	42,100		8.85	−5.11		
		−858			28	286
113	40,400		9.74	−5.36		
		−507			32	281
118	37,900		12.37	−5.87		
		−613			23	297
120	36,700		13.06	−6.23		
		−654			3	352
135	26,800		13.17	−7.03		
		−350			13	314
142	24,400		14.23	−8.05		
		−584			12	293
149	20,300		15.51	−8.60		
		−609			5	213
166	10,000		16.30	−7.39		

Note: These data were calculated from the corrected trajectory for Flight #6.

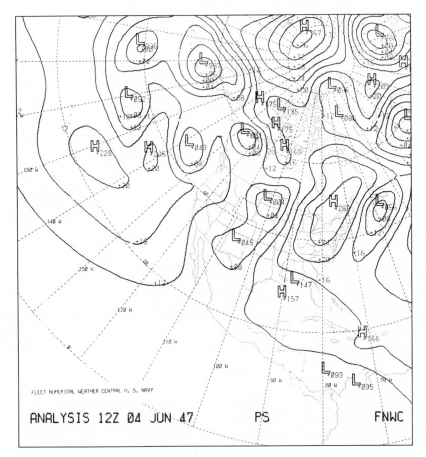

Figure 4. Section of the Navy Fleet Numerical Weather Central's Northern Hemisphere surface pressure map for 0500 MST, 4 June 1947. A region of low pressure extends from northern Mexico to North Dakota.

from New Mexico to North Dakota. The winds aloft on the 500-mb surface (at a nominal altitude of 18,000 ft, or 5.5 km) over New Mexico were from 225° (the southwest). The axis of the associated low-pressure trough aloft was to the west, over Oregon. The clouds reported in Crary's diary during the early morning hours on 3 and 4 June probably were associated with this weather disturbance.

Later, Sam McCown, at the National Climatic Data Center (NCDC) in Asheville, North Carolina, was able to find the Weather Bureau forms 1083 (Original Record of 6-Hourly Synoptic Observations) and the WBAN-10 forms for surface weather observations from the reporting

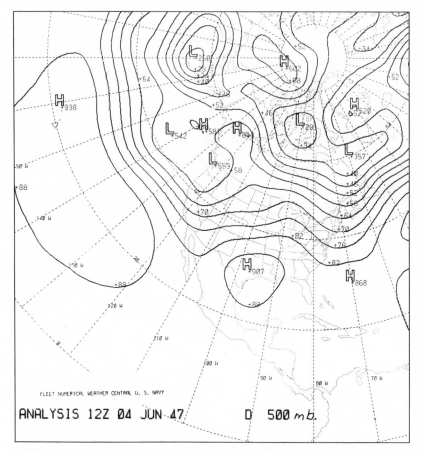

Figure 5.   Section of the Navy Fleet Numerical Weather Central's Northern Hemisphere 500-mb pressure map for 0500 MST, 4 June 1947. The winds at the nominal 18,000-foot (5.5-km) altitude level over New Mexico were blowing from the southwest.

stations in West Texas and in southern New Mexico during the first week of June 1947. ("WBAN" stands for Weather Bureau/Army/Navy.) These records show disturbed weather with towering cumuli and thunderstorms over the Pecos River region of West Texas on the afternoon of 3 June. However, at the same time over Engle, New Mexico (about 50 mi, or 80 km, west northwest of Alamogordo Army Air Field), the sky was mostly clear until around 2230 MST that evening, when a broken layer of five-tenths altostratus and one-tenth cirrus clouds moved over the station. The cirrus increased to six-tenths of the sky coverage, and the altostratus clouds over Engle disappeared before the more complete observation was made at 0230 MST on 4 June. The cirrus was reported as "scattered" at 0300 MST, when the next routine observation was taken.

The weather station at Alamogordo operated only during the working day. The first observation on 4 June was taken at 0730 MST, when sky coverage of two-tenths scattered cirrostratus clouds was reported at an estimated altitude of 20,000 feet (6 km). The El Paso observer recorded two-tenths altocumulus at an estimated altitude of 12,000 feet (3.7 km) from 0126 to 0226 MST on 4 June. Thereafter the sky was more or less clear until noon. At Columbus, New Mexico, upwind of Alamogordo at the time, the four-tenths altostratus cloud deck at 2314 MST on 3 July disappeared after 0211 MST on 4 July, leaving some scattered cirrus clouds over the Columbus area.

Winds Aloft over Central New Mexico, June 1947

While searching the NCDC records, Sam McCown also found the pilot balloon measurements from the weather stations in New Mexico and West Texas for June 1947. Among them were the rawin (radio [or radar] winds aloft) measurements from White Sands Proving Ground. These measurements were made in support of the V-2 rocket program by Captain John R. Smith, an Air Weather Service officer charged with supplying the weather information needed at the proving ground. We had earlier been able to obtain copies of two reports on his operations that he sent to the Air Weather Service in May and August 1947. In those reports (Smith 1947a,b), he described the equipment available to him and how he used it.

During the periods before and after each planned rocket firing, Captain Smith's crew launched 2,000-gram balloons carrying 400-MHz rawinsondes that were tracked with the SCR-658 radio-direction finder (essentially an electronic theodolite). The purpose was to obtain air temperatures, pressures, humidity data, and wind information. In addition, Smith used similar balloons to carry single corner-reflecting ML-307 radar targets to obtain another measure of the winds aloft. These targets, discussed later in this chapter, were tracked with an SCR-584 radar (the same type used by the Watson Lab people at Alamogordo) and with Askania phototheodolites.

On days when V-2 operations were not planned, Smith's crew launched 400-MHz radiosondes beneath smaller balloons that did not go as high as the 2,000-gram balloons. These flights were usually tracked with the SCR-658 direction finder. In the NCDC collection of pilot balloon wind reports was the Winds Aloft Summary Report form, WBAN-22, which

TABLE 4

Winds Aloft over the Alamogordo Area for 3 and 4 June 1947

Altitude (m)	3 June ascent		4 June ascent		Interpolated wind data for 0300 MST, 4 June			
	Direction (points)	Speed (m/s)	Direction (points)	Speed (m/s)	Direction (points)	Speed (m/s)	Direction (°)	Speed (mph)
1,260	08	04	09	04	8.75	4	197	9
1,500	09	04	11	06	10.5	5.5	236	12
2,000	10	05	11	07	10.75	6.5	242	15
2,500	11	06	11	12	11	10.5	247	23
3,000	10	09	11	07	10.75	7.5	242	17
4,000	09	12	10	15	9.75	14.25	219	32
5,000	10	20	10	16	10	17	225	38
6,000	10	21	10	25	10	24	225	54
7,000	10	19	11	21	10.75	20.5	242	46
8,000	10	15	10	26	10	23.25	225	52
9,000	10	30	10	22	10	24	225	54
10,000	10	16	11	21	10.75	19.75	242	44
11,000	10	25	11	23	10.75	23.5	242	53
12,000	10	32	11	24	10.75	26	242	58
13,000	10	40	11	36	10.75	37	242	83
14,000			11	34	10.75	35.5	242	79

Note: Station, Orogrande, New Mexico, 32 miles (51.5 km) south of Alamogordo AAF; latitude 32°24′ N, longitude 106°9′ W; altitude, 1,260 meters (4,134 ft). The rawin ascents started at 0900 MST each day and were tracked by an SCR-658 radio direction finder operating at around 400 MHz. See text for more information about the measurements.

contained the wind data at standard levels above Orogrande, New Mexico, for balloons launched each morning at 0900 MST during much of June 1947. (The rawinsonde station at Orogrande was one of the facilities Captain Smith operated in support of the V-2 missile launches. It was about 32 miles, or 51.5 km, south of our launch area on Alamogordo Army Air Field.)

An extract from the Winds Aloft Summary Report form, WBAN-22, for June 1947 from Orogrande is shown in Table 4. The standard levels in altitude for which the winds were reported were at 500-meter (1,640-ft) intervals until the 3,000-meter (9,840-ft) level was reached; thereafter, the winds were reported at each successively higher 1,000-meter (3,280-ft) level until the balloon burst. The wind speeds were reported in meters per second. The directions from which the wind came were reported in compass points, with 16 points to the full 360° azimuth circle. Therefore, the measured winds from any direction within a 22.5° azimuth sector were reported as all coming from the same compass point.

Winds Aloft over Alamogordo, 4 June 1947

The weather disturbances on 3 June were coupled to a trough aloft that trailed behind the surface low-pressure area shown in Figure 4. This situation occurs in a baroclinic atmosphere and is caused by horizontal temperature gradients on the surfaces of constant pressure (Holton 1979:138). From the NCDC pilot balloon wind records on the afternoon of 3 June, ahead of the trough aloft, the winds at the 20,000-foot (6-km) level were from about 205° at 45 mph (20 m/s) over El Paso and 40 mph (19 m/s) over Albuquerque. As the trough approached, the winds aloft veered clockwise, coming more from the west. The Orogrande rawinsonde launched at 0900 MST on 4 June showed that the mean tropospheric wind then came from an azimuth of about 240°. The axis of the trough probably passed over central New Mexico on the morning of 5 June, causing the mean wind vector to veer further clockwise in azimuth. The tropospheric winds above 20,000 feet that acted on Flight #5 (launched at 0516 MST on 5 June) came from an azimuth of about 265°. The winds aloft continued to shift clockwise after the trough passed to the east; the winds aloft acting on Flight #6 (launched at 0509 MST on 7 June) came from about 285°.

An examination of the pilot balloon wind records made at Orogrande on the morning of 4 June suggests that the winds aloft around the 6-km (20,000-ft) level were veering at the rate of about 5° per hour between 0811 and 1020 MST. Using this observation as an indicator, I interpo-

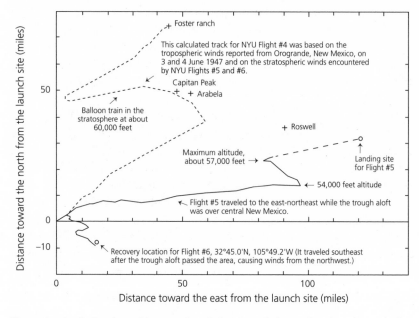

Figure 6. A calculated possible ground track for NYU Flight #4 plotted on the tracks for Flights #5 and #6. Foster Ranch is at about 33°56.35'N, 105°18.36'W (the location of the quarter-section marker on the border between Sections 19 and 30, T4S, R16E).

lated between the 4 June rawin record at 0900 MST and the one on 3 June in an effort to obtain a measure of the tropospheric winds that might have acted on a balloon train launched soon after the skies cleared around 0300 MST of 4 June. Those interpolated measurements of winds aloft are listed in Table 4.

There are, of course, many uncertainties associated with this analysis of the 4 June events. The launching time is not known, but given that Crary's diary shows that he was ready for the launching soon after midnight on 3 June, and given that the clouds that caused the launch delay went away at around 0230 MST on 4 June, I am sure that we would have launched as rapidly as possible thereafter. Crary's diary indicates clearly that we launched a "cluster of balloons" that morning. My memory of the tracking of the balloon train to the vicinity of Arabela places another constraint on the timing: the only winds during this expedition that would have carried the balloons to the northeast toward Arabela occurred on 3 June and early on 4 June.

Another uncertainty has to do with the compass point granularity in the Orogrande WBAN-22 wind direction reports. Because one compass

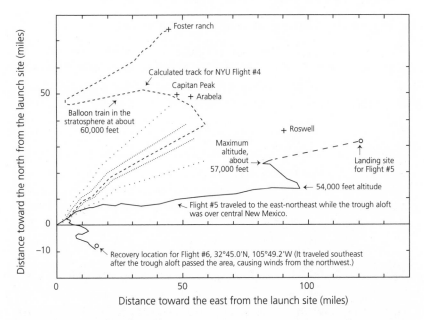

Figure 7. A plot showing the possible errors in the calculated ground track for NYU Flight #4, arising from the granularity in the Orogrande rawin report. The lines with the more widely spaced dots around the calculated trajectory show the limits of the possible uncertainty (±11.25°) due to the reported tropospheric wind directions' being specified to the nearest compass point. The lines with the more closely spaced dots show the limits of the probable uncertainty in the trajectory up through the troposphere.

point covers 22.5° in azimuth, there is an uncertainty of up to 11.25° in each of the actual, reconstructed wind directions. However, when a trajectory is made up by summing the successive displacements of the balloon train as it passed through many different levels, in each of which the uncertainty in wind direction was 11.25°, from simple statistics the probable uncertainty, θ, in the azimuth angle at the last point on the trajectory is

$$\theta = \frac{\pm 11.25°}{\sqrt{N-1}}$$

where N is the number of levels with winds of this directional uncertainty. Because 17 levels were used in constructing the tropospheric trajectory shown in Figure 6, the probable uncertainty arising from the wind direction granularity in the azimuth of the highest point in the troposphere on ascent is 11.25°/4, or about 2.8°. The effect of this uncertainty on the calculated trajectory is shown in Figure 7.

A Possible Ground Track for NYU Flight #4

The calculated track illustrated in Figure 6 was obtained by assuming that the Flight #4 balloons behaved much as did the Flight #5 balloons on the next day. That is, Flight #4 was assumed to have a normal rate of rise in the troposphere of about 600 feet per minute (3 m/s); and it was assumed to have entered the stratosphere, where it was carried more or less to the west, as both Flights #5 and #6 were.

In our early ballooning, we learned about an interesting phenomenon: during the summer months, the winds in the stratosphere over midlatitudes and northern latitudes invariably flow from the east and are not affected significantly by tropospheric weather changes. This phenomenon is caused by the annual formation of a hemispheric high-pressure system (an anticyclone) centered approximately over the North Pole. The result of solar heating, this system develops soon after the spring equinox. (In the winter months, the opposite flow occurs—the stratospheric winds blow from the west around a cyclonic vortex that forms over the Pole. This vortex is created by the subsidence of stratospheric air as the tropospheric air beneath is cooled by radiation to space. The polar air sinks and flows outward over the earth's surface, behind polar fronts in outbreaks of Arctic air.) Flight #5 gave us our first experience with these surprising summertime stratospheric winds. The surprise was repeated when Flight #6 entered the stratosphere.

In the years that followed, we observed many ground tracks similar to the one calculated for Flight #4. Most of the later high-altitude balloons launched during the summer months were initially carried to the east by the winds in the troposphere, but after ascending into the stratosphere, they were blown to the west, often for hundreds of miles. And as they descended at the end of the flights, they were carried back toward the east, again by the winds at lower levels. The calculated trajectory for Flight #4 is consistent with many of the trajectories produced by our subsequent balloon ascents into the stratosphere.

The long flight duration inferred from these calculations would have been possible if the balloons had been launched early in the morning, in the darkness an hour or more before local sunrise (which, with the mountains to the east, began at about 0515 MST). Neoprene balloons like these would usually burst after about 6 hours' exposure to sunlight. But until the sunlight caused the first balloons to burst, the ballast drops from the dribbler would have tended to make the balloons rise slowly in the stratosphere. After some of the balloons burst, the Flight #4 train would have started to descend. Its rate of descent would have increased greatly after the remaining balloons reentered the troposphere and as more balloons burst.

For the train's landing site, I used the location of the debris that was given by Karl Pflock, an independent investigator of the Roswell Incident. According to Pflock,[2] the midsection of the debris was identified as being located at the quarter-section marker that is midway on the boundary between Sections 19 and 30 in Township 4 South (from the New Mexico Baseline), Range 16 East (from the Principal Meridian of New Mexico). The coordinates of the quarter-section marker are 33°56.35'N and 105°18.36'W. This identification was provided by J. O. Payne and independently by Loretta Proctor and Juanita Sultemeier—all surviving neighbors of W. W. Brazel, the rancher who said that he found the debris on 14 June 1947.

A qualitative test of the calculated trajectory can be obtained by use of the azimuths from Alamogordo to the landing sites for Flight #5, launched around the time of passage of the trough aloft, and for Flight #6, launched well after the trough's passage. Flight #6 was recovered at a location at an azimuth of 114.5° from Alamogordo. Flight #5, launched two days earlier while the axis of the trough was about over central New Mexico, landed at an azimuth of 75°, or about 40° counterclockwise from where Flight #6 was recovered. From this shift in trajectories associated with the later phases of the trough aloft passage, I expect that a balloon launched still earlier—while the axis of the trough aloft was to the west of the Alamogordo area and producing winds aloft from the southwest—would have had a trajectory that would carry it into the northeast, perhaps another 40° counterclockwise at an azimuth of around 35°. It is of interest that the location reported for the debris field on the Foster ranch lies on an azimuth of 31° at a distance of 86.4 miles (139 km) from the North Area of the Alamogordo Army Air Field.

Because we planned to make all of these early cluster flights with the Flight #2 configuration we adopted after our learning experiences in Pennsylvania, I think that Flight #4 used our best equipment and probably performed about as well as or better than Flight #5. From this analysis, it appears highly probable that Flight #4 landed to the north of the Capitan Peak–Arabela area, where it was last reported. The plot of the possible ground track shown in Figure 6 is based on the information listed in Table 5.

The calculated possible track is consistent with a report by Major Jesse Marcel, the Roswell Army Air Field intelligence officer who saw the

TABLE 5

Possible Trajectory for NYU Flight #4

Altitude (ft)	Rise rate (fpm)	Time (min)	Wind speed (mph)	Wind from (°)	u (mph)	v (mph)	x (mi)	y (mi)	HDO (mi)	Azimuth (°)
4,069	100	0.0	9	197	2.6	8.6	0.0	0.0	0.0	0.0
4,921	600	2.8	12	236	9.9	6.7	0.3	0.2	0.4	56.0
6,562	600	5.5	15	242	13.2	7.0	0.9	0.6	1.1	59.7
8,202	600	8.3	23	247	21.2	9.0	1.8	1.0	2.1	63.3
9,843	600	12.4	17	242	15.0	8.0	2.9	1.5	3.3	62.8
13,123	600	17.8	32	219	20.1	24.9	4.8	3.8	6.1	51.7
16,404	600	23.3	38	225	26.9	26.9	7.2	6.2	9.5	49.3
19,685	600	28.8	54	225	38.2	38.2	10.7	9.7	14.4	47.8
22,966	600	34.2	46	242	40.6	21.6	14.4	11.7	18.5	51.0
26,247	600	39.7	52	225	36.8	36.8	17.8	15.0	23.3	49.8
29,528	600	45.2	54	225	38.2	38.2	21.2	18.5	28.2	48.9
32,808	600	50.6	44	242	38.8	20.7	24.8	20.4	32.1	50.6
36,089	600	56.1	53	242	46.8	24.9	29.0	22.7	36.8	52.0
39,370	600	61.6	58	242	51.2	27.2	33.7	25.1	42.0	53.3
42,651	600	67.0	83	242	73.3	39.0	40.4	28.7	49.5	54.6
45,932	600	72.5	79	242	69.8	37.1	46.7	32.1	56.7	55.6
49,213	450	79.2	66	242	58.3	31.0	53.3	35.5	64.1	56.3
52,000	350	83.4	38	242	33.6	17.8	55.6	36.8	66.7	56.5
52,100	70	95.5	20	242	17.7	9.4	59.2	38.7	70.7	56.8
53,700	40	125.5	17	144	−10.0	13.8	54.2	45.6	70.8	49.9
54,500	40	166.8	14	115	−12.7	5.9	45.5	49.6	67.3	42.5
57,000	27	231.6	10	100	−9.8	1.7	34.8	51.5	62.2	34.1

58,000	21	317.3	10	80	-9.8	-1.7	20.7	49.0	53.2	22.9
60,600	20	384.8	12	80	-11.8	-2.1	7.5	46.7	47.3	9.1
60,700	15	389.8	12	80	-11.8	-2.1	6.5	46.5	46.9	7.9
60,750	-300	396.0	12	80	-11.8	-2.1	5.3	46.3	46.6	6.5
57,000	-400	404.4	10	100	-9.8	1.7	3.9	46.5	46.7	4.8
54,000	-500	409.4	14	144	-8.2	11.3	3.2	47.5	47.6	3.8
52,000	-600	413.6	38	242	33.6	17.8	5.5	48.7	49.0	6.5
49,000	-700	420.2	66	242	58.3	31.0	12.0	52.2	53.5	13.0
42,651	-800	430.4	83	242	73.3	39.0	24.4	58.7	63.6	22.5
32,808	-850	438.1	54	242	47.7	25.4	30.5	62.0	69.1	26.2
29,528	-900	441.7	54	225	38.2	38.2	32.8	64.3	72.2	27.0
26,247	-900	445.4	52	225	36.8	36.8	35.0	66.5	75.2	27.8
22,966	-900	449.0	46	242	40.6	21.6	37.5	67.9	77.5	28.9
19,685	-900	452.7	54	225	38.2	38.2	39.8	70.2	80.7	29.6
16,404	-900	456.3	38	225	26.9	26.9	41.5	71.8	82.9	30.0
13,123	-900	460.0	32	219	20.1	24.9	42.7	73.3	84.8	30.2
9,843	-900	463.6	17	242	15.0	8.0	43.6	73.8	85.7	30.6
6,562	-900	465.8	15	242	13.2	7.0	44.1	74.1	86.2	30.8
5,900	-900	466.2	12	236	9.9	6.7	44.1	74.1	86.3	30.8

u = eastward-directed component of the wind at the indicated level.

v = northward-directed component of the wind at the indicated level.

x = balloon displacement toward the east (sum of products of the mean eastward wind component in the altitude interval with the time interval required for the balloon train to rise through the specified layer).

y = balloon displacement toward the north (sum of products of the mean northward wind component in the altitude interval with the time interval required for the balloon train to rise through the specified layer).

HDO = horizontal distance out from the launch site in the North Area of the Alamogordo Army Air Field.

Azimuth = direction to the train from the launch site.

debris on the Foster ranch in early July 1947. Marcel reported that the debris was laid out on a line oriented toward the northeast, with most of the debris in that direction. With the winds prevailing over New Mexico on 4 June, a descending train of balloons would have been dragged toward the northeast after it touched down, and the equipment at the bottom of the train that caught in obstructions on the ground would have been torn off. During the recovery of subsequent flights, we found torn fragments of radar targets spread over the ground when the balloons that carried them were dragged by surface winds after returning to Earth.

When the wind information is coupled with the similarities between the debris described by the eyewitnesses and the materials used in our balloon flight trains (the balsa sticks; the "tinfoil"; the tape with pastel, pinkish purple flowers; the smoky gray balloon rubber with a burnt odor; the eyelets; the tough paper; the aluminum rings 4 inches, or 10 cm, in diameter; and the black box), NYU Flight #4 cannot be excluded as a likely source of the debris that W. W. Brazel found on the Foster ranch in 1947.

Apparently, much of the equipment carried on that flight was not recovered. Brazel made no mention of finding the pressure switches, the sonobuoy microphone, or the nylon flying line, 600 feet (183 m) long, that connected the balloons in the train. I suspect that the remaining balloons in the train lifted off and blew away to the northeast after the radar targets, the dangling fragments of the balloons that had already burst, and the aluminum rings at the bottom of the train were detached as the surface winds blew the train over the ground when it first touched down on the Foster ranch. In any event, to my knowledge, no recovery of the upper portions of the Flight #4 balloon train was ever reported.

AN ANALYSIS OF THE ROSWELL INCIDENT DEBRIS

In an interview on 8 July 1947, published the next day in the *Roswell Daily Record* and reprinted in McAndrew (1995: app. 1), Brazel described in considerable detail the debris he had found on the Foster ranch. Five points can be cited linking the wreckage he describes to the NYU balloon flights. In the discussion that follows, quotes attributed to Brazel are from that interview.

Point 1: The Color of the "Rubber"

First of all, Brazel reported that "the rubber was smoky gray." In 1947, the official, normal method of carrying a radar target aloft for wind measurements by all the weather services was to attach it to a pilot balloon.

According to TM 11-2405, the official army technical manual on meteo-rological balloons, the largest pilot balloon was the 100-gram size. All of the pilot balloons were pigmented to allow the meteorological observers a choice of the color that would give the best contrast and visibility when the balloon was viewed against either blue sky or against clouds over-head. The ML-160(A) models were black 100-gram pilot balloons that often were used to carry the pilot balloon radar targets aloft. As far as I can determine, the field artillery weather units that used these radar targets were not supplied with the larger sounding balloons, and the Army Air Force weather stations that used the 350-gram balloons to make radiosonde observations were not supplied with radars or with tar-gets. However, during 1947 and 1948 the NYU Balloon Group and the White Sands Weather Detachment used Dewey and Almy "DAREX" sounding balloons in great quantities. We flew multiple radar targets of the ML-307 configuration repeatedly beneath clusters of unpigmented sounding balloons.

As I remember, these early sounding balloons became dirty-gray or brown after stretching and exposure to solar ultraviolet light during their ascent to high altitudes. The balloons usually burst within about 8 hours or less as a result of the degradation caused by exposure to sunlight. Af-ter several weeks of additional exposure to sunlight, the upper surfaces of the fragments on the ground turned black with a gray sheen. (The sheen was caused by the exudation of plasticizer from within the balloon film, under the influence of the solar heating.) The layers of film that were shielded from direct sunlight darkened more slowly, so the debris recov-ered after a few weeks often was mottled in appearance. The photo-graphs by J. Bond Johnson of the balloon debris in Brigadier General Ramey's office on 8 July have that mottled character.

Brazel's report indicates to me that sounding balloons were used to carry pilot balloon radar targets. The NYU group and then-Captain John Smith's detachment at White Sands Proving Ground were the only people flying these targets on sounding balloons at that time in the Southwest. However, now-Colonel Smith thinks that his targets were not reinforced with the flowered tape that was used on the NYU corner reflectors.

Point 2: The Quantity of the "Rubber"

Brazel made a statement about picking up a quantity of rubber that "made a bundle about 18 or 20 inches long and about 8 inches thick [46–51 cm long, 20 cm thick]." Three or four of the 350-gram sounding balloons would have to have been involved in order to supply that much "rubber." However, when a normal sounding balloon bursts, about all that arrives at the earth attached to the payload (the radiosonde, for example) is the neck of the balloon. The bursting of the balloon removes most of the envelope, and the subsequent rapid descent with or without parachute tears away most of the brittle remainder in the cold upper air.

Brazel's report suggests to me that he recovered the debris from a flight of a cluster of balloons that returned to Earth with some of the balloons still inflated after others had burst in flight. When that type of landing occurred, as it did in several of our flights, the instrument landing was gentle, with no crash. But with some still-inflated balloons in the upper portions of the train, the assembly was usually dragged by the surface winds until the remaining balloons burst or some of the payload snagged on vegetation or rocks and became detached from the train. When part or all of the load was dropped, the remaining balloons sometimes had enough buoyancy to reascend, carrying the remnants of the train aloft and downwind until more balloons burst and the sequence repeated. In either situation, appreciable amounts of the balloon debris were usually found downwind of the landing sites.

The amount of balloon envelope material that Brazel reported is far more than would have returned to Earth attached to any Air Weather Service or Weather Bureau radiosonde, rawinsonde, or radar target (if the weather services had targets to fly, which is unlikely). The only usable explanation for the recovery of such a large amount of balloon envelope "rubber" under these circumstances is that multiple balloons were used and that the flight train landed relatively slowly, with some of the balloons still inflated.

Point 3: The Weight of the Debris

Brazel estimated that "maybe five pounds [2 kg]" of rubber, tinfoil, paper, tape, and sticks were recovered. All of the material that he reported fit the description of balloon and radar target debris. To provide about 5 pounds of such material, about four or five of the balloon-and-target combinations could have been required, because the weight of a ML-307C/AP ruggedized pilot balloon target is listed as being only 100 grams (3.5 oz) and each of our sounding balloons weighed a nominal 350 grams (12 oz). It is unlikely that any Air Weather Service balloon flight would have carried multiple targets, because a single target would have provided a sufficient echo for tracking by the SCR-584 radar, for which the target was designed. (For example, Captain Smith indicated, in his 7 May 1947 report to the Air Weather Service, that he used single targets for his high-altitude wind measurements.) Furthermore, the weight of multiple targets would have been more than a single pilot balloon of the type supplied for use with these targets could have carried. If the Brazel story were a cover-up that used radar targets extracted from some Air Weather Service hidden stock (as has been suggested by some ufologists), the natural approach would have been to conform to the normal usage and report the finding of a single target. The Brazel interview report is not the story that would have described the normal end of a rawin flight, but it is consistent with what Brazel would have reported if he found the debris from one of our flights that carried multiple targets.

Brazel's report and the published pictures of the Roswell debris (see Weaver 1995: attachment 16) both suggest to me that pieces of more than one target were recovered at the landing site, indicating that two or more targets were carried by sounding balloons in a nonstandard flight. The NYU group was flying nonstandard clusters of 350-gram sounding balloons carrying multiple radar targets from Alamogordo Army Air Field during June and early July 1947. (However, the Army Air Force people at Roswell could not have known about this unorthodox practice in time to coach Brazel—as is alleged by some ufologists—before his 8 July interview.)

Point 4: The Absence of a Reward Tag

No reward notice was found on the recovered material. Our Balloon Group put no return tags or reward notices on our early flights, because we never expected or needed to see them again. And later we never put return or reward tags on flights from which we did not want to recover any of the parts. This was particularly true for our radar target flights because the targets were invariably damaged during their landings, such that they were not reusable. Accordingly, the targets were throwaways. We got the idea of putting reward tags on our instrumented flights after our experience with the recovery of Flight #5; the first time we used tags was on Flight #6, which was launched on 7 June.

Some ufologists have advanced the thesis that because the debris carried no reward tag, it could not be related to weather instruments. However, rather than supporting that thesis, the absence of such a tag is consistent with the idea that the debris was that of Flight #4.

Point 5: The Markings on the Tape

Brazel reported that "considerable scotch tape and some tape with flowers printed on it had been used in the construction." That statement got my attention immediately in June 1992, when first I learned of the Brazel interview, because the radar targets that we used in 1947 were constructed using a considerable amount of tape to attach the radar-reflective panels to the balsa-wood structural members, and that tape had abstract, pinkish purple, flowerlike figures printed on the back. My best memory of the construction and of the appearance of the flowerlike figures is given in my drawing reproduced in Weaver (1995: attachment 21). It has been at least 40 years since I last saw one of those targets with that tape, so my representation of the markings on the tape cannot be considered completely accurate. Recently, however, Herbert Crowe and Colonel Albert Trakowski, who were involved with the work of the Balloon Group in 1947, have confirmed my remembrance that our targets carried tape with pinkish purple figures printed on them, approximately as I have shown in the drawing.

I remember these so well because the purpose of these figures puzzled me every time that I saw one of these targets. I was always curious about their significance because the printing served no function that I could find. One interpretation of the situation is that tape with this printing happened to be available when the targets were being assembled and some tape was needed to reinforce the joint between the balsa wood struts and the reflective sheeting.

According to Irving Newton, the weather officer who identified the debris in General Ramey's office on the afternoon of 8 July 1947 as being that of a weather radar target, the debris included tape with the pinkish purple flowered markings. This was the first time Newton had ever seen such tape on targets, although he had used similar targets to make wind measurements for the naval bombardment during the invasion of Okinawa in April 1945. Similarly, Colonel Smith does not remember any such printing on the targets he flew from White Sands. (We still have some unused radar targets, manufactured in 1953, that have essentially the same geometric configuration as the targets that we flew in 1947. However, no reinforcing tape and no markings were used in these later, more rugged ML-307C/AP targets.) It now appears that the NYU group used some uniquely marked targets supplied from Evans Signal Laboratory that were left over from the development program.

Brazel's mention of tape with flowers printed on it and Marcel's discussions of pinkish purple symbols on the structural members in the debris are reasonably good descriptions of the pinkish purple figures on the unique targets that we flew from Alamogordo in June and early July 1947. The markings on the target-reinforcing tape reported by all the people who saw the debris link those targets uniquely to the NYU group like the now proverbial smoking gun. No other group outside of Evans Signal Lab had these targets. Furthermore, given that none of our group even heard about the recovery of the debris until long after it was taken to General Ramey's office on 8 July 1947, it is entirely unlikely that one of our uniquely marked targets could have been taken from our stock in the North Hangar at Alamogordo and substituted for the "real" debris, as some ufologists allege. Prior to our departure on 8 July 1947, none of the military had access to our supplies. No military people were associated with our day-to-day activities at the time; we were a civilian group that had little, if any, contact with the military officials at Alamogordo.

CONCLUSION

Each of the five points discussed in my analysis of the debris is consistent with what would have been recovered if the debris that Brazel found was from one of our balloon flights that carried radar targets. Taken together with reconstructed winds that prevailed on 4 June 1947, those five points make a strong case that supports the hypothesis explaining the origin of Brazel's debris as being debris of NYU flight #4.

This analysis began in 1992, long after the Roswell Incident and about 40 years after the NYU Balloon Group was disbanded. But after launching the balloons in 1947, I had no further involvement in the events associated with the Roswell Incident until I had a visit in 1979 from William Moore, one of the authors of *The Roswell Incident*. In Appendix 2 of this book, I recount my more recent experiences with ufologists, during the period 1979–1995.

EPILOGUE

The education our Balloon Group obtained while making these early flights was useful when the first constant-volume, polyethylene balloons were delivered by H. A. Smith late in June 1947. We launched our first successful constant-level balloon flight on 7 July 1947, at the end of our second expedition to Alamogordo. The balloon floated for more than 7 hours at a controlled level around 17,000 feet (5.2 km) and landed that afternoon 19 miles (30.6 km) west of Roswell Army Air Field. In September 1947, an H. A. Smith balloon, launched from Alamogordo during our third expedition, made an estimated 10-hour flight and was recovered in Croft, Kansas, 555 miles (893 km) downwind. During that expedition, we received improved lightweight balloons, 20 feet (6 m) in diameter, from General Mills. One of them, launched on 12 September, landed in Marietta, Oklahoma. Another General Mills 20-footer, launched on 21 November, was recovered from Mount Albert, Ontario.

On 4 March 1950, two days after Balloon Group members William D. Murray and Martin Koenig and their associates launched NYU Flight #146 from Alamogordo, it was recovered 7,000 miles (11,300 km) away, in Myrdal, Norway. NYU Flight #149, a balloon 19 feet (6 m) in diameter, was launched on 14 March 1950 and landed in northeastern Tunisia. The long distances that these balloons traveled when floating in the region of strong winds near the tropopause made their planned use in monitoring distant explosions impractical, because the balloons rapidly disappeared over the horizon, far from the ground-based telemetry receivers. For this and related logistic reasons, despite some limited success in detecting the pressure waves over New Mexico from the nuclear tests at the island of Eniwetok in 1948, the development of acoustic monitoring with constant-level balloons (i.e., Project Mogul) was discontinued in the early 1950s. New and more successful techniques had been developed for long-range monitoring of the Soviet atomic activities by collecting and analyzing airborne radioactive debris.

On the other hand, after 1950 many other agencies became interested in using plastic balloons and sponsored their further development at General Mills, at the University of Minnesota, at Winzen Research, Inc., at Raven Industries, and at the National Center for Atmospheric Research. As a result, great improvements were made in the design of plastic balloons. In the years since, the new balloons have carried many people and heavy scientific payloads high into the stratosphere. Some unmanned flights have traveled around the earth with flight durations of many weeks. Recently, a solo crossing of the Pacific Ocean was made under a hybrid balloon sustained by helium and hot air. Now, about 50 years after the inception of these balloons, several groups are attempting to circumnavigate the planet with nonstop manned flights. Some of the balloons involved in these efforts have diameters exceeding 350 feet (107 m) and are designed to carry 3-ton (2700-kg) loads. Jean Piccard and Otto Winzen would have been delighted with the outcome of their early efforts, as I am with ours.

CHAPTER FOUR

ROSWELL AND RELIGION

BENSON SALER

he corpus of Roswell myth variants described and analyzed in Chapters 1 and 2 does not suggest the existence of what we might conventionally term a religion. Nor, insofar as I know, has the Roswell Incident become the focal *mysterium* or central celebratory event of any cult.

There are, to be sure, religious groups that pivot on putative contacts with extraterrestrials (see, for example, Lewis 1995), and reports of the Roswell Incident may buttress the faith of their members. But those reports are not definitive of any such group or of any religion.

Yet the Roswell myth suggests certain elements that we elsewhere associate with religion. By treating them, so to speak, as "religious" elements that occur outside of the conventional purview of religion, we might hope to achieve some interesting perspectives on both religion and the narratives themselves. That, at any rate, is the aim of this chapter.

The first sections of the chapter are devoted to formulating a conceptual model of religion that is appropriate for analyzing such "religious" elements. Then, in the context of that model, the religious-like features of the Roswell myth and related aspects of the UFO subculture are examined and discussed.

CONCEPTUALIZING RELIGION: AN ORIENTATION

I argue elsewhere (Saler 1993) that much is to be gained by moving away from conventional definitions of religion. Such definitions typically stipulate one or more conditions that must be met if something is to be labeled a religion.

A Conventional Definition

Anthropologist Melford E. Spiro (1966:96) defines religion as "an institution consisting of culturally patterned interaction with culturally postulated superhuman beings." For "the sake of brevity," he remarks, we may "refer to these beings as 'gods' " (1966:92).

Spiro's definition stipulates two distinguishing features that must be present if something is to be recognized as a religion: there must be cultural postulation of superhuman beings, and there must be some set of culturally formulated patterns for interacting with those beings. The labeling of religion as a social institution is a consequence of its meeting conventional definitions of social institution, which assign great weight to cultural postulation and patterning.

Spiro's definition resonates with what many persons in our society generally deem religion to be. Thus his definition is not, for most of us, counterintuitive. That is a matter of importance to Spiro (and to me), because as Spiro (1966:91) points out, religion "is a term with historically rooted meanings," so that a definition of it ought to satisfy "not only the criterion of cross-cultural applicability but also the criterion of intra-cultural intuitivity."

Yet while Spiro's definition clearly satisfies the latter requirement because it is consonant with understandings of religion that are widely diffused in our society, some critics argue that it does not adequately satisfy the former requirement, the requirement for cross-cultural applicability. Two examples of the diversity of criticisms on that score are cited below, one that does not mention Spiro explicitly but includes him nonetheless, and one that is specifically concerned with Spiro's definition.

Criticisms

Talal Asad (1983), an anthropologist, criticizes Clifford Geertz (1966), another anthropologist, for proffering a seemingly universal definition of religion as if it were culturally neutral—that is, as if it were not culturally loaded but could be applied equally across all cultures. In point of fact, Asad (1983:245) charges, Geertz's characterization of religion "has a specific Christian history." It makes belief central to religion, and it presents religion paradigmatically, Asad writes, as "essentially a matter of meanings linked to ideas of general order (expressed in either or both rite and doctrine)" and having "universal functions." Geertz (1966:26), for ex-

ample, maintains that "the basic axiom underlying . . . 'the religious perspective' is everywhere the same: he who would know must first believe."

If we accept Asad's charges respecting Geertz, we might also apply
them to Spiro. Spiro (1966:94), indeed, insists that "the belief in superhuman beings and in their power to assist or to harm man . . . is the core
variable which ought to be designated in any definition of religion." An
emphasis on belief (and, more generally, on meaning), as Asad notes, is
historically a part of religious developments in the Christian West.
Among various non-Western peoples, analogs to what we call religion
may lack comparable emphases, and belief in God may not be central.

A claimed example of a lack of theistic emphasis is given us by Martin Southwold, a British social anthropologist. Southwold engaged in
ethnographic fieldwork among villagers in Sri Lanka. Most of the people
whom Southwold studied belonged to the Theravada branch of Buddhism. Although Southwold's villagers extolled the Buddha as a great
teacher who had attained enlightenment, they did not worship him as we
in the West understand worship. They did not hope or expect that he
might now personally intervene in their lives. He himself had passed into
nirvana and so could not be the recipient of supplications. Before he did
so, however, he pointed the way to salvation through his teachings, and
it is by following his teachings that one may hope to attain salvation. According to Southwold, the Sri Lankan villagers among whom he lived did
not regard the Buddha as a living god and personal savior.

Spiro (1966:92), in discussing Theravada Buddhism (he himself did
fieldwork among Theravada Buddhists in Burma), maintains: "With respect to supermundane goals, the Buddha is certainly a superhuman being. Unlike ordinary humans, he himself acquired the power to attain Enlightenment and, hence Buddhahood. Moreover, he showed others the
means for its attainment. Without his teachings, natural man could not,
unassisted, have discovered the way to Enlightenment and to final Release."

Southwold rejects Spiro's argument. He maintains that Spiro's assertion is "sheer equivocation, exploiting the vagueness of the word 'superhuman.' " Indeed, Southwold (1978:365) continues, even if the Buddha
might seem to be superhuman in some respects, he is "quite definitely . . .
not . . . godlike in the sense required by the theistic conception" of religion. "We have in Buddhism (which in fact is not wholly unique),"
Southwold writes, "a well-authenticated instance of a system of religious
behaviour without a central concern with godlike beings" (1978:367).
He concludes that theism is a contingent but not a necessary feature of

religion. Furthermore, because it is a formal requirement of the kind of definition offered by Spiro that all cases of religion must share the same stipulated distinguishing feature(s), Spiro's definition is refuted by Theravada Buddhism.

In fairness to Spiro, it must be noted that in addition to arguing for the superhuman status of the Buddha, he also points out that in Buddhist societies people typically participate in the elements of other religious systems (such as a religion associated with beings called nats in Burma) that coexist with Buddhism. "Hence," Spiro (1966:94) argues, "even if Theravada Buddh*ism* were absolutely atheistic, it cannot be denied that Theravada Buddh*ists* adhere to another belief system which is theistic to its core."

Now, all of this talk about Buddhism may strike the reader as rather removed from an interest in Roswell and religion. It does, however, provide some background for making what I regard as an important point in considering Roswell and various "flying saucer" cults. My point has to do with how we might most productively conceptualize religion for purposes of understanding and appreciating both religions and phenomena such as the Roswell myths. We can begin, I think, by first considering an alternative to both Spiro's and Southwold's handling of Buddhism.

Spiro recognizes considerable diversity among Buddhists in Burma, so much so, in fact, that Buddhism there, as he describes it (Spiro 1982), is really a family of religions rather than some monolithic system of doctrines and other conventions. Some Buddhists adhere to teachings expressed in sacred writings known as the Pali Canon, teachings that do not assign gods any role in the achievement of salvation. Others depart from those teachings in significant ways. In his 1966 essay, nevertheless, Spiro generalizes about the distribution of convictions respecting the superhuman status and powers of the Buddha. He seems to attribute much the same convictions about superhuman status and power to all forms of Buddhism save for "atheistic Buddhist philosophies," the teachings of which, he asserts briefly, ought not to be confused "with the beliefs and behavior of a religious community" (Spiro 1966:93).

Southwold also greatly generalizes. He describes the ideas of the Buddhist villagers whom he studied in Sri Lanka, and then he generalizes his understandings of their beliefs to Theravada Buddhists at large.

Not only do Spiro and Southwold strike me as overgeneralizing descriptively, but they agree in effect on treating the matter of theism and Theravada Buddhism as posing a question that entails response within a binary frame. The question seems to be, Is Theravada Buddhism theistic or not? The two authors differ in their respective responses, Spiro answering yes and Southwold answering no. Contrary, however, to the position that they mutually appear to take on this particular issue, I think that a question about theism and Theravada Buddhism need not be resolved bivalently.

Family Resemblances

Philosopher W. D. Hudson (1977) avoids a totalizing either-yes-or-no position regarding Theravada Buddhism and theism. He does so by invoking the "family resemblances" concept of philosopher Ludwig Wittgenstein (1958, 1969).

According to Wittgenstein, the instantiations of a category need not all share in common some one feature or some specific conjunction of features. In a famous example, Wittgenstein (1958:I.66) maintains that all of the things that we call games do not share some one distinguishing feature. A group of things comprehended by a category may contain some members that share no distinguishing features at all with some of the other members of the same group. But in such cases, those members that share no features in common will typically overlap in at least some features with still other members of the group, just as the members of a human family tend to overlap in features such as eye color, shape of the chin, and so forth. These other members serve as intermediaries that link together the members that share no features with one another, rather like the intermediary links of a chain that connect more peripheral links.

Hudson (1977:238) applies this understanding to statements that can be made (predicated) about Buddhism. Some forms of Buddhism, he allows, may well be "atheistic" with regard to the important matter of salvation, as some students of religion have asserted. But others are not (especially in that branch of Buddhism known as Mahayana Buddhism, the dominant form of Buddhism in China and Japan). Hudson concludes that although theism cannot be said or predicated of all forms of Buddhism, it can be predicated of Buddhism in general, and so is among the family resemblance predicates of Buddhism.

Perhaps I can render this strategy more vivid by supplying a comparable example respecting the category "game." Not all games involve team competition (e.g., solitaire), but many do (e.g., baseball). We can say that team competition is among the predicates or statements that we voice in general about the category "game" even though it is absent in certain games.

Now, what this implies with respect to developing a conceptual model of religion is this: We can think of religion as involving a pool of features or predicates that mutually apply to our model. But not all of these features or predicates will be found in all religions. Indeed, it is not necessary for all religions to have the very same features or predicates. Those phenomena that we label as religions will overlap and crisscross, and so what we recognize as religions will constitute a family, the members of which are differentially linked together by resemblances.

Conceptualizing religion in this way implies certain intellectual consequences. First, religion is no longer a bivalent matter of "yes or no"—something, anything, either is or is not "a religion"—but a multivalent matter of "more or less." Some things that we call religion may seem more religious to us than others.

Second, there is no sharp cutoff point for distinguishing religion from nonreligion. Rather, we have some clear, well-elaborated examples of religion, and then we have cases that are increasingly less clear-cut with respect to our conceptual model. If, therefore, a scholar wishes to call a rather peripheral candidate (e.g., communism) a religion, that scholar will have to convince other scholars by reasoned arguments rather than definitional fiat.

Third (and here we come at last to Roswell!), some phenomena that virtually everyone agrees are not religions are nevertheless likely to exhibit certain elements or aspects that we elsewhere identify as religious elements or aspects. We have some idea of their functions and importance in religions, and the possibility exists that by exploring their roles among phenomena that we do not ordinarily or mainly think of as religions, we may enrich our understandings of those phenomena. The idea, indeed, that a wide variety of phenomena may include religious elements suggests an interesting dimension to such phenomena, one that might be most profitably explored by treating it explicitly as a religious dimension.

A MATTER OF BELIEF

Before beginning a topical analysis of the religious dimension of the Roswell myth, it will prove useful to enter some cautionary remarks respecting the matter of belief.

Many people in our society tend to think of religion as being, first and foremost, a matter of belief, with ritual deemed the enactment of belief. Some students of religion call this a Protestant bias, because of the emphasis on belief and inwardness found in the teachings of prominent Protestant theologians. Or, more generally, they term it a Christian bias

(Asad 1983), given the importance that contemporary Christians, many Roman Catholics included, generally attach to belief when conceptualizing religion. In consonance with the emphasis placed on belief, religious groups are often idealized as communities of believers (Smith 1962).

At the same time, however, many members of Western societies recognize that not all persons identified with a religious group accept or internalize the tenets of their religion with equal commitment or intensity. Some persons associated with contemporary religious groups are for the most part unbelievers or disbelievers, sometimes retaining their religious affiliations more for social reasons than for theological or spiritual ones. So although religion may be conceptually idealized in terms of belief, experience has taught many of us that religious labels do not always indicate what individuals actually believe.

The matter is further complicated if we take account of disagreements among philosophers respecting the nature of belief.

A long-enduring philosophical tradition maintains that belief is a state of mind, that is, a mental occurrence or event. According to the mental state theory, a belief is a proposition that someone holds in mind and deems to be true. The act of believing, then, is assenting mentally to the truth of some proposition. This is probably how many nonphilosophers in our society also think of belief, to the extent that they may render their notion of belief explicit.

Some twentieth-century philosophers (e.g., Ludwig Wittgenstein, Gilbert Ryle, and others), however, prefer to think of belief in a different way. They view belief largely as a disposition to think, feel, or act in a certain way under appropriate circumstances (see Price 1969). Belief in that sense is not a mental state or a mental experience that can be readily introspected but rather a likelihood that will have a characteristic expression given the circumstances that facilitate or elicit that expression.

Today some philosophers hold that some beliefs may be propositions that we consciously hold in mind and assent to, whereas others are dispositions. Furthermore, in addition to acknowledging the possibility of a "will to believe," as suggested by William James ([1897] 1956), some posit a disposition or readiness to believe (Audi 1994).

Without going any further into technical arguments among philosophers respecting belief, suffice it to say that belief is a far more complex matter than some may suppose. We ought to bear that in mind when we consider questions about belief in Roswell myths and other accounts of extraterrestrial contacts.

We can note that two factors especially facilitate the development of beliefs about extraterrestrial contacts without actually assuring conviction. First, our own successes in space exploration—landing humans on the moon and sending unmanned probes to other planets—have rendered us sensitive to the possibility that other intelligent life-forms in the universe, if such there are, might also be involved in the exploration of space. Second, science fiction, especially as disseminated by television, has provided many of us with a common vocabulary and set of idioms for talking about extraterrestrials, spaceships, and the like.

The first facilitating factor might be limited or weakened by what scientists tell us about the physical and biological difficulties that living organisms would encounter in traversing great distances in space. But not everyone knows of those scientific considerations. And some who do know nevertheless dismiss them, on the grounds that beings more advanced than us scientifically might well overcome the obstacles to space travel that our scientists now envision.

The second facilitating factor—science fiction—is widely recognized to be the product of creative imaginations. Nevertheless, it is so widespread and popular that many of us—believers, disbelievers, and unbelievers alike—have recourse to its terms and idioms. We share a universe of discourse respecting space travel and extraterrestrials. And for some, use of that vocabulary becomes increasingly habitual and facile.

This touches on an interesting fact about our culture that deserves notice. Writers, filmmakers, and others have created, and disseminated to millions, fictive worlds that many of us often talk about as if they were real—not only worlds of outer space but others as well. Vampires are a good example.

Many people in our society share certain "mainstream" notions about vampires, notions stemming from the most widely diffused literary and cinematic subtraditions about the "undead." Thus, for example, vampires are confined to their coffins or other resting places during daylight hours (although in some books and films they do go out in the daytime, albeit sometimes without the physical strength or other powers that they enjoy nocturnally); vampires turn away from religious symbols such as the cross (although in some accounts this is not the case, or it is the case only if the person administering the symbol is of strong faith); the undead are repelled by garlic; and so on. It is probably correct to suppose that most of us who knowledgeably discuss vampires with our friends do not believe in the actual existence of vampires. But we sometimes talk intelligibly as if we did, and a visiting anthropologist from some distant place might mistake our talk for firm conviction. (One wonders to what extent something similar may compromise descriptions of other cultures in the ethnographic literature.)

When it comes to extraterrestrials, however, talk is probably far more indicative of widely spread convictions about their reality—or likely reality—than in the case of vampires. Some persons, indeed, strongly and repeatedly avow convictions about extraterrestrial contacts, including abductions. And pollsters and others report that sizable percentages of the U.S. population deem it likely not only that extraterrestrials exist but that some of them have monitored our planet. Members of the latter group are not claiming conviction; rather, they are asserting opinions about possibilities and probabilities. Members of the former group, however, appear to be true believers, and they include proponents of the Roswell myth. How might we account for them?

There is, of course, the proverbial problem of getting "inside" someone's mind. The question is sometimes raised, How do we know that people really believe what they say? That is the sort of question that occurs to people who tacitly or explicitly endorse the mental state view of belief—the notion that belief is a proposition entertained in the mind and to which someone mentally gives assent. For disposition theorists, however, belief is signaled by an articulated statement, act, or expressed feeling that is interpreted to be the realization of a disposition; no question is asked about what might consciously and experientially be going on in someone's mind.

For our purposes, we will say that those who believe in the Roswell myth or in other alleged extraterrestrial contacts are those who publicly say that they do and/or who act in other ways that we interpret to be consonant with convictions about the reality of extraterrestrial contacts. Yet although this is in keeping with a dispositional conceptualization of belief, I do not want to rule out the mental state or occurrence view of belief.

Not only does the mental state concept of belief correspond to the sense in which many people in our society use the term "belief," but it is also clearly the case that some people do publicly and explicitly register assent to propositions contained in the Roswell myth and in other accounts of extraterrestrial contacts. Although I cannot be certain that they are not engaging in dissimulation—perhaps even directed at themselves— their public behavior suggests beliefs of the kind that are envisioned in the mental state theory of belief.

Yet though that seems to be the case, believers may nevertheless harbor lingering doubts as to the truth of what they proclaim. Later in this chapter, I discuss Leon Festinger's theory of cognitive dissonance (and the suggested example of some missionaries who attempt to still their own doubts by converting others). And in Chapter 5 we raise the possibility that the efforts of some apparent believers to prove (perhaps through expensive government investigations) that a flying saucer crashed at Roswell may actually suggest a lack of full certitude. These are the sorts of considerations that bedevil the transition from a purely theoretical account of the mental state theory to the identification of real-life examples of it. The problem is ultimately epistemological: although we can make shrewd guesses, we are very unlikely to have full warrant for declaring that another person subjectively assents to the truth of some proposition.

We can, of course, speak safely of avowed beliefs, thus avoiding commitment to the unwarranted supposition that all expressed statements of what we take to be belief are sincerely uttered. The authors of this book do so in their respective chapters. But by doing so, we narrow the distance between the state and dispositional accounts of belief, if not actually converting the former into the latter.

We can preserve the state theory to this extent, however: in the absence of evidence to the contrary, the principle of charity (Wilson 1970; Hollis and Lukes 1982) inclines us to accept people's statements, their avowed beliefs, as expressing propositions to which they probably assent. At the same time, we ought to entertain the possibility that they hold their beliefs with different intensities of attachment, perhaps occasioned by lingering doubts, so that some persons are more susceptible to being persuaded to drop their beliefs than others are. Furthermore, we may reasonably suppose, based on our experiences, that people come to their beliefs in different ways. In short, there is very probably considerable heterogeneity in the attainment and holding of beliefs among those who endorse Roswell and kindred myths.

Among the various factors that dispose people to accept belief in Roswell and kindred myths is the appeal of those myths to the imagination. Believing in extraterrestrial contacts may well be more exciting for some than rejecting or ignoring such beliefs. In addition, asserting such beliefs may, in some social circles, make one a more interesting person. Being a myth proponent can figure in efforts at self-affirmation and self-aggrandizement. Such people may then become the traditors described in Chapter 2. In a minority of cases, moreover, being a myth proponent can have a cash value with respect to remunerated books, articles, and lectures. And of course, some suppose that there is real evidence to support the Roswell myth, even if they may be subject to lingering doubts on that score.

Somewhat more difficult to understand are those persons who join flying saucer cults or who claim to have been abducted by aliens. Putative
abductees are beyond the purview of this chapter because of special com-
plexities in their cases (e.g., the use of "hypnotic regression therapy," the
seeming sexual focus that plays a role in some abduction stories, and so
forth). But in the pages that follow, I do have some things to say about
flying saucer cults, and I assert that at least some of them strongly resemble what most of us call religions. How are we to understand the beliefs
of their members?

Studies to which I will refer suggest that people who join flying saucer
cults usually do not experience sudden, dramatic conversions. Rather,
they are often persons on some sort of a "spiritual" or life-fulfilling quest,
and they may drift from one group to another, gradually picking up the
vocabulary, and more or less endorsing the beliefs, of fellow members
during their time of affiliation.

In that respect, they resemble persons described by the anthropologist
Tanya Luhrmann (1989). These are individuals (many with university degrees) who join groups dedicated to magic in contemporary Britain.
Luhrmann insists that the present-day magicians whom she studied
"*have* beliefs" as distinct from merely speaking a newly learned language
(1989:310). Attracted to groups of magicians for various reasons, they
increasingly do what others in the groups do, and they gradually acquire
"beliefs" through what Luhrmann calls a process of interpretive drift:
"the slow, often unacknowledged shift in someone's manner of interpreting events as they become involved with a particular activity" (1989:312).

When we turn to heterogeneous contemporary American society, we
find that segments of it nourish the quest for new and fulfilling beliefs.
Religion for numbers of Americans is increasingly a matter of finding a
rewarding lifestyle. As such, identifying suitable beliefs becomes an exercise in choice and experimentation. Catholics become Jews, Jews become
Buddhists, and so on, at least for a time. And some join New Age cults or
seek to commune with wise aliens from distant worlds.

Underlying both the heterogeneity in belief content and the diversity
in intensity of belief is our remarkable human capacity—and apparent
need—to believe. We can convince ourselves of almost anything.

While preparing this chapter, I read a newspaper article that provides
a relatively exotic—but nevertheless intelligible and almost familiar—example of the realization of our capacity (under certain circumstances) to
believe or to say we believe things that seem to be impositions on the
senses. Writing in the *New York Times* (1 September 1996, pp. 1, 14),

John F. Burns reported that wolves were terrorizing villagers in a region of the state of Uttar Pradesh, India. According to the Indian police, 33 children were carried away and killed by wolves in recent months, and another 20 were seriously mauled. Numbers of Indian villagers, however, avowed that the wolves were not really wolves: they were either were-wolves or Pakistani infiltrators who disguised themselves as wolves.

Sita Devi, a 10-year-old girl whose 4-year-old brother was carried away and killed, gave this testimony: "It came across the grass on all four paws. . . . As it grabbed Anand, it rose onto two legs until it was tall as a man. . . . Then it threw him over its shoulder. It was wearing a black coat, and a helmet and goggles." Her grandfather, who had driven a truck in Calcutta for some 50 years before retiring to his natal village, remarked: "As long as officials pressure us to say it was a wolf, we'll say it was a wolf. But we have seen this thing with our own eyes. It is not a wolf: it is a human being."

What we believe, what we believe we remember as eyewitnesses, and what we are willing to say we believe are contingent on a host of factors. Under the rules of evidence that guide our courts, eyewitness testimony is admissible. But it is sometimes the stuff of myths, nevertheless.

A RELIGIOUS DIMENSION OF ROSWELL: NONHYPOTHETICAL TRUTHS

I begin considering religious or religious-like elements that attach to talk about the Roswell Incident by elaborating on a matter discussed in Chapter 2: namely, that true believers are strongly resistant to accepting any account of the Roswell Incident that does not involve the crash or breakup of an alien spacecraft. Alternative explanations of the debris found by William W. Brazel are dismissed. Indeed, recent revelations to the effect that there actually may have been something of a military effort at a cover-up—one intended to protect the secrecy of Project Mogul—are themselves dismissed as further efforts by the government to conceal the truth about Roswell. By affirming a continuing government conspiracy, proponents of the Roswell myth in effect render their claim about a crashed flying saucer an example of the kind of statement that some students of religion call a nonhypothetical truth.

In a widely read and widely praised essay published in 1966, anthropologist Clifford Geertz attempts to characterize what he calls the religious perspective and to distinguish it from three other perspectives: commonsensical, scientific, and aesthetic. What he says about the religious perspective, and how it differs from other ways of thinking about things, can, with some qualifications that I will enter, enhance our appreciation of the efforts of numbers of believers in flying saucers to render nonhypothetical the "truths" that they proclaim (in Chapter 2 of this book, Ziegler refers to such "truths" as "practicably unfalsifiable").

The commonsensical perspective, according to Geertz, is a way of "seeing," whereby objects and events are accepted as being what they seem to be. It also encompasses a desire to master the world for one's own ends or, at the very least, to adjust to the world.

In the scientific perspective, Geertz (1966:27) maintains, the commonsensical "givenness" of the world vanishes, and the pragmatic desire to master the world for one's own ends is suspended. Instead, the scientific perspective champions "disinterested observation" and analysis through the modality of formal concepts.

The aesthetic perspective, like the scientific perspective, suspends the "naive realism" and pragmatic motives of common sense. But instead of endorsing the scientific perspective's emphasis on raising questions about the credentials of everyday experience, it tends to ignore that experience in favor of a focus on appearances and an absorption in "things, as we say, 'in themselves'" (Geertz 1966:27).

The religious perspective differs from all of the above. Unlike common sense, it goes beyond the ordinary realities of everyday life. Indeed, Geertz avers that its "defining concern" is to be found in its acceptance of wider realities, in its faith in them. Like the scientific perspective, the religious perspective also questions the realities of everyday life. But it does so, Geertz (1966:27–28) writes, "not out of institutionalized skepticism which dissolves the world's givenness into a swirl of probabilistic hypotheses, but in terms of what it takes to be wider, non-hypothetical truths." And unlike the aesthetic perspective, the religious perspective does not seek to disengage from questions of factuality in favor of intentionally creating "an air of semblance and illusion." On the contrary! It is profoundly concerned with fact and with establishing an aura of thoroughgoing actuality. "It is this sense of the 'really real,'" Geertz (1966: 28) declares, "upon which the religious perspective rests and which the symbolic activities of religion as a cultural system are devoted to producing, intensifying, and so far as possible, rendering inviolable by the discordant revelations of secular experience."

"The basic axiom underlying" the religious perspective "is everywhere the same," in the view of Geertz (1966:26): "he who would know must first believe." Talal Asad (1983, 1993), who is perhaps Geertz's most trenchant critic, rejects Geertz's "basic"—and universalist—axiom. Asad argues (and I agree with him) that the qualities of what we call belief differ depending on context, so that "the form and texture and function" of belief may well vary from one case to another. Geertz's putative "basic axiom," Asad (1983:248) maintains, "is *not* everywhere the same."

My own approach to characterizing religion incorporates Asad's point and, in a manner of speaking, formalizes it. Geertz's talk about nonhypothetical truths, a concern for "the really real," and the "axiom" that he who would know must first believe is applicable to some religions. But we need not suppose that those things are necessary for all religions. They are explicitly evident in various expressions of the Christian family of confessions, but they may be implicit or of little or no significance in other phenomena that, on other grounds, we tend to label religions.

Take, for example, talk about godlike beings in the myths of the Wayú, or "Guajiro," of northern Colombia and Venezuela, an Amerindian population among whom I did fieldwork. Those myths describe the doings of powerful nonhuman (but very anthropomorphic) beings—beings who, in the narratives, often interact with humans and affect their lives in determinate ways. Many of the stories involve a masculine figure named Juya and a feminine figure named Pulowi, and the relationships between them are connected in the myths to fecundity, aridity, birth, death, and many other things of great interest and importance to the Wayú. But as French anthropologist Michel Perrin (1987) points out, there are no cults to these beings. People do not pray to them, worship them, or attempt to propitiate them in real life. Indeed, I was told by some of my own informants that these beings are not "real" in the sense that I am real.

Juya, Pulowi, and other mythic beings have a certain "truth" to them, the truth of capturing and expressing various realities in the existential experiences of the Wayú. And although stories about them are therefore valuable for reflection as well as being entertaining, and although they provide a useful and aesthetically pleasing idiom for talking about a variety of concerns, these godlike beings do not in themselves constitute or represent the "really real." They point to, or otherwise express, experientially validated truths—the truths, if you will, of common sense. But that can be done, and often is done among the Wayú, in other idioms.

Because we Westerners tend to associate religion with superhuman or godlike beings, we might suppose, on first learning about the beings of Wayú myth, that we have encountered the core of Wayú religion. That, however, would be an erroneous supposition. The religious concerns and rituals of the Wayú are largely addressed to the transformed spirits of their own dead (see Perrin 1987; Saler 1988), not to godlike beings of myth.

Juya and Pulowi represent nonhypothetical truths in the sense that the Wayú do not test mythic claims about them. In this case, of course, no one sees any need to test such claims, because the claims are not taken to express ultimate metaphysical truth about the beings themselves.

But in many other things, the Wayú, like us, accept purported truths on authority, or perhaps authority coupled with seeming experiential validation, in effect treating those truths as nonhypothetical. That is, the Wayú, like us, do not challenge the truthfulness of those "truths," except perhaps when circumstances and vital concerns combine in such ways as to motivate them to do so.

Much of what people in our society claim to know is also taken on authority, authority sometimes reinforced by experiences. Most of us, for example, do not ourselves challenge the assertions of our medical authorities except in special circumstances. We accept the microbe theory of disease and much else without attempting to test the truth of such theories ourselves, although many of us suppose (and hope) that persons qualified to do so have accomplished effective testing.

For many persons in our society, moreover, religious claims are accepted largely on authority, though perhaps to some extent authority reinforced by experience and underwritten by psychological longings and hope. Spiro (1978), indeed, argues that beliefs in gods or godlike beings are plausible for many persons because of their experiences as infants and very young children.

Before attaining competence in language and acquiring culture, we humans typically experience interactions with powerful beings—our parents or others, who feed us, change us, carry us, and in other respects nurture and protect us. Infants and young children are especially dependent on others for their very survival as well as, of course, their comfort. Although they cannot intellectually process experiences of the intervention of powerful beings (parents and others) without language and culture, the experiences are real and produce impressions. Later in life, Spiro argues, when they learn of the superhuman beings recognized by their cultures, those beings are likely to seem plausible to them on the basis of their own experiences, which they could not intellectually process early in life.

Proponents of the Roswell myth accept the putative existence of powerful aliens who overcome the limitations that our science currently posits regarding travel in space and time. Indeed, Roswell proponents seem to deem the existence of such beings plausible. In part, I think, they do so for the very reasons that Spiro gives regarding the seeming plausibility that other persons sense in the culturally postulated existence of the gods of traditional religions. Roswell proponents are also motivated to some extent, I suspect, by dependency longings, a topic that I treat in the next section of this chapter. Here, however, I want to focus on the matter of nonhypothetical truths and Roswell.

Although nonhypothetical, or "practicably unfalsifiable," truths are central to numbers of religions, some religions nevertheless do incorporate allowances for what would count as fatal evidence against their core tenets. Thus, for example, Paul writes to the Christians in Corinth, "And if Christ be not risen [from the dead], then is our preaching vain, and your faith is also vain" (1 Cor. 15:14).

Frequently, however, doctrines are shielded from falsification by ascribing them to singular (and therefore incomparable) validating contexts, by claiming to accept them on the basis of unique authority, or in some other way. Early in the third century A.D., for example, Tertullian declares of Christ's resurrection, "it is certain because it is impossible" (*De carne Christi* 5.4). One must accept the resurrection on faith. Various Christian theologians, moreover, maintain that true and enduring faith comes from God, not from ratiocination or social authority, so that if you do not accept the central truths of Christianity, it is because God has not selected you to receive his grace.

At least some proponents of the Roswell myth, though often extolling their commitments to empiricism and scientific ideals, have effectively rendered nonhypothetical the "truth" that they proclaim. They allow that should empirical study of the debris collected near Roswell show that the materials are of earthly origin, then in accordance with the canons of evidence that they endorse, the claim that an alien spacecraft broke up or crashed near Roswell would be refuted. But by alleging a continuing government conspiracy and cover-up, they discredit any such proof in advance.

They maintain that the government, which is the custodian of the evidence, would tamper with that evidence were it forced to produce it. Thus, should the government make public any materials of an earthly origin, it would be because the government had substituted such materials for the original ones. In consequence, the assertion that there is material evidence for the existence of an alien spacecraft cannot be falsified to the satisfaction of at least some of its proponents.

Effectively rendering claims to truth nonhypothetical is by no means restricted to religion. Numbers of people employ various stratagems for preserving convictions of diverse sorts, especially to the degree that those convictions may function to order the world and to situate the self. Many such convictions are outside the purview of what we conventionally call religion. In our society, nevertheless, we sometimes say that such convictions are sacrosanct—that is, they have an imputed sacred character. We occasionally speak, indeed, of the sacralizing of some of our most important existential and causal ideas and theories, ideas and theories that are not identified as specifically religious.

Sacralizing involves efforts to render convictions inviolable to trespass or falsification. That in effect is what some proponents of the Roswell myth have done. To the extent that they have sacralized and thus empowered a narrative by rendering it impervious to refutation (at least insofar as they are concerned), they have provided the Roswell myth with a religious-like dimension.

ALIENS AS SUPERHUMAN BEINGS

The aliens of the Roswell myth share a general characteristic with other aliens posited by believers in flying saucers: they are superhuman. That is, they have powers that far exceed human powers. At the very least, these are superiorities in intellect and technology. They are inferred from suppositions to the effect that aliens have traversed vast distances and, for the most part, cloaked their existence while monitoring (or intervening in) the affairs of earth. These powers, moreover, could presumably be made use of (or are being made use of) in ways that affect human life, for good or for ill.

Superhuman and Religion

The reader may recall Spiro's substantive approach to the definition of religion. Spiro (1966:94) insists that "the belief in superhuman beings and in their power to assist or to harm man . . . is the core variable which ought to be designated by any definition of religion." Religion, as Spiro defines it, is "an institution consisting of culturally patterned interaction with culturally postulated superhuman beings" (1966:96). If we were to accept that definition, and if we were to suppose that the Roswell myth authorizes and pertains to an actual institution of the sort described by Spiro, then the myth would point to a religion.

While that would be pushing matters too far in the case of Roswell, given that the myth is not definitive of or embodied in cultic practices, there are culturally organized groups that represent themselves to be engaging in patterned interactions with aliens, a matter that I discuss later in this chapter. Here, however, I want to focus on the superhumanness of aliens as a general posit of those who affirm the reality of extraterrestrial beings.

Heterogeneity, Superhuman, and Supernatural

It is important to point out that there is considerable heterogeneity in convictions, claims, and agendas among those persons who maintain that extraterrestrials have visited our planet.

Many persons who allege alien contacts endorse the idea that extraterrestrials are superior to humans in scientific achievements. However, some of those persons—in all probability a minority of those who affirm the reality of aliens—go beyond suggesting that aliens are superhuman in intellect and technology. They suggest, indeed, that at least some of the aliens are supernatural and not merely superhuman. That is, in keeping with contemporary, popular acceptations of the term "supernatural" in Western societies (Saler 1977), they suggest that aliens are able to transcend the ordinary course of nature. Rather than merely being able, because of their superior science and technology, to manipulate the forces of nature in ways that we cannot, aliens, because of their own superior natures, are not bound by the laws of nature in the ways that we are bound.

Some who support the idea of aliens as supernatural depict them as angelic beings (Saliba 1995:26, 32). Indeed, such notions are consonant with other similarities between angels and aliens noted in Chapter 2. For the most part benign and solicitous of human welfare, though sometimes obliged to chastise or restrict humans in order to accomplish some higher plan, angelic aliens are sometimes represented to be fulfilling transcendental missions. These missions may be depicted as mandated by the God of traditional Western religions, or they may be attributed to the workings of divine forces or beings described in vocabularies that diverge from mainstream Judeo-Christian phraseologies.

Others who view aliens as supernatural depict them as demonic. Some who depict aliens as demonic do not explicitly invoke a Christian frame of reference (Clark 1995:28), but others put extraterrestrials within a Christian context. Some fundamentalist Christians declare that aliens are minions of Satan. They claim, moreover, to take comfort from the idea that increased alien activities, as surmised from growing reports of sightings and contacts (including abductions), point to the increasingly overt intervention of the Antichrist in our world, which in their reading of the Book of Revelation is a necessary preliminary to the Second Coming of Jesus Christ (Saliba 1995:41).

And still others, who at times talk of extraterrestrials as if they were supernatural, declare themselves to be mystified regarding the purposes of the visitors and to be uncertain as to their ultimate effects on humanity.

The Term "UFO"

The heterogeneity indicated by the above considerations only skims the surface of differences among persons who declare it likely or certain that our world has been visited by beings from other worlds. Even the term "UFO" is a matter of disagreement. For instance, as early as 1957, Isabel L. Davis attempted to distinguish, with reference to terminology, between those who thought that unusual sightings are mysteries that should be probed empirically and rationally, and those who evinced conviction, on the basis of claims about close sightings and actual contacts, that the flying objects are spacecraft from other worlds: "To the skeptics, flying saucers still deserve the name of UFOs—*Unidentified* Flying Objects. To the believers, on the other hand, thanks to the extensive information they claim to have received from their extraterrestrial friends, the saucers are no longer UFOs but IFOs—*Identified,* fully identified, Flying Objects. The two terms are mutually exclusive. An object cannot be identified and unidentified at the same time" (Davis 1957, quoted by Clark 1995:23). Clark (1995:24) distinguishes between "ufologists" and "saucerians": "Saucerians spoke in an occult-tinged language which, consciously or unconsciously, echoed the supernaturalistic doctrines of Swedenborg, Blavatsky, Gut Warren Ballard, and N. Meade Layne. Where ufologists spoke of 'UFOs,' saucerians had flying saucers, spaceships, scoutcraft, motherships, ventlas, and vimanas."

If we adopt the terminological distinctions offered by Davis and Clark, then the Roswell myth variants in Chapter 1 pertain to the "UFO" vocabulary, and the chief expositors of the Roswell myth described in this chapter can be labeled "ufologists." The term "flying saucer," however, is widely used by persons of different persuasions and commitments, and it is often employed as a synonym for "UFO."

The Term "Flying Saucer"

The term "flying saucer" came into currency shortly before the Roswell Incident came to the attention of the press. On 24 June 1947, Kenneth Arnold, a businessman and deputy sheriff of Boise, Idaho, saw nine disk-shaped objects while flying a plane to Yakima, Washington. He told reporters that the motion of those objects put him in mind of "a saucer skipping over water" (Jacobs 1975:36–37), and the press coined the term "flying saucer."

The creation of the category "flying saucer" was undoubtedly of importance in the development of the Roswell myth and the larger narrative fabrics to which it pertains. Categorization and labeling are processes that organize and give meaning to experiences that might otherwise be treated by uncertain vocabularies and disparate analogies.

By categorizing, an act of classifying, we construct and legitimate with respect to a broader context of classifications and understandings. Once a category has been created, its figured or potential instantiations have a certain reality, regardless of whether or not one actually expects to encounter them outside of discourse and the imaginings and memories that the category facilitates. Wide acceptance of category terms, moreover, contributes to the maintenance of a community that talks about things in a common vocabulary, even if the members of that community use the vocabulary to express different interpretations and expectations.

Flying Saucers and Superhuman Beings

Regardless of differences of opinion with respect to the designation "UFO," it is clearly the case that many persons who declare belief in extraterrestrial contacts, or who maintain that they have an open mind on the possibility of such contacts, use the term "flying saucer(s)." Flying saucer, moreover, is a category that implies a certain commitment. That is, if one believes in the existence or the possibility of flying saucers, one commits oneself to belief either in the existence of extrahuman intelligence in the cosmos or in the possibility of it.

The category "flying saucer," as widely employed, denotes a conceptualized spacecraft, a machine. Machines, as most of us conceive of them, are devices made to serve some purpose. And purpose implies intelligence, intelligence that consciously anticipates ends and that deliberately works to achieve those ends.

Widespread use of the very category "flying saucer" frames debate and serves to limit heterogeneity of opinion. It plays a role in structuring argument along these lines: (1) Do flying saucers exist independently of the beliefs of persons who affirm that they do? This question is tantamount to the question of whether or not there is mind other than human (and perhaps divine) mind in the cosmos. And (2) if flying saucers exist, does the mind that they indicate differ from the divine (or satanic) mind envisioned by traditional Western religions?

Those who affirm the existence of flying saucers or proclaim that they have an open mind on that issue may tend to favor distinctive opinions about the nature of extrahuman mind in the cosmos, but all of those persons are affirming, or allowing the possibility of, at a minimum, superhuman mind. By "superhuman mind," I mean mind capable of constructing flying saucers and sending them to our world, thus overcoming problems in physics (and perhaps in biology) that we humans are now incapable of overcoming. In short, at a minimum, the category "flying saucer" implies superhuman beings (who may or may not be supernatural). To assert or allow for the existence of the former is to assert or allow for the existence of the latter.

Superhumans and Dependency Longings

Among persons who maintain that Roswell provides material evidence for an extraterrestrial spaceship, as among those who affirm the existence of flying saucers generally, there is speculation as to the intentions of the putative visitors. Some of these people are optimistic, with their optimism ranging from the cautious to the enthusiastic. They suppose, or at least hope, that the visitors are favorably disposed to humans. In some cases they imagine that the visitors have problems of their own for which they seek solutions in our world—a favored scenario at the moment has to do with reproduction, with the aliens engaged in breeding experiments intended to produce alien-earthling hybrids (Bryan 1995). And in some cases there is also hope that with alien help we humans may be able to end war, famine, disease, poverty, and perhaps even death itself.

These hopes, and the wistfulness with which they are sometimes expressed, are reminiscent of traditional longings in Western religiosity. Among other things, these hopes often give voice to dependency longings.

Dependency, psychologically speaking, is the looking to others for the satisfaction or fulfillment of one's own needs and desires. Children, of course, are very dependent, materially and psychologically, on their parents or other persons senior to themselves. But our culture values the increasing emancipation of persons as they mature. Maturity, indeed, is idealized as the ability to stand on one's own: to earn one's own living, to make one's own decisions, and to accept responsibility for the consequences of doing so. Many of us, nevertheless, harbor dependency longings that we express from time to time. Although these in great measure may be unconscious or disguised, we are also consciously aware, at least occasionally, of our own desires to have others take care of us, make decisions for us, and promote our welfare.

Traditional Western religions answer to dependency longings. They maintain that a benign, omniscient, and omnipotent creator looks upon his human creatures as his children, whom he guides and sustains. He is their father in heaven, the ultimate source of their daily bread. Though a righteous judge, he is also merciful. And as a celestial king, he is protective and supportive of his faithful subjects, their sole and ultimate savior.

Similar dependency longings are now directed to superhuman extraterrestrials. Though often more limited, expressed in a less overtly spiritual vocabulary, and focused on specific material conditions—war, disease, and so on—they remind us strongly of traditional religious longings for immortality, incorruption, and impassability (freedom from suffering).

Extraterrestrials and Explanation

Religions play a multiplicity of roles in human societies. Among their most important traditional functions, according to numbers of scholars, are explaining or accounting for the world, including human social arrangements, and vouching for a moral order.

But in Western societies religion has gradually—although unevenly—yielded to science in the matter of explaining the world. I say unevenly mainly because numbers of religionists (who nowadays are often popularly and indiscriminately labeled "fundamentalists") continue to cling to supernaturalist explanations. Many other Westerners, however, now look to science. Although some who accord primacy to science in the matter of explaining the world repudiate religion, large numbers of others continue to find value in religion, and they continue to support it in various ways.

Some persons continue to look to religion for moral guidance and justification (Wallace 1966:256–264). Religions typically vouch for moral codes in ways that science does not. Some people are attracted to religion because of its "communion" aspect, its emphasis on valued social relationships with nonhuman beings (Horton 1960:222), all the more so, I suspect, where there are strong dependency longings. Some persons hope for a "salvation" beyond the powers of our sciences. Numbers of people find religion an effective way of relating to their fellow human beings in morally defined and socially approbated ways, perhaps especially when they find themselves otherwise powerless socially, politically, and economically. And many, no doubt, find religion attractive because of various sorts of combinations of the above considerations.

The erosion of religion's explanatory powers, nevertheless, has weakened religion among those people who increasingly accord explanatory functions to science. The relative vitality of fundamentalist Christianity in the United States, I think, owes much to the faith that many of its adherents continue to invest in biblical narratives as acceptable accounts of the world and how it came to be. Religion is less multiplex and less totalizing for those who do not.

Yet ironically, large numbers of Westerners who cede explanation of the world to science know relatively little about science. Many have a poor understanding of scientific methods and perspectives, and scant knowledge of scientific theories. They deem science prestigious and hold its derivative technology to be effective and desirable, yet their comprehension of both science and technology is, at best, superficial. This state of affairs can sometimes lead to an interesting cultural development.

Among those persons who have no real understanding of scientific methods, theories, and philosophy, yet who look to science rather than to religion for explanations of the world, there is something of a culturally mediated disposition to support pseudoscientific quests and explanations. That is, in a culture that values science and its derivative technologies, many persons are disposed to entertain uncritically what they suppose to be scientific explanations. That may particularly be the case when they can comprehend those explanations, which can happen when putative scientific explanations are actually closer to traditional religious narratives than to the formulations of normal science. While affirming a commitment to science and making use of some of the vocabulary of science, people may well endorse myths that are not subject to procedures and efforts at refutation that are of crucial normative and prescriptive importance to science.

The Roswell myth and kindred myths pivot on an extraterrestrial hypothesis. But it is a hypothesis that is not falsifiable: how could one disprove the existence of extraterrestrials? Rather, it is accepted by some persons in preference to alternative explanations, partly, we may conjecture, because of its mythic associations. For modern Westerners, moreover, it has a certain contemporary plausibility. Donald Menzel (1972: 125), who dates the idea of flying saucers to 1947, the year in which Kenneth Arnold saw what looked like saucers during his flight over the state of Washington, remarks that the time was ripe for the concept of extraterrestrial spacecraft. "Man," he reminds us, "was already contemplating space exploration. So why not space travel in reverse?"

SITUATEDNESS
A Metaphysical-Cosmological Dualism

In a book titled *God the Problem,* the theologian Gordon Kaufman (1972:42) writes of a "fundamental metaphysical-cosmological dualism found in the Bible (as well as in traditional metaphysics) and in virtually all Western religious thought." He continues, "There is the division of reality into 'earth' and 'heaven'—that which is accessible to us in and through our experience and in some measure under our control, and that beyond our experience and not directly open to our knowledge or manipulation."

That dualism might be amended or refined to include the subterranean, to which various European folk traditions assign dangerous and usually malevolent beings. But even where supernatural personages or forces are said to dwell under ground, in the recesses of caves, or deep below the surface of the sea, they are still, in one sense or another, part of the earth, even though not under our control. The devil, for example, though popularly imagined to have his throne in infernal regions, is also sometimes labeled "prince of the world."

The "fundamental metaphysical-cosmological dualism" to which Kaufman refers has been expanded by the Roswell myth and by kindred myths to include extraterrestrials who travel in spaceships. Space beings are not under human control. For the most part, moreover, they make efforts to minimize either our experiences of them or our memories of having had such experiences. (Saucerians who participate in flying saucer cults, however, often maintain that extraterrestrial beings reveal themselves in various ways to cult leaders and sometimes to initiates, a matter that I treat later.)

Heaven and Space

One of the most interesting aspects of claims about the existence of flying saucers has to do with where those machines are situated in the narratives that have developed about them. Except for what is probably a relatively small number of fundamentalist Christians, the culturally conceived locus of flying saucers is not heaven. Rather, they are situated in space (Jacobs 1975; Peebles 1994; Bryan 1995). And the transition in interest from heaven to space that is signaled by beliefs in, and speculations about, flying saucers is one of a number of expressions of cultural change in Euro-American societies during the last several centuries.

In Renaissance paintings of heaven, that realm is characterized by serenity, beauty, and joy, in keeping with mainstream Christian traditions about salvation. It is a place of benevolence and innocence, a celestial garden. But as various observers point out (e.g., Jacobs 1975; Peebles 1994), space is different.

As many persons have come to imagine space—to a great extent in consequence of numerous science fiction novels and stories, films, and TV programs—it is not consistently one thing or another. Though sometimes beautiful, joyful, and serene, it also departs radically on occasion from Renaissance images of heaven. It is sometimes portrayed as exotic to the point of being weird and decidedly stressful or otherwise off-putting, a far cry from the peace and joy of that reconciliation between God and humans that Christians traditionally represent as heaven.

Space is sometimes ugly, dangerous, and conflict laden. As some imagine it, it is populated by Klingons and other menacing intelligences, empires that strike back, frightful microbes and voracious blobs, obsessive and uncaring machines, alien psychopaths, and our own missiles and other weapons, as well as old-fashioned human greed, fear, intolerance, and itchy trigger fingers, now projected onto a high-tech and galactic stage. It also has its attractions, of course. It is the setting for stirring adventures, fantastic sex, far-out architecture and designer clothes, and other enticements that might well appeal to us planet-bound earthlings. When we consider its problems as well as its attractions, however, we are forced to conclude that space, unlike heaven, is rather much of a mixed bag.

Cultural Significance of the Transition in Interest from Heaven to Space

A diverse group of persons have written about the investments in time, energy, and personal commitment that others have made in UFOs and flying saucers. Some commentators have suggested that many of the claims made about extraterrestrial ships and beings are founded on religious longings and fantasy projections. What is new, some say, is that those longings and projections are now partially expressed in idioms and icons popularly associated with science, technology, and science fiction (e.g., Sagan 1996). There is evidence to support that interpretation, at least in some cases (Peebles 1994; Lewis 1995). The matter of idioms and icons, however, is actually a very complex cultural affair. It deserves to be treated as such and to be explored in its multifactorial richness.

For my purposes, it is useful to explore further what may be involved in the shift in interest from heaven to space as evinced by the assertions and speculations of numbers of ufologists and others. "Space" here refers to more than space as structured by a few abstractly conceived coordinates. It is, rather, a set of cultural constructs.

In viewing some (but not all) UFO and flying saucer myths as suggesting a transition in cultural interest from heaven to space, some caveats need to be entered. Such a shift is hardly complete or thoroughgoing. Space and heaven, as presently figured, are not mutually exclusive, bipolar opposites. They overlap in various ways. And in contemporary Western imaginings, which are demonstrably heterogeneous, they mutually support each other's intelligibility in different ways and in different degrees among those who evince interest in them. Furthermore, the transition is still in process, and it is not always linear. Some persons, indeed, go back and forth in their imaginings, with interesting zigs and zags in their conceptualizations and assertions.

When we examine mainstream Christian imaginings of heaven, those imaginings may strike us at first as suggesting that heaven, traditionally conceived, constitutes a tripartite social hierarchy. At the apex is the godhead, the celestial sovereign. And then there are two classes of the creator's creatures: unfallen angels (pure spirits or intelligences) and once-fallen humans who have been restored to God's grace by that grace (and who gaze beatifically upon their creator either—opinions differ—as disembodied souls or as souls united with their resurrected and glorified bodies).

But when we inquire into the political economy of heaven, we find that there is none. Heaven is a place totally devoid of discord or strife. We normally recognize discord and strife to be concomitants of pluralism, and the absence of the former suggests the absence of the latter. Heaven is metaphysically tripartite. But to the extent that we might even speak of it politically, it is clearly monolithic: a perfect totalitarian order.

Space, on the other hand, is popularly conceived to be pluralistic. It is thought of as such metaphysically, of course, but the discord, strife, danger, and unrealized potentialities attributed to it vivify its pluralism. Its heterogeneous denizens have very different intellectual capacities and understandings, they differ in their emotional possibilities and expressions, and their agendas are assumed to be quite diverse, all the more so because they are often hermetic or difficult if not impossible to comprehend.

Space is a screen that can serve for the projection and displacement of xenophobic, racial, and ethnic biases. But beyond its possible psychological utility for individuals in that regard, it is interesting as a set of contemporary cultural constructs. Indeed, there is something remarkably realistic about it, even when viewed as fantasy. Its pluralism and other characteristics suggest some of the conflicts and contradictions that we increasingly recognize in present-day life on this planet: multiculturalism, polyphony, heightened ethnic and religious divisiveness and fragmentation, multinational corporations and trade, increasing utilization of new informational and other technologies, growing resemblances in material cultures and in dispositions to treat nonmaterial phenomena as commodities, depthlessness, increasing recourse to spatial images and logic, and heightened sensitivities to contingency, pastiche, social pathology, and menace (Lyotard 1984; Jameson 1991).

Whereas Western political theorists and activists in the past might aspire to create social orders that would increasingly approximate to Western images of heaven, in the hope that human society might eventually become something in the nature of "a celestial organism," that aspiration is decreasingly viewed as a realistic possibility outside of certain distinct contemporary circles. So-called fundamentalist Muslims, Jews, and Christians, some other religionists (including some saucerians), and what are in all probability shrinking numbers of more secular utopians may continue to deem it a goal worthy of their prayers and political actions. But many other persons, including numbers who continue to believe in heaven as a postmortem destination for themselves, are decidedly less inclined to suppose that something like heaven on earth is a prospect for the near future.

Many persons in our society continue to hope for a future life in heaven. To them, heaven, so to speak, is not dead. But for many of those hopefuls, heaven is in heaven, and the kingdom of God on earth is unlikely to be established by ballot, revolution, conversion, or direct extrahuman intervention. For a number of the hopefuls, and for a number of those who disbelieve in heaven even as a postmortem possibility, space as constructed by science fiction writers and ufologists is a more arresting metaphor for the future than heaven. In fact, widespread and growing interest in space suggests the ongoing construction of new tropes through which people attempt to come to terms with readjustments in their expectations, hopes, and fears.

The Roswell myth is part and parcel of the new figuration of space, and ufologists have assigned it an important role in that figuration. Proponents of the myth assert that Roswell—with its putative metallike substances that are unlike any earthly metals, mysterious writings that resist decoding, and harvest of alien cadavers—provides material evidence for the undeniable reality of space as configured by kindred mythologies. That space, though pluralistic and menacing, at the same time offers prospects of new marvels and new solutions to old problems. It represents, indeed, an effort at enchantment. And Roswell constitutes an effort to put enchantment on a solid empirical footing.

EMOTIONAL TONES

In a famous work, *The Varieties of Religious Experience,* William James ([1902] 1929:29) maintains that there "seems to be no elementary religious emotion, but only a common storehouse of emotions upon which religious objects may draw." Many contemporary students of religion agree with him. Religionists, nevertheless, may tend to associate certain emotions from that common storehouse with distinct religious events. They sometimes suppose, for example, that feelings of solemnity, awe, joy, solidarity with fellow communicants, and so forth are especially appropriate—and often to be expected—in the case of certain rituals or liturgies. People, to be sure, may experience such emotions outside of what we deem religious settings or occasions, but perhaps some of their most vivid memories of those emotions are connected to religious events.

Awe and Joy

Some flying saucer myths explicitly connect awe to extraterrestrial contacts. The connection is well portrayed, for example, in the movie *Close Encounters of the Third Kind.* Toward the end of that presentation, a huge alien mothership, preceded by an earth-alien musical duet of pattern-establishing tones, descends on a Wyoming landscape in a haze of lights. Awaiting it are a sizable number of human scientists and technicians, professionals whom we might suppose are among the most rational and hardheaded of earthlings. But close-ups show them to be overcome by awe or rapture. Their emotions in this encounter put me in mind of the feelings that many Christians attribute to the disciples who witnessed Jesus' transfiguration on the mount and that many Hindus attribute to the warrior chief Arjuna when, as related in the *Bhagavad-Gita,* he beheld Krishna's divine form.

A very interesting treatment of the emotions is given in the movie *E.T.* Throughout most of that film, government agents are in search of an extraterrestrial who was accidentally stranded on our planet when his spaceship, here to gather plant samples, departed. The government squad is depicted as decidedly sinister in its implacable and heavy-footed search: a sort of Southern California gestapo that is likely to do unspeakable things to the lovable alien should he/she/it fall into their hands. The government agents, moreover, are something in the nature of an extension of adults, for in this film children are pure in heart and clear-sighted whereas adults are typically silly, sinister, or both. But at the end of the story, when E.T.'s shipmates descend to take the alien home, the chief government agent reveals himself to be really a grown-up kid. He confesses that he has long desired contact with aliens and that he is overcome with awe and joy that such has occurred. Rather than being an American Heinrich Himmler, he is actually a Huck Finn with a high civil service rating.

Other Emotions

Various films and other narratives associate other emotions with human-alien contacts, drawing on the gamut of emotions that we recognize conventionally. Motion pictures such as *The Thing from Another World* (1951) and *Earth vs. the Flying Saucers* (1956) capitalize on anxiety, fear, and horror. Such emotions are also evoked in numbers of contemporary abduction accounts, though sometimes laced with eroticism and other feelings. Common themes in abduction accounts are the powerlessness of the victims, their vulnerability to exploitation, and the indifference to human dignity and pretensions of autonomy that is a marked aspect of alien hegemony. These are postmodernist themes, evocative of postmodernist sentiments. From some observers' perspectives, we might suppose, assertions that such themes and sentiments are elicited by hypnotizing quite ordinary people could better be deemed assertions about hypnotic progression rather than regression.

Roswell and Emotions

Turning to the Roswell myth, we find that it encapsulates and expresses a limited fan of emotions. The strongest emotions implied in various versions of the myth are anger and hostility directed against the U.S. government. These would seem to be occasioned by beliefs about the government's alleged efforts to cover up the truth of Roswell. A possible interpretation, however, might counter that such hostility toward the government—hostility against hegemonic power—stems from a variety of situations and conditions and that the Roswell myth itself is something of a projection of hostilities that were already in place and that had, and that still have, a decided capacity for growth.

A fairly extreme expression of hostility, coupled with an undertone of fear, is found in the television film *Roswell*. In this cinematic version of the myth, one of the aliens recovered at the crash site was still alive. He was cared for in a U.S. military installation, and shortly before he died of apparently crash-induced traumas, he communicated telepathically with Secretary of Defense James V. Forrestal. Shaken by what the dying alien told him, and alarmed in other respects by his own government's policies, Forrestal decided to tell his fellow citizens what he knew about alien contacts. The film hints broadly that Forrestal was murdered in order to prevent him from doing so. In some other accounts it is openly asserted that he was killed by the CIA in Bethesda Naval Hospital and that his death was made to look like a suicide (Peebles 1994:275).

The Roswell myth incorporates a double conspiracy theory. First, the aliens, for reasons of their own, conspire to conceal their existence from earthlings, though they occasionally fail to do so (as in New Mexico in 1947). That is why they don't land their ships on the White House lawn or drop in on the editors of the *New York Times*. Second, the U.S. government, perhaps in collusion with other national governments, conspires to keep the public as ignorant as possible of alien sightings and contacts. Such double-dipping in conspiracy theory constitutes something of an exercise in suspicion, anxiety, fear, and hostility.

In other respects, the Roswell myth serves to underwrite, if only indirectly, emotions associated with kindred myths. To the extent that people connect their feelings and behaviors to what they deem reality, they are better able to justify those feelings and behaviors to themselves. Roswell is of great importance to numbers of persons because they maintain that it provides solid empirical evidence of the existence of extraterrestrials. It testifies, in their opinion, to the reality of beings from space. By so doing, it helps to warrant the emotional postures that kindred narratives dispose their proponents to take.

FLYING SAUCERS AND RELIGION

I have referred above to kindred narratives, that is, to narratives about flying saucers that resemble the Roswell myth, at least to the extent of affirming the reality of flying saucers. These narratives, however, are quite diverse. Some are part and parcel of what many Westerners would call religions. Other narratives, however, are in effect antireligious, for they advance materialist interpretations of the central narratives of traditional Western religions, thus attempting to desupernaturalize them. Still other kindred narratives, though in themselves neither distinctly religious nor antireligious, can be used either to support religion or to attack it.

Desupernaturalizing Religion

One genre of narratives, while maintaining that flying saucers are real enough, attempts to use their posited reality to strip biblical and other religious myths of their supernaturalist elements. Erich von Däniken's *Chariots of the Gods?* (1969) and R. L. Dione's *God Drives a Flying Saucer* (1969) are examples.

Such works generally suggest that extraterrestrial beings visited Earth long ago; that some of the feats they accomplished with their very advanced technology so impressed earthlings that the latter, sometimes at the deliberate promptings of the former, worshiped the aliens as gods; and that biblical stories and other ancient myths recount some of those happenings as if they were supernatural events. Thus, for example, the Hebrews were brought out of Egypt as part of a breeding experiment, what Moses and his followers actually saw at Sinai was a flying saucer, the birth of Jesus resulted from artificial insemination, and so on and so forth.

These narratives constitute contemporary examples of what is called euhemerism. Euhemerus, a Sicilian Greek who was born around 330 B.C., claimed that many of the gods of Greek mythology originated as exceptional human beings whose remarkable and beneficial achievements eventually resulted in their deification. The tenet associated with his name holds that myths about divine personages are based on real but distorted events. For the euhemerist, a major purpose in analyzing myths is to distill history by boiling off exaggeration.

Persons who seek to desupernaturalize biblical and other religious stories by reinterpreting them as involving extraterrestrials are engaging in a euhemeristic enterprise, but some (e.g., von Däniken) seem to do so with marked animosity toward certain traditional religions. Indeed, their interpretive efforts sometimes appear to be harnessed in the service of atheism. That, however, may not have been the case for the original Euhemerus. Although Plutarch (1970), a Greek writer and priest of Delphi, denounced him as a quack and accused him of disseminating "all manner of atheism throughout the world," Euhemerus as portrayed by Diodorus Siculus (1956) seems to have accepted the sun, moon, and stars as genuine deities while casting doubt on the divine origins of the Olympian gods.

Flying Saucer Myths in Religion

Whereas some religionists have incorporated flying saucers into traditional Western religions by asserting either that they are angelic messengers sent by God or minions of the devil, other people have created distinct religions that pivot on flying saucer myths. The doctrines of these flying saucer religions typically draw on a diversity of sources, including traditional religions, spiritism, theosophy, other occult dispensations, and science fiction.

One of the earliest detailed studies of these new religions was published in 1956 by Leon Festinger, Henry W. Riecken, and Stanley Schachter, under the title *When Prophecy Fails: A Social and Psychological Study of a Modern Group That Predicted the Destruction of the World*. The group studied was located in the midwestern part of the United States. The authors took pains to conceal the exact location, and they used pseudonyms for the participants and for the two towns where most of the participants lived.

The studied group revolved around "Mrs. Marian Keech" of "Lake City." For at least 15 years prior to the emergence of her flying saucer religion, Mrs. Keech had read in the literatures of—or otherwise experimented with—theosophy, dianetics, the I AM movement, and other enterprises and projects intended to provide "cosmic" knowledge and knowledge of one's self. She attended lectures on flying saucers and seems to have developed a keen interest in them. She eventually began to receive messages from her deceased father by means of automatic writing. Her father, however, seemed a poor correspondent, for the messages that he sent her from the beyond were relatively trivial. Things picked up when Mrs. Keech began to receive automatic writing messages from "the Elder Brother" and some other spiritual beings headquartered on the planets "Clarion" and "Cerus."

Eventually, Mrs. Keech began to receive messages from the "superior being" Sananda, who revealed himself to have been the historical Jesus and who figured as an important link to traditional forms of Christian revelation and millennialism. The teachings of Sananda and other superior beings collectively referred to as the Guardians attracted a small number of adherents, mainly from "Lake City" and nearby "Collegeville," the domicile of Mrs. Keech's most devoted supporters, "Dr. and Mrs. Armstrong." The adherents would gather from time to time to learn of and discuss the latest messages transmitted through Mrs. Keech. They also prepared themselves for the new life promised them by the Guardians.

Sananda, among other things, was the commander of a spaceship. Superior beings had long used such vehicles to visit Earth and other planets, and one was now being readied for the benefit of Mrs. Keech and her followers. The Guardians had decided to destroy Lake City and much of the rest of the lands of the earth by flood just before dawn on 21 December, and they communicated their decision to Mrs. Keech by automatic writing. (This prophecy was later transmitted by earthly means to a local newspaper, which published it in late September.) But while catastrophe would overwhelm humanity on the appointed day, Mrs. Keech and her followers were to be saved by Sananda and other superior beings, who would transport them by flying saucer to a paradisical planet. Some of the adherents prepared for their upcoming evacuation in various ways, including the giving away of many of their worldly possessions.

When the prophesied flood did not occur, some of the adherents repudiated Mrs. Keech and her messages. Others, however, closed ranks around her in heightened solidarity and became, if anything, more fervent in their expressed endorsements of the messages. Mrs. Keech and the faithful Armstrongs, moreover, now sought new converts and attention from the newspapers with an enthusiasm and intensity notably greater than that exhibited prior to 21 December. Further, they proposed various reasons for the failure of the flood to occur, most notably the idea that the Guardians had postponed the catastrophe because of the faith and devotion of those adherents who truly respected the messages that had been communicated through Mrs. Keech.

This study, fascinating as a scholarly inquiry into the religious imagination and its social dimensions, is also of importance for the history of psychological theory. It constitutes a milestone in the development of Leon Festinger's famous theory of cognitive dissonance. Briefly described, that theory maintains that when individuals become conscious of a dissonance or inconsistency between two or more of their opinions, beliefs, or claims to knowledge, they will experience psychological discomfort, and they will make efforts of various sorts to reduce or eliminate the dissonance that produces the discomfort. In advancing that theory, Festinger attempts to describe the different strategies and tactics that people tend to employ in their efforts to avoid, reduce, or eliminate dissonance, and the likely conditions or factors that might promote one sort of effort rather than another.

In the case of religious movements such as the one described in *When Prophecy Fails,* efforts to reduce dissonance between belief in a prophecy and knowledge that the prophecy has not been fulfilled may sometimes take the form of increased proselytizing. The cognitive principle at work, Festinger, Riecken, and Schachter (1956:26) suggest, is that "if more and more people can be persuaded that the system of belief is correct, then clearly it must, after all, be correct." This principle may also be involved in the case of missionaries who attempt to still their doubts about the doctrines they endorse by making efforts to convert others to them.

During the last half century, a number of flying saucer religions have developed in the United States and elsewhere. Many of them center around a medium or channeler who receives messages from space. In others, such as "the Group," started by Marshall Herff Applewhite and Bonnie Lu Nettles—aka Bo and Peep, aka Pig and Sow, aka Do and Te, aka Do and Ti, aka the Two, aka TeDo—the founders or core members themselves claim to be superhuman, supernatural, or superior (more highly evolved) beings (Balch and Taylor 1977; Balch 1995).

Most scholars have no problem, I think, in deeming the flying saucer groups described above, and many like them, religious groups, in keeping with common acceptations of the adjective "religious" and the noun to which it relates. Indeed, they are reminiscent of more traditional Western religions in their postulations of superhuman or supernatural beings, their metaphysical-cosmological dualism (this world and another), the emergence of a sacred canon (teachings from superior beings), an eschatology regarding the end (literal and/or figurative) of earthly life as we know it, promises of salvation of some sort (perhaps on another planet or astral plane), ritualized and sacralized social activities (attending lectures, discussing messages received, and so forth), the fellowship among believers, the evocation of powerful emotions such as awe and rapture, the use of and reverence for sacred symbols, and the like.

Although flying saucer religions are sometimes described as cults, in recognition of their small memberships and doctrinal deviations from the mainstream, there is no doubt that they are genuine religions for persons who sincerely invest themselves in these groups. This, of course, may not be the case for all who join; to join is not necessarily to be committed (Lofland and Stark 1965; Balch 1995). Many persons who join are in search of spiritual experience, and in the course of their quest they may be attracted to one group after another. But for those who do become committed, these flying saucer religions can be fulfilling, at least for a time. Among the things required to perpetuate these religions are sustaining myths. And those, it seems, are in significant degree matters of experiment, of trial and error.

The Roswell myth is neither Revelational nor euhemeristic. It neither supports some particular religion nor attacks one. But it can be used to do either, if it is skillfully woven into a larger fabric of meanings. It can be described as a facilitating and supportive narrative—but what it may facilitate and what it may support depend on how it is used.

The Roswell myth is not a religious myth. Nor, in itself, does it point to any religion. It does, however, contain elements that remind us of religious elements, for we sometimes encounter them in contexts that we clearly deem religious. It suggests the existence of beings that are superior to humans in science and technology and who therefore are potential threats or boons to human existence. It expresses dependency longings. It incorporates a metaphysical-cosmological dualism that affirms an interest in space. It is redolent of mystery, yet in effect it has been rendered nonhypothetical. And it suggests that our right to know, the very cornerstone of our dignity as mature human beings, has been compromised and deliberately subverted by a conspiracy of establishments, military, scientific, and governmental—and that salvation of a sort depends on unmasking the conspirators and proclaiming the knowledge that they seek to conceal.

And what ultimately is this gnosis or knowledge, the acquisition of which will enhance our dignity? It is knowledge, finally, that we humans are not the only intelligent beings in the universe and that we can hope for contact and communion with other intelligent beings. Hope is not vain, because the others, who are presently alien, are not indifferent to us. They are monitoring us, as the saucer crash in New Mexico indicates.

Roswell is an effort at enchantment in an increasingly postmodern world, one of many efforts to rescue decentered selves by proclaiming that the universe, after all, is not indifferent to us. Its future, I think, will not depend on efforts to refute it. Its future, rather, will depend on the kindred narratives with which it becomes associated, and on their powers or lack of powers to sustain themselves in the imaginations of those persons who are open to such stories. And therein lies its pathos, for it is only in their imaginations that the truly unempowered are empowered.

CHAPTER FIVE

THREE IMAGES OF ROSWELL

CHARLES A. ZIEGLER AND BENSON SALER

ach chapter in this book is intended to support an assertion made in the Introduction—that is, as a cultural phenomenon the Roswell Incident can best be understood as an example of a modern myth. In the discussions that follow, we explore the extent to which that intent has been fulfilled. We do so by assessing some of the analytical findings that have been presented in the context of certain facets of the Roswell Incident that are not examined explicitly in the previous chapters but, nevertheless, are among the primary determinants of its cultural significance.

More specifically, we describe three images of the Roswell Incident: the public image projected by the media, the scholarly image conveyed by the writings of skeptics, and the believers' image promulgated in letters, commentaries, and articles by members of the UFO community. In a final section we discuss the significance of these images in terms of societal effects.

THE PUBLIC IMAGE: A CASE OF MISTAKEN IDENTITY

We believe that the media have played, and continue to play, an important role in reinforcing the status of the Roswell Incident as a myth. To describe this role, it is useful to begin by analyzing the degree to which various segments of the media can influence the public.

In our society a story may receive considerable media attention. The conveyed image of such a tale, in terms of its genre and subject matter, is shaped in the first instance by the originator and secondarily by the media. Some segments of the media may accept and promulgate the originator's image, while other segments may reject it and promulgate an altered version of this image based on a critical evaluation. What may be called the public image of such a story is the version that predominates in those segments of the media that reach the largest number of people.

We emphasize that we define "public image," not as the way a story is *perceived by,* but rather as the way it is *presented to,* the largest number of people. For example, the tabloids have a circulation that ranks among the highest of the print media segments, typically numbering a few million readers, and television routinely reaches audiences numbering in the tens of millions. In contrast, the readership of newspapers usually numbers in the hundreds of thousands and that of specialist journals in the thousands. Thus, if a story attracts the attention of the tabloids and television, the predominant image projected by those media segments becomes its public image, because the audience they reach is vastly greater than the audience reached by other media segments.

The Roswell Incident is, of course, such a story, and the predominant image of this story projected by the tabloids and by television docudramas is that of the originators. According to the findings of Chapters 2, this means that the public image of the Roswell story involves, as it were, a case of mistaken identity. In other words, the type of tale that the Roswell story represents has been misidentified in its public image. A society as complex as our own produces stories of many types, but only two are relevant to understanding this misidentification: the exposé and the folk narrative.

As a tale type, the exposé may be defined as a story that results from the uncovering of hitherto hidden events by investigators exercising their skills in the tradition of America's open society in order to satisfy the public's right to know. This is an activity that gains special piquancy if it proceeds in the face of perceived stonewalling by a person, group, or institution (e.g., the government) with a vested interest in keeping the events hidden. The history of such exposés can be traced back to the birth of the Republic, but for many Americans the Watergate affair may be prototypical.

Like the exposé, the folk narrative is also a story, but it represents a different tale type. As its definition in Chapter 2 indicates, the term "folk narrative" refers to a tale that stems from and expresses the traditions and beliefs of a community, and in our society such traditions and beliefs often constitute an embedded subculture.

The embedded subculture is a type of social phenomenon with a long history in the United States, where the spectacle of individuals coalescing around some special interest to form a "community" has always been a significant feature of the cultural landscape. Although the physical aggregation of members may occur, it is not essential to such groupings, which often involve individuals scattered throughout the general population who are linked by traditions and beliefs related to their special interest. Such traditions and beliefs constitute a subculture that is embedded within the complex of the more generally recognized traditions that constitute the larger national culture. In the eyes of the public, such embedded subcultures appear to range from the benign (e.g., the ham radio community) to the pernicious (e.g., the militia movement).

The findings of Chapters 1 and 2 point to the conclusion that the originators of the Roswell stories consistently presented them as examples of the first type of story (the exposé), but the stories are actually examples of the second type (the folk narrative of an embedded subculture). This misidentification is ascribable, in the first instance, to the traditions of the UFO subculture itself, which dictate that narrative elements of its folklore must be expressed in the format of an investigative report. The originators' image of the Roswell Incident as a genuine exposé has been rejected by skeptics, who maintain that the Roswell stories are based on flawed investigatory methods. These criticisms, which have appeared in some newspapers and specialist journals, promulgated an altered image of the Roswell Incident—that of a counterfeit exposé.

Of overriding significance for the public image of the Roswell Incident, however, is that the originators' image of the story as an exposé not only has been accepted uncritically but also has been enthusiastically embraced by the tabloids and by some television networks. For these media segments, the idea that the Roswell Incident may represent a counterfeit exposé appears to be irrelevant, because that possibility is not examined in their presentations.

This media stance on UFO phenomena is not new. In his 1959 book *Flying Saucers,* the psychoanalyst Carl Jung noted that an interview in which he expressed skepticism about UFOs was later published in a distorted form that made him appear to be a believer. He responded with a statement giving his true opinions, but that statement was ignored. Jung (1959:x) opined that "one must draw the conclusion that news affirming the existence of UFOs is welcome, but that skepticism seems undesirable." And he went on to ask a rhetorical question: "Why should it be more desirable for saucers to exist than not?"

Insofar as certain media segments in the United States are concerned, a clue to an answer to Jung's question is offered by Alexis de Tocqueville. His remarks about American culture, made in the first half of the nineteenth century, display a cogency unwithered by time. He observed, "The love of wealth is . . . to be traced, as either a principle or accessory motive, at the bottom of all Americans do; this gives to their passions a sort of family likeness."

If de Tocqueville is correct, one reason for the tabloids and television to deem it more desirable for UFOs to exist than not is that, as tales of the bizarre and unusual, stories involving "real" UFOs are eminently profitable. Because the image of the Roswell Incident as an exposé reinforces the reality of UFOs, the uncritical acceptance of this image by some media segments may be ascribed, at least in part, to an economic motive. But the existence of such a motive does not necessarily imply cynicism on the part of those media representatives who appear to have adopted the stance of true believers. For example, Paul Davids, the executive producer and cowriter of one widely aired television docudrama that treats the Roswell Incident as an exposé, has written articles in UFO journals (Davids 1994, 1995) that strongly suggest that his belief in the reality of extraterrestrial visitations may be sincere.

Whatever the mix of economic and ideological motives that may lie behind the treatment accorded to the story of the Roswell Incident by various media segments, the resultant public image of the story is that of an exposé, a public image that creates the impression that the events portrayed are real. We have argued that this public image is a case of mistaken identity. Paradoxically, however, to the extent that this image has tended to maintain a coterie of avowed believers, the tabloids and television have played a significant role in reinforcing the status of the Roswell Incident as a myth, inasmuch as the existence of such believers is one of the criteria for that status.

THE SCHOLARLY IMAGE:
A CASE OF DUBIOUS HISTORICITY

A coterie of avowed believers is necessary (but not sufficient) to make a story a myth. Another condition that must be met—according to the stipulative definition of "myth" in Chapter 2—is that the story not be treated as factual in the annals of our society. That the Roswell Incident fulfills this condition is a matter of common observation. For example, encyclopedias and almanacs record events such as the 1863 Battle of

Gettysburg, the 1912 *Titanic* disaster, and so on, but not a 1947 flying saucer crash at Roswell. Ostensibly, this omission has occurred because the epistemological standards used by the scholars responsible for such mainstream histories differ from those used by ufologists and other Roswell believers.

The word "ostensibly" appears in the statement above in deference to the ufologists' assertion that there is no such difference in standards and that their Roswell findings are not treated as factual because of a bias against phenomena that fall outside the narrow paradigmatic thinking that prevails within the scholarly community. Indeed, the application of scholarly epistemological standards in some contexts and by some practitioners sometimes appears to contravene ideals about open-mindedness that are widely accepted in our society. And insofar as this has occurred with regard to the Roswell Incident, the complaints of ufologists are understandable.

It appears, however, that the cause of such complaints may not be bias, in the pejorative sense of this word, but merely that scholarly epistemological standards impose boundaries on open-mindedness. To some extent, the location of these boundaries is a judgment call. Thus, even within the scholarly community there is not perfect unanimity on where to draw the lines in assessing new findings and claims. Nevertheless, shared elements in the training of its members and the peer review process, which make the scholarly community self-monitoring, tend to produce a consensus on how these boundaries should be drawn. Evaluations of the Roswell stories in the context of this consensus thus project what may be termed the scholarly image of the Roswell Incident. Evaluations of this sort (cited in Chapter 2) have been published as critiques of one or more of the Roswell stories, and they consistently convey an image of the transfigured Roswell Incident as an event of dubious historicity.

Such critiques vary in length and detail, but in overview it is possible to discern in them two salient evaluative approaches that are evocative of the scholarly perspective. These approaches can be labeled "comparative" and "interpretive." The first involves comparing the informational pattern displayed by the sequence of Roswell stories with the pattern known to be characteristic of genuine exposés. The second involves making a choice, based on epistemological principles, between the interpretations of validated historical events presented in the Roswell stories and alternative interpretations.

The first, or comparative, approach makes use of the fact that a definitive informational pattern has been observed to be characteristic of investigative reports based primarily on testimony about past events, events whose objective reality has subsequently been established by other means (e.g., physical evidence). Namely, in a genuine exposé the stories that result from successive investigations of the same past events generally produce a picture of these happenings that becomes increasingly clear with each story. Key elements in the early stories are not usually contradicted in later stories, but more details are filled in as each story emerges.

The Roswell stories do not display this pattern. Instead, successive stories about the Roswell Incident display substantive changes in which key elements in the early stories are contradicted in later stories. Over the years, as each of the "investigative reports" on the Roswell Incident has appeared, the picture of this incident has become more clouded. The reports provide dramatically different answers, not only to questions about details such as the shape of the alien spaceship, but also to more fundamental questions such as when and where the crash occurred and whether there was one crashed saucer or two.

Such disparities lead scholars to suspect that there is no underlying template of objective reality to which these stories conform; in other words, the informational characteristics of the Roswell stories are indicative of a narrative based on pseudoevents. Another dimension to this assessment is added by the analysis in Chapter 2, which demonstrates that changes in successive Roswell stories can be correlated with changes in the relevant beliefs of the UFO subculture. This correlation supports the view that the Roswell Incident, as depicted by these stories, is a folk narrative masquerading as an exposé.

The second, or interpretive, approach relies on the fact that there are references in the Roswell stories to a set of events whose historicity is confirmed by contemporary documents. These events can be related to a mosaic of relevant scientific fact and theory to form an interpretation of the events that is alternative to that presented in the Roswell stories. This alternative interpretation (i.e., the events are related to a crashed radar reflector) may then be compared with the first interpretation given in the Roswell stories (i.e., the events are related to a crashed saucer) in terms of situational logic—that is, the way these events are linked through hypotheses to form an explanation.

It is also possible to conceive of a third interpretation, namely, that the Roswell Incident may have involved both a crashed saucer and a crashed radar reflector. In fact, according to Chapter 1, this is precisely the scenario of Version 6 of the Roswell myth. The name of the game is to decide which of these three interpretations is most likely to correspond to objective reality. Making this decision involves principles of logic and epistemology, one of which is called Ockham's razor.

Ockham's razor was first enunciated as a principle some six and a half centuries ago in the scholarly language of the day by the English cleric and philosopher William of Ockham: *Frustra fit per plura quod fieri potest per pauciora*. In practice, this means that in explaining a thing or looking for its causes, we must not assume more entities than are needed to account for it *(entia non sunt multiplicanda sine necessitate)*. This applies to the making of hypotheses, the introduction of too many real distinctions, and so forth.

Ockham's razor can be combined with other principles. For example, when combined with the principle of sufficient reason, it yields the following rule: To explain a phenomenon by two causes or to postulate two distinct entities when one suffices is without sufficient reason. Such rules of the game (not a lack of open-mindedness) dictate that most members of the scholarly community will choose interpretation number two (a crashed radar reflector) because it contains fewer hypotheses and because those that it does contain are consonant with existing scientific fact and theory (e.g., as described in Chapter 3).

This outcome, although it suffices to dissuade most scholars from treating the first and third interpretations as objectively factual in their writings, by no means proves the falsity of these interpretations with certitude. The rules of the game are designed not to uncover truth but to guard against error. Like all communities, the scholarly community has its own subculture, and one of its values is that top priority should be given to keeping the fund of "knowledge claims" (i.e., statements wherein someone claims to know something) as error-free as possible by using the most stringent epistemological standards.

Because the status of a story as myth depends, in part, on a judgment made by the scholarly community, it is necessary to discuss our conception of this community and the way it works. The scholarly community is made up of individuals who actively participate in preserving, transmitting, reassessing, and augmenting the fund of knowledge claims. Because this is the primary criterion for membership, some of its members have had little formal education and some are independent scholars who are institutionally unaffiliated. In the United States, however, the overwhelming majority of its members hold advanced degrees, are affiliated with some accredited institution, and belong to a professional society. Currently, they represent a small fraction of the adult population. They have divided themselves up in accordance with their special interests, which are reflected in the names given to the broad categories of scholarship: the physical and biological sciences, the social sciences, the humanities, and the arts.

In practice, the active participation of scholars in augmenting the fund of knowledge claims usually takes the form of publishing their findings and theories in peer-reviewed books and journals and in assessing the findings and theories of others. From the perspective of the scholarly community, these findings and theories may be mostly accepted, mostly rejected, mostly held in abeyance pending further information, or mostly ignored in the writings of the members (which, in effect, corresponds to casting a vote). Scholars make their assessments of findings and theories mostly on the basis of evidence and the kinds of rules of the game described previously. Their assessments, however, are also colored by personal interests (often economic) and by the usual mélange of passions and eccentricities to which flesh is heir. In other words, their assessments are influenced by all the things that contribute to human fallibility.

Nevertheless, at any given time, what we have described as the fund of knowledge claims, which has its physical existence largely in the form of scholarly books and journals, consists of those portions of these texts that reflect findings and theories that fall in the "mostly accepted" category, as determined by the process just described. There are a lot of "mostlys" involved in this process, so how much credence can we give to this so-called fund of knowledge claims?

Because the assessment process we have described is used by all the members of the scholarly community, including scientists, the fund of accepted knowledge claims includes the kind of knowledge used in building bridges, designing airplanes, and concocting medicines. It thus consists of the kind of knowledge claims that we literally bet our lives on when we walk across a bridge, fly in an airplane, or swallow a pill. But the fund includes other kinds of knowledge claims as well.

In finer detail, the assessment process that renders claims to knowledge acceptable depends on evidence, logic (which we have been calling the rules of the game), and interests (all those things that lead us to espouse an idea independent of, or perhaps in spite of, logic and evidence). Even if we assume that the practitioners in each of the categories of scholarship are equally skilled in logic and equally in thrall to their interests, the reliability of their findings will vary because the nature of the evidence on which their judgments rest is not the same. If we scan the evidence adduced by practitioners in the physical and biological sciences, the social sciences, the humanities, and the arts, we find that in a hazy area between the biological and social sciences, it starts to change from the concrete (things we can see, hear, smell, and feel, albeit sometimes only with instruments) to the increasingly abstract.

The public at large seems to be aware of this. The authority that the public recognizes in the pronouncement of a geophysicist that a dam is about to rupture is at quite a different level from that accorded to the prediction of a political scientist that the future government of Russia will remain democratic or the assertion of an art scholar that Picasso will always be regarded as a great painter. These examples suggest that the word "reliable," when applied to a knowledge claim, refers to its usefulness in predicting outcomes. The track record of scientists is unexcelled in this regard, not because they are more logical or less biased by interests than are other members of the scholarly community, but because of the nature of the evidence they are able to use in their assessments. Members of the public, who primarily want the kind of information that will enable them to exercise some degree of control over their lives and their environment, will no doubt continue to consider scientific knowledge claims to be more authoritative than other kinds, even though some scholars question this idea.

In the last few decades there has been a movement within the scholarly community to dethrone science. Some nonscientist-scholars have put forth abstract arguments that putatively demonstrate that scientific knowledge claims are not more authoritative than other kinds. Most scientist-scholars have ignored these arguments, perhaps because they are unaware of them. A few, however, have responded vigorously by rejecting them, as for example, in the 1994 books *Higher Superstition,* by Paul Gross and Norman Levitt, and *Uncommon Sense,* by Alan Cromer. The pros and cons of this debate need not concern us here, but the existence of this controversy has been made relevant to any discussion about UFOs.

This relevance stems from the fact that the authors of some books about UFOs and a broad variety of paranormal phenomena have attempted to prove their claims about these phenomena by citing the work of scholars who have in effect changed the rules of evidence in order to debunk the authoritative nature of scientific knowledge claims. The point that needs to be made is that there is no evidence that, within the scholarly community as a whole, the ideas of these scholars fall in the "mostly accepted" category, although some ufologists and popularizers of the paranormal have made that assertion to buttress their arguments.

Because the top priority of the scholarly community is keeping the fund of accepted knowledge claims as error-free as possible, occasionally findings and explanations that are true may not survive the evaluative process. They may be rejected, at least until additional evidence is found. A story (considered apocryphal by some) aptly illustrates this point. Early eighteenth-century savants dismissed the tales of peasants who declared that stones fell from the sky in an area where a meteor was sighted near the earth. The savants reasoned that it was far more likely for peasants to lie than for stones to fall from the sky. Only later, with the acquisition of physical evidence, did scholars accept the reality of meteorites.

This story is sometimes cited to support the assertion that scholars are biased against phenomena that cannot be encompassed by familiar paradigms and that this bias can lead them to ignore important discoveries. In the eyes of scholars, however, the savants in this story have nothing to apologize for nor did the epistemological standards fail to operate as designed. What the story illustrates is that this design makes the accretion of accepted knowledge claims a contingent and sometimes slow process, but according to the values of the scholarly subculture, this is a small price to pay to ensure that the fund of such knowledge claims is as reliable as human fallibility allows.

It is also noteworthy that one of the themes of Chapter 2 can be restated in a way that is analogous to the meteorite story (i.e., it is more likely for traditors to lie than for flying saucers to fall from the sky). Can this analogy be extended, and if so, what does it portend for the status of the Roswell Incident as a myth? To answer this question it is pertinent to note that the definition of "myth" in Chapter 2 is independent of the objective factuality of the narrative—rather, it involves the scholarly community's assessment of factuality. According to the norms of this community's subculture, such assessments are always tentative.

As the meteorite story illustrates, explanations and findings that initially fail to meet scholarly epistemological standards may, if new evidence surfaces, meet those standards and become part of the fund of accepted knowledge claims. Thus, if unambiguous physical evidence of a saucer crash at Roswell is found, the status of the existing Roswell stories will change from history-like versions of a myth to mythlike versions of history. Past experience with crashed-saucer stories, however, suggests that such evidence will remain elusive and that the present scholarly image of the Roswell Incident, together with its concomitant status as a myth, will endure.

THE BELIEVERS' IMAGE:
A CASE OF EMBATTLED TRUTH

The commentaries and letters of readers that have been published in UFO journals indicate that most of these individuals claim to believe that the government recovered a crashed saucer near Roswell in 1947, on the basis of a generic form of the scenarios presented in the various versions of the Roswell myth. In other words, they seem to have selected a relatively bland assortment of ideas that tend to be common to all the versions while ignoring those that are unique to one version. Their commentaries thus project an image of the Roswell Incident that does not include things like two crashed saucers (Version 4), an elongated alien spaceship with batlike wings (Version 5), a saucer crashing into a balloon-borne radar reflector (Version 6), and so on.

Believers have also contributed lengthy articles to UFO journals in which they reject the criticisms of skeptics. In some cases these articles are written by individuals who hold doctorates from accredited universities and who are, as it were, card-carrying members of the scholarly community as well as being members of the UFO community. They are familiar with the scholarly rules of the game and display great dexterity in using these rules to advocate the factuality of their conception of the Roswell Incident or of other UFO phenomena. In doing this, they often draw upon their disciplinary specialties.

For example, an engineer (Galganski 1995) has written an equation-filled paper that uses mathematical modeling techniques in an attempt to show that the debris found on the Foster ranch could not have been that of a balloon-borne radar reflector. A historian (Jacobs 1992) has produced a book that attempts to demonstrate the factuality of selected elements in alien abduction stories by applying conventional methods of determining historicity such as the unlikelihood that noncollusive witnesses will tell similar lies. And sociologically oriented scholars (Rodeghier and Chesney 1994, 1995) have contributed articles that depict the history of the recent government investigation of the Roswell Incident in a way that provides an organizational context for believing that the allegation of a government conspiracy, which is found in all the Roswell stories, is factual.[1]

The spectacle of individuals who participate in two subcultures and who selectively make use of the norms, values, and traditions of both to achieve personal goals (in this case the protection of a cherished belief) is a familiar one to anthropologists. This practice can be observed in small-scale non-Western populations and is endemic in our complex society, in which virtually everyone participates in two or more subcultures (e.g., professional, religious, and so forth). Nevertheless, this practice imparts an aura of defensiveness to articles and commentaries in UFO journals. Such writings, in turn, project a believers' image of the Roswell Incident as an embattled truth.

That image, moreover, has been confirmed by the actions of believers who have demanded government cooperation in their continuing effort to prove the reality of various UFO phenomena. There is a long history of such demands by the UFO community, which in 1972 prompted Harvard University astrophysicist Donald Menzel to note that UFO studies (e.g., the Condon investigation) had absorbed government resources that would otherwise have been used for scientific research. And he warned against the importunities of UFO organizations: "Do not take these amateur groups lightly. They can do considerable harm to science with their vociferous demands for costly studies. I hope the silent majority will speak up against this situation" (Menzel 1972:145). His fears now seem somewhat overdrawn, but the recent example of the costly government investigation of the Roswell Incident once again raises the question of whether or not such expenditures are justified.

In this regard, it seems worthwhile to quote the remarks of an Air Force officer involved in answering the FOIA (Freedom of Information Act) requests of UFO buffs, many of whom he characterizes as "'serial/shotgun' requestors who oftentimes make the same request to different offices at the same time or the same request over and over." He laments that "FOIAs must be handled 'out of hide,'" meaning that "although Congress has directed that we provide a service to the public (usually for free) they give us neither the people nor the money to accomplish this task; which seems to be growing every year, even as our budget and personnel are cut." In a humorous, half-serious reductio ad absurdum, he adds that the Air Force "somewhere in the near future . . . will reach the point where we will quit working on *current* activities because we will have to devote all our time to answering requests for records of *past* activities; thereby becoming the world's only armed research service."[2]

Clearly, there are public costs associated with the efforts of members of the UFO community to prove the reality asserted by their beliefs. Insofar as the money spent on the recent government investigation of the

Roswell Incident is concerned, this expenditure seems particularly point-less if—as is suggested in Chapters 2 and 4—there is no form of government evidence against the crashed-saucer hypothesis that the UFO community would find acceptable. Nevertheless, the question of why believers are so zealous in seeking to prove the reality affirmed by their belief about the Roswell Incident deserves further discussion. Because such a discussion necessarily involves the convictions of believers, it is necessary to begin with an expository note about avowed and subjective belief.

Throughout this book we have used avowed belief as the criterion for categorizing individuals as believers, because it is the kind of belief we can identify from their verbal and written statements. But avowed belief (as we know from introspection) does not necessarily reflect our inner convictions—our subjective belief—which is likely to be revealed by our actions.

The actions of believers, such as their defensive writings and their past efforts to obtain government support to prove that their belief is in accord with the facts, suggest strongly that their avowed belief may not be identical to their subjective belief. These actions may indicate that although they want to believe that the recovery of a crashed saucer near Roswell is a historical event, in the same way that they believe, say, that the sinking of the *Titanic* is a historical event, they have failed to achieve a level of certitude about the Roswell Incident that would allow them to do this. The key question is, Why do they want to believe? The Roswell-as-myth approach may supply an answer to this question and also throw some light on the ancillary issue of the nature of the reality underlying the believers' image of the Roswell Incident.

As Chapter 4 makes clear, some myths (and the Roswell myth is an example) are not religious, in the conventional sense of this term, but they may express religious-like themes involving issues that are as real as death and the creation of worlds. Myths, by definition, deal with transcendental issues related to the human condition, a condition that is perhaps most aptly expressed by poetic imagery. For example, one view holds that life "is a tale told by an idiot, full of sound and fury, signifying nothing." Many of us cannot accept this idea, but nevertheless at some level we are aware that our lives are spent, as it were, on the edge of an abyss overlooking a void. We get through the day by "forgetting" that the abyss exists or, if we are occasionally reminded of its presence, by recourse to stories that fill in the void. Myths are these stories, and they are based on an aspect of reality that most of us prefer not to face, except through the medium of stories that provide comforting answers to the sometimes terrifying questions this reality evokes.

Myths vary enormously in subject matter and detail, but the central themes they address are relatively few in number. The theme is usually implied rather than stated, and it is often perceived as the answer to an unframed question. Hence, we can become more aware of the transcendental issue involved in a myth by first interpreting its theme and then stating the question to which the theme is the answer. For example, the subject matter of the Roswell stories is strikingly different from that of the angel stories described in Chapter 2, but the implied theme is the same: We are not alone in the universe. The transcendental issue involved becomes more apparent when we transpose the theme into a question: *Are* we alone in the universe?

All myths put us in touch with reality. Their implicit themes shift our humdrum worldview, forcing us to acknowledge that we are part of a reality so awesome that we desperately need the comfort of a mechanism that translates this reality into familiar human categories. The subject matter of the myth is that mechanism. Ironically, the trick of this mechanism is that it provides its jot of comfort only to true believers. In other words, it is necessary to believe in the reality of the myth's subject matter (e.g., UFOs or angels) in order for the myth to work. When myths are seen in this context, it becomes understandable that believers want the Roswell Incident to be real.

Some who find the subject matter of a myth, whether it be gods, angels, or UFOs, to be fantastical and unreal have derided the "faithful." But there is a terrible reality about myths that evokes feelings of empathy in many nonbelievers, feelings that are perhaps tinged with envy of the faithful for the comfort they derive from their belief. This kind of empathy, for example, seems to inform C. D. B. Bryan's book *Close Encounters of the Fourth Kind*. Although Bryan does not characterize alien abduction stories as versions of a myth (which they indeed appear to be), it seems that he is referring to his growing appreciation of the underlying reality in these stories when he states that "my perception of the abduction phenomenon has changed." And Bryan (1995:5) goes on to say, "I no longer think it is a joke. This is not to say that I now believe UFOs and alien abductions are *real*—'real' in the sense of a reality subject to the laws of the universe as we know them—but rather that I feel something very mysterious is going on."

In the *Times Book Review*, Dean Koontz wrote approvingly of the empathetic tone of Bryan's book: "No one should want to trade his rare kindness for yet another tome written by a sarcastic cynic." And he makes known his own feelings of empathy and his explicit recognition of the transcendental issue involved by noting wistfully that Bryan's work "left me not merely with an open-mindedness toward the subject of alien abduction but with the hope that many abductees are in fact telling the truth and that we are not alone in the universe."[3]

Perhaps one of the more useful functions of a myth is that it can serve to remind believers and nonbelievers alike that they are searching for answers to the same questions.

PORTENTS AND OMENS

That there are three images of the Roswell Incident rather than two is significant. If only the scholarly and believers' images existed—promulgated by specialist journals that reach a small fraction of the population—the Roswell Incident would have remained merely one among the many UFO phenomena whose reality has been debated by believers and skeptics over the years. It owes its pride of place—in having reached a relatively large fraction of the population—to its public image. What does this image portend? And does it matter? One clue to the answers can be found in studies of the role of the mass media in our society.

For example, based on their decades-long research, the authors of the 1994 book *Prime Time* conclude that "Madison Avenue and Sunset Boulevard have long since displaced classical mythology and the Bible as signposts of our cultural geography" (Lichter, Lichter, and Rothman 1994:4). Their findings emphasize that television has become a major factor in shaping our culture and that, over the years, the gradual increase in the use of the video vérité format has produced a qualitative change in television's social role. In that regard, they find that print media segments run a poor second to television in recasting reality as mass entertainment. They point out that television viewers have become "accustomed to the bastard genre of news and entertainment known as 'infotainment' through a steady stream of tabloid television series and docudramas." They continue, "But the 1990s mark the historical moment when such developments reached a critical mass, and the rapid accumulation of quantitative changes produced a qualitative change in the social role. . . . Today, the merger of information and entertainment has become so rapid and widespread as to threaten the very distinction between fact and fiction" (1994:4–5). According to critics of the video vérité approach, it not only blurs the line between fact and fiction but also sacrifices evenhandedness to achieve a dramatic impact; in other words, only one side of a story is told in an effective manner.

The issue of one-sidedness becomes apparent when we examine the three images of the Roswell Incident. Both the scholarly and believers' images necessarily present a view of the Roswell Incident as having two sides: the scholarly image, because it is an assessment of the believers' interpretations; the believers' image, because its defensive aura implies the existence of an alternative perspective. Television docudramas, on the other hand, are dramatizations of only the believers' interpretation of the Roswell Incident, dramatizations that convey few hints that this interpretation is controversial. To be sure, some television talk shows have included skeptics among their "talking heads," but the dramatic impact of the shows is far less than that of docudramas. Hence, the public image of Roswell, which is largely a creation of television, is predominantly one-sided.

The public image, of course, reaches vastly more people than either the scholarly or the believers' images, which have been promulgated only in specialist books and journals. Thus the public image of the Roswell Incident, an image created in large part by the video vérité format of television, appears to be a contributing factor in the acceptance of the idea that alien beings have landed on the earth. According to a recent survey (Gallup and Newport 1991:145), 27 percent of adult Americans hold this belief, a figure that represents tens of millions of people.

That so many people in our society are willing to accept unfounded ideas when embodied in one of television's video vérité products is, according to some students of the media, an example of a phenomenon they call media-driven public credulity. To explicate this term, it is helpful to return to the claim of the authors of *Prime Time,* which was quoted earlier—namely, that the blurring of fact and fiction in television's video vérité products had, by the 1990s, proceeded to the point that "such developments reached a critical mass," a point at which a qualitative change occurred in the social role of the popular culture purveyed by such products.

The authors borrowed the term "critical mass" from nuclear physics to convey the notion of many small quantitative increments adding up to a qualitative change. In nuclear physics, critical mass is the amount of fissionable material needed for a chain reaction to become self-sustaining, an amount that is truly capable of producing qualitatively different effects than smaller quantities. The critical mass analogy thus conveys the idea that television's video vérité approach is no longer something that is a reaction to the public demand for an entertaining format, but rather it has become a self-sustaining enterprise that seeks to ensure its continued existence by creating a public demand for its wares in a cycle of credulity feeding upon credulity.

This progression in the development of video vérité products appears to be part of a more general pattern described by historian Daniel Boorstin. He points to shortcomings in the conventional view that human needs create an environment in which new products of technology either flourish or languish, depending on whether they meet these needs. The products of technology "are only sometimes invented in response to fixed environmental needs," Boorstin (1995:159) avers. "More often man-made novelties are ways of inventing needs." And he notes that frequently the power of a product of technology "to survive depends on its ability to bring forth its own environment, or create its own demand" (1995:137).

In applying the above insight, the expression "media-driven credulity" refers to the fact that video vérité "products" no longer merely reflect public credulity but actively create it. This phenomenon involves not only UFOs but also astrology, extrasensory perception, and a host of other ideas that are often subsumed under the heading "paranormal." Quite apart from the question of the objective factuality of stories about UFOs, telepathy, and the like, the frequent projection of an unskeptical one-sided image of these stories in television docudramas affects adversely the public's ability to judge. Indeed, it constitutes a unilateral rejection on the part of some television producers of the public's right to know both sides of the story. Regarding docudramas about the Roswell Incident that portray it as a UFO crash, what appears to be culturally significant about millions of people having apparently accepted the factuality of the story line is not the content of the story per se but rather that it represents a type of story that exemplifies media-driven public credulity.

Does it matter that this kind of credulity exists? Some commentators insist that it does. They claim that media-driven public credulity has created a society in which individuals who opt for "psychic surgery" or some other New Age nostrum instead of validated medical remedies may die unnecessarily, that those who regulate their business affairs in accord with the predictions of psychics instead of proven economic indicators may suffer financially, and so on. For example, in a recent newsletter, the director of an organization that investigates paranormal phenomena quotes an inquiry received from a 14-year-old girl: "I was hoping you could send me some info on reports, abductions and just facts about aliens. I am doing a project on UFO phenomena. I believe [in UFOs] with all my heart. . . . I was convinced I was an alien when I was a child. . . . I guess that is why I am such a believer."[4] The director finds it chilling that such beliefs "are this firmly rooted in the culture," an outcome he attributes to the media. He goes on to assert that the media, especially television, have much to answer for:

> By repeatedly showing the public a television world where psychics can see the future, where astrologers read the stars to make important personal and business decisions, TV programmers make possible real life nightmares. How about the scandal in Orange County, California, where treasurer Robert L. Citron allegedly drove the county into bankruptcy—and used psychics and mail order astrologers to predict interest rates! How about "financial astrologers" who charge up to $10,000 for one consultation? Need more proof of the harm media-driven credulity can do? The United States government spent $20 million on a program called *Stargate*. "Psychics" and "remote-viewers" were paid to use their "powers" to find ships carrying drugs off Florida, spy on nuclear testing in China and the Soviet Union, and look for a kidnapped American general held hostage by terrorists. Yet today the federal government repeatedly shuts down over budget battles and funding cuts for Medicare, Medicaid, education and social services.[5]

He points out that societal effects such as these make a mockery of the claim by television producers that they are merely trying to entertain the public.

Other commentators have taken a less jaundiced view. They characterize the openness of television toward UFOs and the paranormal as merely one of the more overt signs that we are becoming an increasingly tolerant and mature society. They aver that although this openness may produce some negative effects, these are more than counterbalanced by beneficial effects, such as reducing prejudice and comforting those for whom conventional religions have lost their appeal. For instance, psychologist Charles Tart (1989:67) suggests that an openness to New Age beliefs "is a legitimate recognition of some of the realities of human nature." He continues, "People have always had and continue to have experiences that seem to be 'psychic' or 'spiritual.'"

Regardless of which view is deemed correct, it is quite apparent that real societal effects are involved in the phenomenon of media-driven public credulity, a phenomenon that is now largely attributed to the recent qualitative change in the social role of television's video vérité "products." The public image of the Roswell myth is thus significant both as a prominent indicator of the changed role of television "infotainment" in the dynamics of our culture and as an omen of things to come.

THE ORIGINS OF THE ML-307B/AP PILOT BALLOON TARGETS

CHARLES B. MOORE

Before World War II, the only method for measuring winds aloft from the earth used pilot balloons. This so-called pibal method had limited accuracy and utility. It depended on an observer with a theodolite who visually tracked a small balloon that had been inflated so as to give it an approximately known rate of rise. The observer recorded the elevation and azimuth angles to the balloon during each minute of the ascent. After the flight, the observer calculated the balloon's horizontal position as a function of time, using simple trigonometry on the balloon angles and its assumed height. The mean wind for the layer of atmosphere traversed between two successive angle readings was then calculated by determining the vector displacement of the balloon during that interval. The speeds of the winds determined with the pibal technique were often inaccurate. Furthermore, because the measurement depended on the ability of the observer to see the balloon, the technique obviously failed whenever the balloon entered a cloud or was otherwise lost to view.

The need for winds aloft information increased greatly during the war. It was needed for weather analysis, for controlling aircraft operations, and for gunnery. To fill these needs, concerted efforts were made to devise electronic means of locating free balloons for all-weather measurements of the winds aloft. (The official acronym for the winds aloft measured electronically was RAWIN, pronounced "ray-win." In later years, the acronym became a common noun and is no longer capitalized.) Early in the war, the Signal Corps Engineering Laboratories at Fort Monmouth, New Jersey, undertook the development of a radio direction finder to track the balloon-borne radiosondes that were used to obtain air temperature, pressure, and humidity measurements for the weather services. The equipment that was developed was given the Signal Corps nomenclature of Radio Set SCR-658. Production of the SCR-658 took appreciable time; the first working instruments did not reach the military users until the end of 1943.

In December 1942, Captain Joseph O. Fletcher, an Army Air Force pilot, was assigned to the MIT Radiation Laboratory in Cambridge, Massachusetts. Soon afterward, he suggested that winds aloft could be measured with the hundreds of radars that were already in use overseas and, even better, with the recently developed antiaircraft gun-laying radar, the SCR-584. At the "Rad Lab," Fletcher and his associate, Lieutenant John Nastronero, developed and fabricated corner-reflecting radar targets for this purpose (Fletcher 1990). After initial opposition by Signal Corps personnel who were partisan to the still-unavailable SCR-658 radio direction finder, Captain Fletcher was able to carry out demonstrations in 1943 that convinced Colonel Marcellus Duffy and the Signal Corps of the merits of wind measurements with radars. This idea was particularly attractive at the time because many useful antiaircraft fire-control radars were already installed in the combat theaters. Thereafter, Captain Fletcher was transferred to Colonel Duffy's staff, where he continued the development of radars for weather purposes (Kerr and Goldstein 1951) and where he trained many young weather officers in the techniques of using fire-control radars to collect wind measurements. Upon completion of this intensive training, these weather officers were immediately shipped overseas to the theaters of war in the North Atlantic, England, Africa, India, China, the Pacific, and Australia, where their techniques were quickly put to use.

In early 1944, after the SCR-584 radars became available for use within the United States, Major John Peterson, in Colonel Duffy's Army Air Force Liaison Office to the Signal Corps, was able to have several of these radars transferred to the Air Weather Services. Major Fletcher had one of them installed at Colonel Duffy's Weather Equipment Technicians School in Sea Girt, New Jersey, for training and for experimental work. A number of young officers were assigned to him for this work; among them were Second Lieutenants O. J. Tibbets and Edwin J. Istvan, who experimented with various designs for Fletcher's retroreflectors. One early model measured 4 feet by 15 feet (1.2 m by 4.6 m) and was given the Signal Corps nomenclature of Pilot Balloon Target, type ML-306/AP. (The *A* indicated that the equipment was to be airborne; the *P* showed that it was to be used in conjunction with radar.) The Signal Corps versions of

Fletcher's targets were designed to be carried aloft beneath 100-gram pilot balloons.

Another, more successful design for these targets used panels of aluminum foil laminated to a tough paper to make a lightweight, tear-resistant material. The targets were constructed as retroreflectors consisting of three mutually perpendicular panels of the reflective material held by struts of balsa wood. They were made so that they could be folded for shipment and storage, but when assembled for flight, each of these targets resembled a tilted x,y,z coordinate system—all three coordinate axes were at a 55° angle with the vertical line to the balloon from which it was hung. When the targets were illuminated by a radar, a large fraction of the incident radar pulse would be reflected directly back to the source, regardless of the incident angle. Returned signal increases in excess of 1,000-fold over that of an isotropic scatterer of the same cross-sectional area were possible with corner reflectors having three accurately perpendicular panels. The theory behind these devices is described in the MIT Radiation Laboratory Report Series (Nash 1947; Siegbert, Ridenour, and Johnson 1947; Kerr and Goldstein 1951.)

In 1943, Major Fletcher was able to have a number of these early targets fabricated by small manufacturers in Manhattan's garment district. When modifications to improve the design were later made, then-Lieutenant Ed Istvan (now retired Lieutenant Colonel) was assigned the task of procuring more targets for test. He has told me that he found a small company, again in New York, whose people were willing to attempt the fabrication of the targets.[1] At the present time, Ed does not remember the name of the company, but he thinks it was located around East 28th Street in Manhattan.

The Signal Corps Engineering Laboratories finally adopted this design for the corner reflectors in June 1944 and assigned it the meteorological nomenclature of Pilot Balloon Target, type number ML-307/AP. The design drawing (SC-D-14407) for the ML-307/AP target is dated 9 June 1944. Istvan remembers that there were problems with the first production targets. After being launched under a free balloon, they often broke up in flight because of the aerodynamically induced stress. A redesign became necessary. The modifications that were made included placing an aluminum or brass bracket (designed by Istvan) at the target vertex and reinforcing the laminated panel attachments to the balsa struts. Reportedly, the manufacturer used some tape that he had in stock to make this reinforcement. The tape, as Colonel Trakowski remembers, was a source of amusement for him and for Major Peterson because it carried a pinkish purple abstract flower pattern on the backing, which put some art onto utilitarian meteorological targets.

On 21 November 1944 the ML-307/AP modified target was renamed ML-307B/AP. Drawing SC-D-14407 was changed to include Istvan's bracket and to specify, as Item 22, the usage of "Scotch Acetate Film, Type AL as made by Minnesota Mining & Mfg. Co., St. Paul Minn. or equal" for reinforcing the laminated panel attachments. There was no specification whatsoever for markings on the tape nor for any identification of the targets. Air Force Captain James McAndrew, who in 1994–1996 investigated the archive records of these targets from the Office of the Secretary of the Air Force, found copies of the monthly letters of transmittal showing that ML-307/AP targets were being shipped on a regular basis from October 1944 through January 1945 to the Dayton (Ohio) Signal Corps Supply Agency and to Army Air Force Headquarters. The Weather Wing Headquarters in Asheville, North Carolina, was also notified monthly of the receipt of the target shipments in Dayton. However, the archives did not contain the enclosures to these letters, which specified the quantities of targets being shipped.

A final wartime modification of the targets was recorded on 12 March 1945, when Items 17 and 21 (which were not identified) were removed from the drawing and an enlarged view of Lieutenant Istvan's center bracket was added. The target design thereafter was unchanged until 8 January 1951, when the target was extensively redesigned, ruggedized, and given the ML-307C/AP type number.

The targets were widely used for wind measurements by the military during the remainder of the war. For example, in preparation for the April 1945 invasion of Okinawa, an extensive naval bombardment was begun in late March. To supply the necessary wind information to the naval gunners, rawin measurements were made by a small group of weather personnel that landed five days before D day at Zamami in the Kerama Rhetto with a SCR-584, with balloons and with radar targets. One member of this group was Warrant Officer Irving Newton, who later identified the Foster Ranch wreckage as radar target debris.

The use of the targets decreased after the war because few weather stations then were equipped with the expensive radars, which were difficult to maintain in peacetime. However, the SCR-584 radars were used extensively for wind measurements in a thunderstorm research project that began in 1946. The targets used when the thunderstorm research was moved to Ohio added to the unidentified flying object (UFO) reports during the 1947 summer. Around 1 July of that year, residents around

Circleville, Ohio, began finding ML-307B/AP targets on farms in the area. These finds were reported in the Circleville *Daily Herald,* beginning on 7 July of that year. Recently, Joel Carpenter, an investigator into UFO sightings, obtained copies of the *Daily Herald* for the period and sent copies to me.

My search for the source of the targets quickly found that they came from the University of Chicago's Thunderstorm Project (Byers and Braham 1949:12, 13, 268), which operated that summer from around the Clinton County Airport, about 40 miles west of Circleville. This project operated five SCR-584 radars and, beginning in late June, launched 214 of the ML-307 targets carried by 350-gram sounding balloons for wind measurements around thunderclouds.

The significant feature of the Circleville reports is that Carpenter found that the 8 July *Daily Herald* story included the information that "the markings on the newly found gadget are: 'ML-387B-AP, Mfg By Case,'" whereas the 9 July story stated, "That device bears the markings: 'ML 387. B-AP. Mfg. By Chase.'" (The reporting of the number "387" appears to be due to poor printing of the number "307" on the targets. Incidentally, the Circleville reports provide the only record that any of these targets were ever so identified with printed labels prior to 1951.)

Karl Pflock has discovered that on 12 December 1950, after another mistaken identification of a radar target as a "flying saucer," Lieutenant Colonel K. M. Gillette, the commander of the Air Force Fourth District of the Office of Special Investigations at Bolling Air Force Base, wrote a letter to his director that began, "It has been determined that the Air Weather Service, USAF has, in connection with their studies of winds aloft launched Corner Reflectors (Radar Targets). These targets do not bear any stamps, tags or other data which would serve to identify it for what it is." Following this communication, in January 1951, the chief of the Air Weather Service issued this order: "All AWS units which use Corner Reflectors (Radar Targets) will be instructed to indicate on the target that it is a weather target and may be retained by the finder."

Joel Carpenter's subsequent search at the New York Public Library yielded the address in the 1945 telephone directory of a Case Manufacturing Corporation at 336 East 28th Street (telephone MUrrayhill 5-7542), but there was no current candidate in that area to match that business name. As well as we can establish, the Case Manufacturing Corporation on East 28th Street no longer exists. At present, there is a Case Manufacturing Company on Saw Mill River Drive in Yonkers, New York, but it is a stationery company and, according to the manager, was never associated with the targets. New York City ceased publication of its city directory in 1935, and the issue for that year in the Library of Congress contains no useful information on the occupants of 336 East 28th Street in Manhattan. Lieutenant Colonel Istvan thinks, however, that "it is likely that the [manufacturer of the] ML-307B was the Case Mfg. Corp.—336 East 28th St. cited in Joel's 10/28/95 e-mail."[2]

This constitutes the present status of the search into the origins of the ML-307B/AP Pilot Balloon Targets.

LATER EXPERIENCES PERTAINING TO THE ROSWELL INCIDENT

CHARLES B. MOORE

It seems appropriate to recount my more recent experiences with the affair referred to as the Roswell Incident. These experiences started with a visit from William L. Moore, who with Charles Berlitz coauthored the first book on this topic, titled *The Roswell Incident* (1980). Sometime around 1979, Moore had asked me if one of the New York University balloons could have plowed long, deep furrows in the ground where W. W. Brazel found the debris on the Foster ranch in the early summer of 1947. Readers who refer to page 28 in *The Roswell Incident* will note that my reply contained the condition that it was "based on the description you just gave me." Although William Moore showed me no evidence or documents to bolster his story, he told me that some heavy craft had crashed, made long, furrowlike gouges in the ground, lost some parts, then rebounded into the air and left the region. As I remember, he said that the craft finally crash-landed on the Plains of San Agustin about 110 miles (177 km) to the west. His description of the two widely separated crash landings with long, deep furrows in the earth at the first site made a balloon explanation unlikely.

However, on 12 January 1981, after reading the published Berlitz and Moore book, I wrote Moore, taking issue with some of his information and his incorrect identification of my balloon photograph in the book. He never responded to my letter, and the errors are reprinted in the book that is now on the market.

I had long held the opinion (from 1947 until 1992) that the debris from one of the new polyethylene balloons we had launched from Alamogordo in early July 1947 probably was responsible for the press flap about the "flying saucer." We had launched several experimental balloon trains from Alamogordo Army Air Field in two expeditions during June and July of that year. The last flight in the second expedition was NYU Flight #11A, which used a cluster of polyethylene balloons. This flight, launched at 0508 MST on 7 July, was tracked by Watson Lab personnel in a C-54 airplane until the balloons landed at 1427 MST, about 19 miles (30.6 km) due west of Roswell Army Air Field. The equipment had not been recovered when our group left Alamogordo on the morning of 8 July in the C-54, bound for Newark, New Jersey. We heard about the press report of the "flying saucer" recovery during our trip east and concluded that it was probably based on the finding of Flight #11A by people who could not have ever seen polyethylene balloons before.

There was much excitement nationwide about flying saucers in the last week of June and in early July 1947. Rewards were even being offered for the recovery of any flying saucer debris. During that period, the radio station at Alamogordo received many calls about saucer sightings from local residents around Alamogordo who saw our balloons in the sky over the Tularosa Valley. We recognized that our balloons were responsible for these local radio reports, and later we guessed that some of the polyethylene balloons were the basis of the so-called Roswell Incident. But as far as we were concerned, it was a funny example of how the flying saucer furor could get the press excited about a research balloon flight.

I first saw the 1947 *Roswell Daily Record* interview with Brazel in June 1992, after UFO researcher Robert Todd sent me a copy. When I read it, it was clear that no polyethylene was associated with the Foster ranch debris. Rather, Brazel provided an excellent description of how the remains of one of our unorthodox, early-June meteorological balloon clusters carrying multiple, corner-reflecting radar targets would have appeared after some of the balloons burst and the others dragged the lower targets across the ground. They would not have plowed "furrows," but no furrows were reported by Brazel, by Marcel in his Associated Press interview, by Jason Kellahin (the AP reporter who visited the recovery site), by Sheridan Cavitt (the officer who accompanied Marcel), or by Bessie Brazel (William Brazel's daughter, who was 14 years old at the time).

On the basis of this information, which was new to me, I discarded the idea that a polyethylene balloon had been the source of the debris, and I looked at the records from our earlier flights with clusters of meteorological balloons. One of our cluster flights in early June 1947 (Flight #4) was tracked by the crew of a B-17 airplane to the Capitan Peak–

Arabela area. Tracking ceased when its transmitter batteries failed while the balloon train was still airborne at a location about 25 miles (40 km) from the Foster ranch. I think it is likely that this flight provided the debris that Brazel found.

In response to the recent Air Force identification of the program, it should be pointed out that Project Mogul was so highly classified that I did not know until 1992 that it was the name of the project we worked on. In 1947 I had no "need to know," although I eventually acquired a general idea of the purpose for our effort. I "did not remember" the project name when I talked to William Moore around 1979, because I did not know it and had never heard it before. However, as part of my argument to him that one of our NYU balloons caused the incident, I supplied him with the balloon photograph and with a sketch of the Flight #11A balloon train, both of which he used in *The Roswell Incident*.

None of our balloon ascents was ever identified or known as a Project Mogul flight. All of the flights were designated as New York University balloon flights. We prepared the balloon equipment, launched it, and documented the flight performance whenever we obtained altitude information. The project to develop means for detecting a Soviet atomic bomb test, known in September 1947 as the Long Range Detection Program, was tightly compartmented, with the classified portions retained at Watson Laboratories. Project Mogul was a classified part of this program, but the NYU balloon operations themselves were unclassified. Our mission was to develop constant-level balloons, ostensibly for meteorological purposes. Coupled with the development mission was the requirement for our making service flights when requested by the project scientists. On the service flights, the Watson Lab payloads themselves were not classified; by July 1947 the Watson Lab people had decided that no outside person would be able to deduce their purpose if their debris was ever found after they landed. Under these conditions, there was no great urgency to recover our payloads, except when we wanted to find what went wrong.

With all the security around the purpose of Project Mogul, I'm reasonably sure that the Eighth Army Air Force District officers, Brigadier General Ramey and Colonel Thomas DuBose, had no need to know about the project and therefore were not briefed on the Air Materiel Command operations in Alamogordo until after the debris was recovered. They were probably as mystified initially about the origin of the debris as were Colonel Blanchard and Major Marcel. On 8 July 1947 none of the Eighth Army Air Force officers were qualified to answer questions about any balloon flights. In fact, it now appears that General Ramey wanted a second opinion after Warrant Officer Newton's identification of the radar target debris. In response to questions from Robert Todd in 1991, Colonel Marcellus Duffy (who had been responsible for the development of the radar targets and much other meteorological equipment and who also was in charge of Project Mogul in 1947) gave Todd this answer: "While stationed at Wright Air Force Base in 1947, I received a call at home one evening saying that what was currently being described by the press as a 'flying saucer' was being flown to Wright Field and would be brought to my home that evening for identification. I identified 'the flying saucer' as a weather observation balloon. I'm reasonably sure this is the one found by that rancher near Roswell, but can't swear to it."[1] In a letter to Todd a week later, Colonel Duffy wrote that he should have identified the material as "weather observation equipment," perhaps a dropsonde, a corner reflector, a rawin-windsonde, a standard radiosonde, or equipment used in rocket-launched research—he was not sure exactly what kind of weather equipment he had identified. He went on to say that he "didn't attach any great importance to this particular incident at the time."[2]

In 1993, Colonel Trakowski recounted to me a telephone conversation he had with Colonel Duffy late in 1947. At that time, Colonel Duffy "thought it was comical that the people at Roswell had confused a rawin target with a flying saucer."

In recent years the charge has repeatedly been made that the Army Air Force and later the U.S. Air Force personnel have lied about the nature of the debris. In response to repeated questions, retired Major Irving Newton has repeatedly written to UFO researcher Robert Todd and to me, stating that after he identified the debris in General Ramey's office, Major Marcel followed him around and tried to convince him that the debris was that of a flying saucer and that the markings on the tape were alien hieroglyphics.[3] From these letters, it appears that Major Marcel established on 8 July 1947 that the debris on the office floor was the same as that found by Brazel and that no substitution had taken place.

On my part, having been closely involved with this affair, the only untruth that I can identify is in the original press release, in which Lieutenant Walter Haut, without ever seeing the debris, repeated the rancher's belief that he had found a crashed saucer. But after the identification by Warrant Officer Newton in Fort Worth, General Ramey said the debris was that of a weather radar target and a meteorological balloon; that is what Colonel Weaver (1995) said in his report; and that is how some of the debris from the NYU flights with the unique Signal Corps ML-307B targets and multiple meteorological balloons could be described. On the other hand, unknown to any of the NYU balloon crew, the Air Materiel Command officers held a press conference on 9 July 1947 at Alamogordo and stated the debris was theirs (which was essentially true—we worked for AMC under contract W28-099-ac-241). So where is the alleged Air Force lie regarding the weather balloon and radar target identification of the debris?

Another correction that should be made for the record has to do with the effect of sunlight on the neoprene balloon film, an effect that has not been fully and accurately described in the brief accounts that have appeared. When first inflated, the ML-131 balloons that we used, which were made by Dewey and Almy, were ivory in color. After exposure to sunlight for a few hours, they acquired a gray or brownish color (depending on the latex formulation) and usually burst, leaving large fragments of thin film. With about three weeks' exposure to the sun, the upper portions of these fragments became almost black. Additionally, a faint gray deposit, caused by the exudation of the plasticizer in the neoprene, often appeared on the top surface. The neoprene film in the lower layers usually acquired a mottled appearance, the darkness of which depended on how much sunlight had penetrated. Eventually, after several months of exposure, the film fragments deteriorated under the influence of the sunlight, became very fragile, and often crumbled when flexed by the surface winds.

To improve the flight performance of these balloons, we conditioned them before inflation by dipping them into very hot water. This procedure increased the elasticity of the film, which always degraded during prolonged storage. Afterward, however, as a result of the wet heating, the balloons developed an acrid, "burnt" odor due to migration of the antioxidant, antiultraviolet compounds in the neoprene to the surface. This odor was often noticeable thereafter whenever the balloon film was handled. It is interesting that both J. Bond Johnson, the *Fort Worth Star Telegram* reporter who photographed the debris in General Ramey's office, and Warrant Officer Irving Newton, the weather officer who identified the debris, reported odors associated with the debris. Kevin Randle and Donald Schmitt interviewed Johnson in 1989, and in their book *UFO Crash at Roswell* (1991:72) they state that Johnson spoke of "some burnt rubber that was stinking up the place." Retired Major Irving Newton later wrote Todd in response to a question: "I can't be sure, but yes I do think there was a smell of old rubber, rather than burnt rubber."[4]

Newton, of course, had smelled neoprene balloons before and probably would have associated the odor with old balloons rather than with burned rubber.

In conclusion, it now appears to me that the landing of NYU Flight #4 on the Foster ranch around midday on 4 June 1947 probably produced the debris found by William Brazel on 14 June. Brazel's later guess, after he heard about the $3,000 reward offered for pieces of a "flying saucer," apparently infected Major Marcel with the idea and started the affair now known as the Roswell Incident, which has provided the city of Roswell with its main tourist attraction.

NOTES

CHAPTER 1

1. Information about the Balloon Group and its activities in New Mexico in June 1947 has been derived from Moore, Smith, and Goldstein (1948) and Charles B. Moore to Robert G. Todd, 20 May 1993. The statements attributed to Moore in the text are from this letter.
2. Brazel recounted the story of finding the wreckage to local reporters on 8 July. Quotations in this paragraph are from an account of that interview in the *Roswell Daily Record*, 9 July 1947 (reproduced in McAndrew 1995: app. 1).
3. In World War I the United States developed the first unmanned "balloon bombers"—small, cheap, wind-driven balloons carrying incendiary bombs—designed to be launched in enormous numbers from bases in France to destroy forests and croplands in Germany (see Ziegler 1994). The armistice intervened before they could be deployed, but in World War II they were used by the British to bomb German-occupied Europe and by the Japanese to set forest fires in the western United States. More than 9,000 transpacific balloons were launched from bases in Japan to drop incendiaries on North America (see Peebles 1991:51–82).
4. Information and quotes in this paragraph are from the interview cited in note 2.
5. Ibid.
6. Information in this paragraph and the statement attributed to Moore are from Charles B. Moore to Joseph O. Fletcher, 14 January 1993.
7. Information and quotes in this paragraph are from an account of the identification of the wreckage in the *San Francisco Chronicle*, 9 July 1947.
8. Ibid.
9. Ibid.

CHAPTER 2

1. See, for example, columns by Jay Miller, *Las Cruces (N.Mex.) Sun-News,* 16 September 1994, p. 3, and by Tom Teepen, *Albuquerque Tribune,* 6 October 1994, p. 6; and editorials in the *Albuquerque Journal,* 12 September 1994, p. A6, and the *Albuquerque Tribune,* 20 September 1949, p. A8.

2. As quoted in the *Lowell (Mass.) Sun,* 9 July 1947, p. 3, Ramey stated that the alleged flying disk was the "remnant of a weather balloon and radar reflector."

3. Regarding the notion of "responsible member of society" as a "screening" criterion, the tales of Gerald Anderson and Frank Kaufmann were considered credible, in large part, because these men were not only responsible members of society but also veritable pillars of the community. Anderson, a licensed law enforcement officer employed by the state of Missouri as a security guard, was taking night courses toward a degree and was an active member of his church (Whiting 1992:34). Kaufmann, an Army Air Force veteran and a prominent citizen of Roswell had long held a position in the local Chamber of Commerce, eventually becoming its executive vice president, and later worked for a Dallas firm as an industrial and economic consultant (Pflock 1994b:44). Anderson's story figures prominently in Version 4 and that of Kaufmann in Versions 3 and 5. Reconsideration by some ufologists, however, has resulted in Anderson's tale being described as seriously suggesting a hoax (Swords 1992:46) and Kaufmann's as being riddled with discrepancies and invented facts (Pflock 1994b:41–54).

4. According to Todd (1995), a number of the biographical statements made by Marcel (see Pratt 1994:120, 126) appear to be false. Among them are statements that he had received five Air Medals during World War II, was promoted to lieutenant colonel shortly after the Roswell Incident, was a private pilot with 3,000 hours of flying time, and had received a bachelor's degree in nuclear physics from George Washington University (GWU). His Military Record and Report of Separation (copy in the author's collection) indicates that he did not receive five Air Medals and that he never rose above the rank of major. According to the Federal Aviation Administration (FAA), he was not a private pilot, and according to the GWU records office, he did not attend or receive a degree from that institution (R. Delk, Registrar's Office, GWU, to R. G. Todd, 23 October 1995; M. S. Dakota, FAA, to R. G. Todd, 1 February 1996; my thanks to Mr. Todd for providing me with copies of these letters). The possibility that such records may be incorrect cannot be ruled out, but it seems unlikely that the records of all of these disparate institutions should be uniformly incorrect in a way that vitiates Marcel's claims. Two of these false claims, however, have some basis in fact: Marcel did not receive five Air Medals, but he was awarded two; he never served as a lieutenant colonel, but he did hold that rank in the Reserve.

5. Regarding the involvement of members of the UFO community in prompting the recent GAO investigations instigated by Congressman Steven Schiff, it

was suggested that UFO investigator Karl T. Pflock (Version 6), who is a member of CUFOS and MUFON, may have influenced the decision of Schiff to contact the GAO. A conduit for such influence exists in the form of Pflock's wife, who works for Schiff and who, for a time, managed Schiff's Washington office. Steve Brewer, a columnist who checked on the origins of Schiff's request, maintains that Pflock and Schiff denied allegations of untoward influence. According to Brewer: "Pflock said he's talked to Schiff in 'strictly casual conversations' two or three times about his interest in the case. Schiff said he didn't recall these conversations and that his interest was sparked by a 'flurry' of letters from constituents" (*Albuquerque Journal,* 14 January 1994, p. D-3).

6. The Roswell Declaration and its accompanying explanation appeared in a number of UFO publications. For example, see the *Roswell Reporter,* December 1994. This journal is edited and published by D. R. Schmitt and K. D. Randle, the literary traditors responsible for Versions 3 and 5 of the Roswell myth.

7. The decline of public trust in government is documented by surveys. For example, according to Yankelovich (1977:2), trust in government declined dramatically from almost 80 percent in the late 1950s to about 33 percent in 1976. Later surveys reveal that this trend continued into the 1980s (see Lipset and Schneider 1987:3).

8. The hypothetical question I pose has actually been put to ufologist Stanton Friedman (Version 4) by a radio show host. According to Jim Hitzel and Hector Acuma (writing in the *Tucson Weekly,* 20–26 July 1995, p. 17), "The host asked Friedman, 'is there anything the government could bring forward that could convince you that it really was a Project Mogul balloon and not an alien craft?' And Friedman said no there wasn't anything that could convince him of that. He's already made his mind up."

9. See, for example, Goldsmith (1997:237–242) for a discussion of the significance of these discoveries for estimating the probability of extraterrestrial life.

CHAPTER 3

1. Edwin Istvan to C. B. Moore, 24 November 1995.
2. Karl T. Pflock to Moore, 24 July 1993, including a map locating the debris found on the Foster ranch.

CHAPTER 5

1. All of these authors make it quite clear that they are true believers, and their cited work on UFOs has appeared only in UFO journals, not in scholarly journals. At least one scholar, however, folklorist Thomas Bullard, has succeeded in keeping a foot, as it were, in both the UFO and the scholarly communities by maintaining an uncommitted stance on the question of the objective factuality of UFO stories. Thus, although his work on the folkloristic aspects of alien abduction stories was supported by a UFO organization

(FUFOR) and appeared as one of its publications, he was also able to publish a modified version in a scholarly journal. See Bullard (1989).

2. Private communication, 20 July 1994.

3. D. Koontz, quoted in Woolcott (1995).

4. Barry Karr, executive director for the Executive Council, CSICOP (Committee for the Scientific Investigation of Claims of the Paranormal), to *Skeptical Inquirer* subscribers, 23 February 1996, p. 2. Our thanks to Mr. Karr for permission to quote from this letter.

5. Ibid.

APPENDIX 1

1. Istvan to Moore, 24 November 1995.

2. Ibid.

APPENDIX 2

1. Marcellus Duffy to Robert G. Todd, 6 November 1991.

2. Duffy to Todd, 13 November 1991.

3. Irving Newton to R. G. Todd, 18 February 1994; Newton to C. B. Moore, 11 April 1995.

4. Newton to Todd, 18 February 1994.

BIBLIOGRAPHY

Asad, Talal. 1983. Anthropological Conceptions of Religion: Reflections on Geertz. *Man* 18(2): 237–259.

———. 1993. *Genealogies of Religion: Discipline and Reasons of Power in Christianity and Islam.* Baltimore: Johns Hopkins University Press.

Ashcroft, Bruce. 1994. Summary of HQ NIAC Research into the Roswell Incident, Flying Saucers, and Project Blue Book. Air Intelligence Agency, Department of the Air Force. Unpublished report.

Audi, Robert. 1994. Dispositional Beliefs and Dispositions to Believe. *NOUS* 28(4): 419–434.

Balch, Robert W. 1995. Waiting for the Ships: Disillusionment and the Revitalization of Faith in Bo and Peep's UFO Cult. In *The Gods Have Landed: New Religions from Other Worlds,* ed. James R. Lewis, 137–166. Albany: State University of New York Press.

Balch, Robert W., and David Taylor. 1977. Seekers and Saucers: The Role of the Cultic Milieu in Joining a UFO Cult. *American Behavioral Scientist* 20: 839–860.

Bartlett, F. C. 1920. Some Experiments on the Reproduction of Folk Stories. *Folklore* 31:30–47.

Bascom, William R. 1954. Four Functions of Folklore. *Journal of American Folklore* 67:333–349.

———. 1965. The Forms of Folklore: Prose Narratives. *Journal of American Folklore* 78:3–20.

Bauman, Richard. 1986. *Story, Performance, and Event.* London: Cambridge University Press.

Benedict, Ruth. 1931. Folklore. In *Encyclopedia of the Social Sciences,* vol. 6, 228–293. New York: Macmillan.

Berlitz, Charles, and William L. Moore. 1980. *The Roswell Incident.* New York: Grosset and Dunlap.

Boorstin, D. 1995. *Cleopatra's Nose.* New York: Vintage Books.

Bryan, Courtland D. B. 1995. *Close Encounters of the Fourth Kind: Alien Abduction, UFOs, and the Conference at MIT.* New York: Alfred A. Knopf.

Bullard, T. E. 1989. UFO Abduction Reports. *Journal of American Folklore* 102:147–170.

Byers, H. R., and R. R. Braham. 1949. *The Thunderstorm: Report of the Thunderstorm Project.* Washington, D.C.: U.S. Department of Commerce.

Cahn, J. P. 1952. The Flying Saucers and the Mysterious Little Men. *True* (August): 17–19, 102–112.

Clark, Jerome. 1988. UFO Crashes. *Fate* 41(1): 41–56.

———. 1991. Crashed Saucers of the 1950s. In *The Roswell Report,* ed. George M. Eberhart, 92–100. Chicago: Hynek Center for UFO Studies.

———. 1995. Contacts, Encounters, and Animals at the Zoo: A Review of *The Gods Have Landed. International UFO Reporter* 20(5): 23–29.

Clarke, E. T., and S. A. Korff. 1941. The Radiosonde: The Stratosphere Laboratory. *Journal of the Franklin Institute* 232:217–355.

Cox, E. F. 1949. Upper Atmosphere Temperatures from Helgoland Big Bang. *Journal of Meteorology* 6:300–311.

Crary, Albert P. 1947. Personal diary. Reproduced in McAndrew 1995: app. 17.

Creighton, Gordon. 1979. Close Encounters of an Unthinkable and Inadmissible Kind. *Flying Saucer Review* 25:8–12.

Davids, Paul. 1994. Deflating Balloon Claims. *UFO Magazine* 9(6): 10–15.

———. 1995. Forum. *UFO Magazine* 10(1): 37–38.

Davis, Isabel. 1957. Meet the Extraterrestrial. *Fantastic Universe* (November). Quoted in Clark (1995:23).

Degh, Linda, and Andrew Vazsonyi. 1971. Legend and Belief. *Genre* 4:281–304.

Diodorus Siculus. 1956. *The Bibliotheca Historica.* Trans. John Skelton. London: Oxford University Press.

Dione, R. L. 1969. *God Drives a Flying Saucer.* New York: Exposition Press.

Drake, Frank. 1972. On the Abilities and Limitations of Witnesses of UFOs and Similar Phenomena. In *UFOs—A Scientific Debate,* ed. Carl Sagan and Thornton Page, 247–257. Ithaca, N.Y.: Cornell University Press.

Dundes, Alan. 1965. *The Study of Folklore.* Englewood Cliffs, N.J.: Prentice-Hall.

———. 1980. *Interpreting Folklore.* Bloomington: Indiana University Press.

Eberhart, George M., ed. 1992. *The Plains of San Agustin Controversy, July 1992.* Washington, D.C.: Fund for UFO Research.

Festinger, Leon, H. W. Riecken, and S. Schachter. 1956. *When Prophecy Fails: A Social and Psychological Study of a Modern Group That Predicted the Destruction of the World.* New York: Harper and Row.

Fletcher, J. O. 1990. Early Developments of Weather Radar during World War II.

In *Radar in Meteorology,* ed. David Atlas, 3–6. Boston: American Meteorological Society.

Freeman, Eileen E. 1993. *Touched by Angels.* New York: Warner Books.

Friedman, Stanton T. 1991. The MJ-12 Debunking Fiasco. In *The Roswell Report,* ed. George M. Eberhart, 112–118. Chicago: Hynek Center for UFO Studies.

———. 1994. The Roswell Incident, the USAF, and the *New York Times.* Unpublished report, 26 September, distributed by S. Friedman.

Friedman, Stanton T., and Don Berliner. 1992a. *Crash at Corona: The United States Military Retrieval and Cover-up of a UFO.* New York: Paragon House.

———. 1992b. Yes, There Was a Saucer Crash in the Plains in 1947. In *The Plains of San Agustin Controversy, July 1947,* ed. George M. Eberhart, 2–4. Washington, D.C.: Fund for UFO Research.

Friedman, Stanton T., and William L. Moore. 1981. The Roswell Incident: Beginning of the Cosmic Watergate. In *The 1981 MUFON UFO Symposium Proceedings,* 132–153. Seguin, Tex.: Mutual UFO Network.

Galganski, R. A. 1995. A Quantitative Evaluation of the Project Mogul Hypothesis. *International UFO Reporter* 20(2): 3–6, 23.

Gallup, George H. 1972. *The Gallup Poll: Public Opinion 1935–1948.* New York: Random House.

Gallup, George H., and F. Newport. 1991. Belief in Paranormal Phenomena among Adult Americans. *Skeptical Inquirer* 15(2): 137–146.

Geertz, Clifford. 1966. Religion as a Cultural System. In *Anthropological Approaches to the Study of Religion,* ed. Michael Banton, 1–46. London: Tavistock Publications.

Goldsmith, Donald. 1997. *The Hunt for Life on Mars.* New York: Penguin Books.

Gunkel, Hermann. [1901] 1975. *The Legends of Genesis.* New York: Schocken Books.

Hall, Richard. 1991. Crashed Disks—Maybe. In *The Roswell Report,* ed. George M. Eberhart, 101–111. Chicago: Hynek Center for UFO Studies.

Herken, Gregg. 1982. *The Winning Weapon.* New York: Vintage Books.

Hollis, Martin, and Steven Lukes, eds. 1982. *Rationality and Relativism.* Cambridge: MIT Press.

Holton, J. R. 1979. *Introduction to Dynamic Meteorology.* International Geophysics Series, vol. 23. New York: Academic Press.

Horton, Robin. 1960. A Definition of Religion, and Its Uses. *Journal of the Royal Anthropological Institute* 90 (pt. 2): 201–226.

Hudson, W. D. 1977. What Makes Religious Beliefs Religious? *Religious Studies* 13:221–242.

Jacobs, David M. 1975. *The UFO Controversy in America.* Bloomington: Indiana University Press.

———. 1992. *Secret Life.* New York: Simon and Schuster.

James, William. [1897] 1956. *The Will to Believe and Other Essays on Popular Philosophy and Human Immortality.* New York: Dover Publications.

———. [1902] 1929. *The Varieties of Religious Experience: A Study in Human Nature.* New York: Modern Library.

Jameson, Fredric. 1991. The Cultural Logic of Late Capitalism. In *Postmodernism, or the Cultural Logic of Late Capitalism,* 1–54. Durham, N.C.: Duke University Press. First published in *New Left Review* 146 (1984): 53–92.

Jung, Carl G. 1959. *Flying Saucers: A Modern Myth of Things Seen in the Sky.* New York: Harcourt Brace.

Justin Martyr, Saint. [ca. 178] 1948. *The Writings of Saint Justin Martyr.* New York: Christian Heritage.

Kaufman, Gordon D. 1972. *God the Problem.* Cambridge: Harvard University Press.

Kendrick, Frederick. 1992. News and Comments. *Skeptical Inquirer* 16(4): 344–347.

Kerr, D. E., and H. Goldstein. 1951. Radar Targets and Echoes. In *Propagation of Short Radio Waves,* MIT Radiation Lab Series, vol. 13, 593. New York: McGraw-Hill.

Klass, Phillip J. 1983. *The Public Deceived.* Buffalo: Prometheus Books.

———. 1986. Crash of the Crashed Saucer Claim. *Skeptical Inquirer* 10(3): 234–241.

———. 1988. Special Report: The MJ-12 Documents. *Skeptical Inquirer* 12(2): 137–147.

———. 1991. Review of *UFO Crash at Roswell. Skeptical Inquirer* 16(1): 71–75.

Kluckhohn, Clyde. 1959. Recurrent Themes in Myths and Mythmaking. *Daedalus* 88:268–279.

Komarek, Ed. 1994. A Karl Pflock Alert. Unpublished report, 19 October, distributed by E. Komarek.

Kusche, Larry. 1975. *The Bermuda Triangle Mystery Solved.* New York: Harper and Row.

———. 1979. Book Reviews. *Skeptical Inquirer* 4(1): 58–62.

Lewis, James R., ed. 1995. *The Gods Have Landed: New Religions from Other Worlds.* Albany: State University of New York Press.

Lichter, S. R., L. S. Lichter, and R. Rothman. 1994. *Prime Time.* Washington, D.C.: Regnery Publishing.

Lipset, Seymour N., and William Schneider. 1987. *The Confidence Gap: Business, Labor, and Government in the Public Mind.* Baltimore: Johns Hopkins University Press.

Lofland, John, and Rodney Stark. 1965. Becoming a World-Saver: A Theory of Conversion to a Deviant Perspective. *American Sociological Review* 30:862–875.

Luhrmann, Tanya M. 1989. *Persuasions of the Witch's Craft: Ritual Magic in Contemporary England.* Cambridge: Harvard University Press.

Lyotard, Jean-François. 1984. *The Postmodern Condition: A Report on Knowledge*. Trans. Geoff Bennington and Brian Massouri. Minneapolis: University of Minnesota Press.

Malinowski, Bronislaw. 1954. *Magic, Science, and Religion*. Garden City, N.Y.: Doubleday, Anchor Books.

Maltais, L. W. 1991. Affidavit, April 23, 1991. In *The Plains of San Agustin Controversy, July 1947,* ed. George M. Eberhart, 79. Washington, D.C.: Fund for UFO Research.

Mansueto, Anthony. 1994. Visions of Cosmopolis. *Omni* 17(1): 66–69, 110.

Mayor, Adrienne. 1994. Guardian of the Gold. *Archaeology* 47(6): 55–59.

McAndrew, James. 1995. Synopsis of Balloon Research Findings. In *The Roswell Report: Fact versus Fiction in the New Mexico Desert*. Washington, D.C.: U.S. Government Printing Office.

Menzel, Donald H. 1972. UFO's—The Modern Myth. In *UFO's—A Scientific Debate,* ed. Carl Sagan and Thornton Page, 123–147. Ithaca, N.Y.: Cornell University Press.

Moore, Charles B., James R. Smith, and Seymour Goldstein. 1948. Technical Report No. 1: Balloon Group, Covering the Period November 1, 1946, to June 1, 1948. Unpublished report, New York University. Reproduced in McAndrew 1995: app. 13.

Moore, Charles B., R. Todd, M. Rodeghier, and K. Randle. 1995. Project Mogul and the Roswell Crash. *International UFO Reporter* 20(2): 7–9.

Nash, J. P. 1947. Corner Reflectors. In *Radar Aids to Navigation*. MIT Radiation Lab Series, vol. 2, 324–331. New York: McGraw-Hill.

Nickell, Joe, and John F. Fischer. 1991. The Crashed Saucer Forgeries. In *The Roswell Report,* ed. George M. Eberhart, 119–129. Chicago: Hynek Center for UFO Studies.

O'Hara, Maureen. 1989. A New Age Reflection in the Magic Mirror of Science. *Skeptical Inquirer* 13(4): 365–374.

Ortutay, Gyula. 1959. Principles of Oral Transmission in Folk Culture. *Acta Ethnographica* 8:175–221.

Patsuris, Penelope. 1994. The Invasion of the Angels. *TV Guide* (13 August): 16.

Patterson, James, and Peter Kim. 1994. *The Second American Revolution*. New York: Morrow.

Peebles, Curtis. 1991. *The Moby Dick Project*. Washington, D.C.: Smithsonian Press.

———. 1994. *Watch the Skies: A Chronicle of the Flying Saucer Myth*. Washington, D.C.: Smithsonian Press.

Perrin, Michel. 1987. *The Way of the Dead Indians*. Trans. Michael Fineberg. Austin: University of Texas Press. Originally published as *Le chemin des indiens morts* (Paris: Payot, 1976).

Pflock, Karl T. 1994a. Roswell, the Air Force, and Us. *International UFO Reporter* 19(6): 3–5, 24.

———. 1994b. *Roswell in Perspective*. Washington, D.C.: Fund for UFO Research.

Plutarch of Chaeronea. 1970. *On Isis and Osiris*. Trans. J. Gwyn Griffiths. Cardiff: University of Wales Press.

Pratt, Robert. 1994. Interview with Jesse A. Marcel, Sr., December 8, 1979. In *Roswell in Perspective,* ed. Karl Pflock, 119–126. Washington, D.C.: Fund for UFO Research.

Price, Henry H. 1969. *Belief*. London: Allen and Unwin.

Raglan, Lord (Fitzroy R. Somerset). 1934. The Hero of Tradition. *Folklore* 45:212–231.

Randle, Kevin D. 1995a. *The Roswell Crash Update*. New Brunswick, N.J.: Global Communications.

———. 1995b. To Whom It May Concern. Unpublished report, 10 September, distributed by K. Randle.

Randle, Kevin D., and Donald R. Schmitt. 1991. *UFO Crash at Roswell*. New York: Avon Books.

———. 1994. *The Truth about the UFO Crash at Roswell*. New York: Avon Books.

Randle, Kevin D., Donald R. Schmitt, and Thomas J. Carey. 1992. Gerald Anderson and the Plains of San Agustin. In *The Plains of San Agustin Controversy, July 1947,* ed. George M. Eberhart, 13–25. Washington, D.C.: Fund for UFO Research.

Rodeghier, Mark. 1991. Some Thoughts on MJ-12. In *The Roswell Report,* ed. George M. Eberhart, 130. Chicago: Hynek Center for UFO Studies.

Rodeghier, Mark, and Mark Chesney. 1994. The Air Force Report on Roswell: An Absence of Evidence. *International UFO Reporter* 19(5): 3, 20–24.

———. 1995. The Final(?) Air Force Report on Roswell. *International UFO Reporter* 20(5): 7–9.

Sagan, Carl. 1996. *The Demon-Haunted World*. New York: Random House.

Saler, Benson. 1977. Supernatural as a Western Category. *Ethos* 5(1): 31–53.

———. 1988. Wayú (Guajiro). In *Los aborígenes de Venezuela*, vol. 3, ed. Walter Coppens, Bernarda Escalante, and Jacques Lizot, 25–145. Caracas: Fundación La Salle de Ciencias Naturales.

———. 1993. *Conceptualizing Religion: Immanent Anthropologists, Transcendent Natives, and Unbounded Categories*. Leiden, Netherlands: E. J. Brill.

Saliba, John. 1995. Religious Dimensions of UFO Phenomena. In *The Gods Have Landed: New Religions from Other Worlds,* ed. James R. Lewis, 15–64. Albany: State University of New York Press.

Schaeffer, Robert. 1981. Review of *The Roswell Incident*. *Skeptical Inquirer* 5(3): 59–62.

Schmitt, Don, and Kevin D. Randle. 1991. Roswell Investigation Notes. In *The Roswell Report,* ed. George M. Eberhart, 39–43. Chicago: Hynek Center for UFO Studies.

Schnabel, Jim. 1994. *Round in Circles*. Amherst: Prometheus Books.

Schneider, Charles. S. 1947a. Special Report #1: Constant Level Balloon, Covering the Period from January 1, 1947, to April 30, 1947. Unpublished report, New York University. Reproduced in McAndrew 1995: app. 16.

———. 1947b. Progress Report: Constant Level Balloon, Covering the Period from May 1, 1947, to May 31, 1947. Unpublished report, New York University. Reproduced in McAndrew 1995: app. 15.

———. 1947c. Progress Report: Constant Level Balloon, Covering the Period from June 1, 1947, to June 30, 1947. Unpublished report, New York University. Reproduced in McAndrew 1995: app. 18.

Schultz, Ted. 1989. The New Age: The Need for Myth in an Age of Science. *Skeptical Inquirer* 13(4): 375–379.

Scully, Frank. 1950. *Behind the Flying Saucers.* New York: Henry Holt.

Sender, Gillian. 1995. Out of This World. *Milwaukee Magazine* (March): 19–23.

Siegbert, A. J. F., L. N. Ridenour, and M. H. Johnson. 1947. Properties of Radar Targets. In *Radar System Engineering,* MIT Radiation Lab Series, vol. 1, 67–68. New York: McGraw-Hill.

Smith, John R. 1947a. Comprehensive Report of Operations to the Chief, Air Weather Service. Unpublished report, 7 May, White Sands Proving Ground. Copy in the C. B. Moore collection.

———. 1947b. Report of 2000-Gram Balloon Flights. Unpublished report, 20 August, Air Weather Station, White Sands Proving Ground. Copy in the C. B. Moore collection.

Smith, Wilfred Cantwell. 1962. *The Meaning and End of Religion.* New York: Macmillan.

Southwold, Martin. 1978. Buddhism and the Definition of Religion. *Man* 13(3): 362–379.

Spilhaus, Athelstan F., C. S. Schneider, and C. B. Moore. 1948. Controlled-Altitude Free Balloons. *Journal of Meteorology* 5:130–137. Reproduced in McAndrew 1995: app. 14.

Spiro, Melford E. 1966. Religion: Problems of Definition and Explanation. In *Anthropological Approaches to the Study of Religion,* ed. Michael Banton, 85–126. London: Tavistock Publications.

———. 1978. *Burmese Supernaturalism: A Study in the Explanation and Reduction of Suffering.* Expanded ed. Philadelphia: Ishi Publications. Original ed., 1967.

———. 1982. *Buddhism and Society: A Great Tradition in Its Burmese Vicissitudes.* 2d ed. Berkeley and Los Angeles: University of California Press. Original ed., 1970.

Stacy, Dennis. 1994. Review of Karl Pflock's *Roswell in Perspective. Mutual UFO Network Journal,* no. 315:16–17.

Swords, Michael D. 1992. Crash III Summit: Views of the Moderator. In *The Plains of San Agustin Controversy, July 1947,* ed. George M. Eberhart, 39–48. Washington, D.C.: Fund for UFO Research.

Tart, C. 1989. *The Fringes of Reason.* New York: Harmony.

Taylor, Lee R., and Michael R. Bennett. 1985. The Saguaro Incident: A Study in UFO Methodology. *Skeptical Inquirer* 10(1): 69–82.

Thompson, Keith. 1991. *Angels and Aliens: UFOs and the Mythic Imagination.* New York: Addison-Wesley.

Thompson, Stith. 1955. *Motif Index of Folk-Literature.* Bloomington: Indiana University Press.

———. 1964. *The Types of the Folktale.* Helsinki: Academia Scientarium Fennica.

Todd, Robert G. 1995. Major Jesse Marcel: Folk Hero or Mythomaniac? Unpublished report, 5 December, distributed by Citizens against UFO Secrecy, P.O. Box 176, Stoneham MA 02180.

Utley, Francis L. 1961. Folk Literature: An Operational Definition. *Folklore* 74:193–206.

von Däniken, Erich. 1995. *Chariots of the Gods?* New York: Putnam's Sons.

von Sydow, C. W. 1948. Folktale Studies and Philology. In *Selected Papers on Folklore,* ed. Laurits Bodker, 189–219. Copenhagen: Rosenkilde og Baggers Forlag.

Wallace, Anthony F. C. 1966. *Religion: An Anthropological View.* New York: Random House.

Wang, Betty. 1935. Folksongs as Regulators of Politics. *Sociology and Social Research* 20:161–166.

Weaver, Richard L. 1995. Report of Air Force Research Regarding the Roswell Incident. In *The Roswell Report: Fact versus Fiction in the New Mexico Desert,* 8–32. Washington, D.C.: U.S. Government Printing Office.

Whiting, Fred. 1992. Raiders of the Lost Archaeologists. In *The Plains of San Agustin Controversy, July 1992,* ed. George M. Eberhart, 33–35. Washington, D.C.: Fund for UFO Research.

Wilcox, Robert K. 1985. *Japan's Secret War.* New York: Morrow.

Wilson, Bryan R., ed. 1970. *Rationality.* Oxford: Basil Blackwell.

Wittgenstein, Ludwig. 1958. *Philosophical Investigations.* 3d ed. Trans. G. E. M. Anscombe. New York: Macmillan. Original ed., 1953.

———. 1969. *The Blue and Brown Books.* Oxford: Basil Blackwell. Original ed., 1958.

Woolcott, J. 1995. I Lost It in the Saucer. *New Yorker* (31 July): 76.

Yankelovich, Daniel. 1977. Emerging Ethical Norms in Public and Private Life. Unpublished report, 20 April, seminar, Columbia University, New York.

Ziegler, Charles A. 1988. Waiting for Joe-1: Decisions Leading to the Detection of Russia's First Atomic Bomb Test. *Social Studies of Science* 18:197–229.

———. 1994. Weapons Development in Context: The Case of the World War I Balloon Bomber. *Technology and Culture* 35:750–767.

Ziegler, Charles A., and David Jacobson. 1995. *Spying without Spies: Origins of America's Secret Nuclear Surveillance System.* Westport, Conn.: Praeger Publishers.

INDEX

T

Tart, Charles, 167
Taylor, David, 148
Taylor, Lee R., 31
Tertullian, 130
Thompson, Keith, 70
Thompson, Stith, 49, 51
Time, 14
Tocqueville, Alexis de, 153
Todd, Robert G., 27, 37, 58, 176, 178, 179, 184n4
Traditors: deception by, 55–57; definition, 36; literary, 57, 60; personalized legends of, 40–41; rewards to, 54–55
Trakowski, Colonel, 178

U

Truth about the UFO Crash at Roswell, The. See Randle, Kevin D.; Schmitt, Donald R.
UFO community: conflict within, 24; conformance of Roswell myth with beliefs of, 39–40, 42; demands for government cooperation by, 161–62; size, ix, 13. *See also under* Roswell myth
UFO Crash at Roswell, 179
UFO Encounter '95, x–xi
UFOs (unidentified flying objects): beginning of modern era of sightings of, 6; meanings of, 13, 133; origin of term, ix; profitability of, 153
UFO stories: link to angel movement, 70–72; literary classification, 30–32. *See also* Roswell myth
U.S. Air Force: Freedom of Information

Act requests of UFO buffs to, 161; Project Blue Book, 69; research and report on Roswell Incident by, x, 2, 4, 10–11, 29. *See also* Army Air Force
U.S. General Accounting Office (GAO), x, 2, 4, 67, 69, 185n5
Utley, Francis, 35

V

Vazsonyi, Andrew, 72
Venus, 13, 14
von Däniken, Erich, 145
von Sydow, C. W., 36, 57, 59

W

Wallace, Anthony F. C., 136
Wang, Betty, 68
Watch the Skies, xii. *See also* Peebles, Curtis
Watergate, 69
Watson Laboratories, 4, 12, 75, 177
Wayú, 128–29
Weaver, Richard L., 12, 45, 80, 111, 112, 178
White Sands Missile Test Range, 17
White Sands Proving Ground, 25, 81
Whiting, Fred, 24, 59, 60, 66, 71
Wilcox, George, 8, 17, 20, 23, 26, 28
Wilcox, Robert, 30, 32
Wilmot, Mr. and Mrs., 15–16, 48–49
Wilson, Bryan R., 124
Wittgenstein, Ludwig, 119

Z

Ziegler, Charles A., 12